For the Love of
Stephen

For the Love of Stephen

The Story of a Boy Who Was Never Broken

Stuart D. Jones, Ph.D.

Published by

EVERY LIFE
PUBLISHING

2025

Disclaimer

This memoir reflects the author's personal experiences, memories, and interpretations, as well as those of immediate family members and certain individuals referenced herein. While every effort has been made, through personal recollection, interviews, and reasonable research, to ensure accuracy, the events, conversations, and perspectives described are presented as remembered by the author and may be subject to the limitations of human memory.

Except for members of Steve's immediate and extended family—including parents, siblings, cousins, uncles, aunts, grandparents, nieces, and nephews—the names and certain identifying details of many individuals have been changed or omitted to protect their privacy and maintain anonymity. Any resemblance to actual persons, living or deceased, beyond those intentionally included, is coincidental.

No statement in this work is intended to defame, disparage, or harm the reputation of any individual, group, or entity. The inclusion of any person, place, or event is based solely on the author's understanding and recollection, without malice or intent to misrepresent. The author and publisher disclaim any liability for any loss, damage, or perceived harm arising from the content of this work.

To request permission, contact:

Stuart D. Jones, Ph.D.
fortheloveofstephen@yahoo.com

Cover Design by SelfPublishing.com
ISBN: 979-8-89694-938-1 - Ebook
ISBN: 979-8-89694-939-8 - Paperback
ISBN: 979-8-89694-940-4 - Hardcover

Printed in the United States of America
Published by Every Life Publishing

Email: fortheloveofstephen@yahoo.com
Website: www.authorstuartjones.com
Instagram: @AuthorStuartJones
Facebook: AuthorStuartDJones

DEDICATION

To the remarkable family I grew up with, this story is dedicated in part to you—Stephen's symphony in the calm and anchor in the storms. Your unwavering support and unconditional love were the bedrock of Stephen's life journey. It is a testament to the power of family connection and the beauty of belonging.

For my beloved brother, Stephen, my heart's companion and my forever playmate. This story is lovingly dedicated to you and to the beautiful spirit that lit up our lives with your joy, your relentlessness, and your incredible persistence and courage. You lived with a heart full of love, a laugh that could brighten the darkest day, and a kindness that made the world a softer, sweeter place. You weren't just my brother—you were 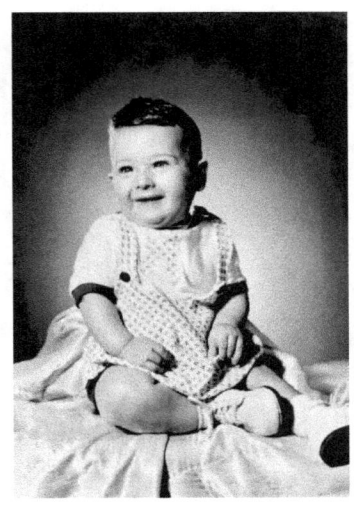 my first best friend, my favorite playmate, and the one who taught me what it means to suspend judgment and love unconditionally. Growing up with you was the greatest gift of my childhood. I will always be grateful that we were born to the same resilient parents and that, in the grand design of things, I got to be your brother. That was—and always will be—one of life's greatest blessings. I miss you more than words can say. And one day, when the time is right, I'll meet you again in Playland—where the toys are abundant, the sun never sets, and laughter never ends.

EACH CHILD IS DIFFERENT

(Author unknown)

I cannot change the way I am,

I never really try,

God made me different and unique,

I never asked him why.

If I appear peculiar,

There's nothing I can do,

You must accept me as I am,

As I've accepted you.

God made a casting of each life,

Then threw the mold away,

Each child is different from the rest,

Unlike as night from day.

So often we will criticize,

The things that others do,

But, do you know, they do not think,

The same as me and you.

So God, in all His wisdom,

Who knows us all by name,

He didn't want us to be bored,

That's why we're not the same.

CONTENTS

FOREWORD

Stephen's story is beautifully told through the eyes of his brother, Stuart. He was born premature in the 1950s and diagnosed as mentally retarded. Today, his condition is labeled Intellectual and Developmental Disability (IDD). His parents refused to put him in an institution, and he was successfully educated in a regular public school classroom. He also had a job he loved in hospital housekeeping.

Temple Grandin, Ph.D.
Photo courtesy of Dr. Temple Grandin, used with permission

Steve was different, not less. You will love his story.

Temple Grandin, Ph.D.
Distinguished Professor of Animal Science, Colorado State Univ.
Author, *The Way I See It: A Personal Look at Autism*
Author | Autism Advocate | Speaker
Subject of the HBO movie, *Temple Grandin,* and the documentary, *An Open Door*

I came to The Arc of Indiana by coincidence rather than connection. My background was public policy. I worked for a United States Congressman and the Indiana House of Representatives before becoming a registered lobbyist. It was when I saw images of people with disabilities being abused in one of our state institutions that I first heard about The Arc.

I reached out to our then Governor, Frank O'Bannon, to learn more about what was happening as I was conflicted by families being scared and angry about the closing of a place that seemed so horrible. It was Governor O'Bannon who told me to contact The Arc of Indiana to learn more. Learn more I did, as I learned about The Arc's mission and met with then Executive Director John Dickerson, who quickly became someone I wanted to learn more from. As luck would have it, I joined The Arc team in 1998 as Director of Government Affairs at a time when Indiana was just beginning to close state-run institutions. At that time, over 20,000 people with intellectual and developmental disabilities (IDD) were on Medicaid Waiver waiting lists with a wait time of 15-20 years.

When my predecessor retired in 2015, I became CEO. Fast forward over two decades, and

I have been fortunate to work for The Arc of Indiana for over twenty-seven years.

Fortunately, so much has changed during these years for people with IDD. Our state is a much better place for people with disabilities to live a good life and have opportunities for greater independence. I am so very proud to work for an organization that has carried the torch for so much good, not only in our state but in our nation. Every single piece of landmark legislation impacting people with IDD has passed due to the efforts of The Arc. National laws, including the Americans with Disabilities Act and the Individuals with Disabilities Education Act, and state laws requiring newborn screening and establishing First Steps early intervention services, continue to make a difference in the lives of so many.

The Arc is an organization that is led by people with disabilities and their families. We work alongside them to impact policy and create opportunities. We were founded by families who demanded more for their children with IDD at a time when medical professionals pushed them to place their child in an institution and go on with the rest of their lives.

The Arc calls those families who said "NO!" to medical professionals *pioneers* as they bravely set out on a path not well traveled. Keith and Phyllis Jones were *pioneers*. All the opportunities and programs available today for people with IDD exist because *pioneers* before us pushed us to dream of a world of inclusivity.

When Dr. Stuart Jones asked me to read his manuscript and potentially write this foreword, I knew that I would be reading the story of what thousands of people with disabilities have gone through throughout their lives - stories where people with disabilities provide grace and kindness, while others show meanness and greed.

For the Love of Stephen is a beautiful tribute to a man, a son, a brother, a husband, and, more importantly, a beautiful human being who showed the world how special someone with a disability can be. Stephen was not special because he had special needs, but because he was truly special in the way he lived his life with laughter and love. I hear all the time how thankful families are to have someone with a disability in their life, as it has led them to people they otherwise would likely have never met. It also led them to see the world through the eyes of their loved one, a world full of love as well as hate.

In the world we live in today, we all need to take a moment to hear or read about some good. For those of you about to flip the page, be prepared to laugh, cry, feel happiness, and sorrow. Some parts are difficult to read, but necessary to reflect the realities we live in.

I could say this is a quick, easy read, but it is not. Some parts will and should disturb you, especially learning about our Indiana history and what our state leaders thought was "okay." You will find yourself re-reading portions to make sure you read them right the first time.

I would expect this book was difficult to write, though some of it may have been therapeutic. To revisit some of the horribleness had to open up semi-healed wounds. *For the Love of Stephen* is a look into the life of a wonderful man. Thank you, Dr. Stuart Jones, for writing it.

Kim Dodson
Photo courtesy of Kim Dodson, used with permission

Enjoy this great read!

Kim Dodson
CEO, The Arc of Indiana

PROLOGUE

In Every Life, a Light

For as long as humankind has walked the earth, there have been individuals whose minds, bodies, and senses danced to a different rhythm—children not broken, but beautifully unique. These individuals with exceptionalities have been present throughout history like human constellations in the dark and quiet sky—sometimes misunderstood, often unseen, but always there. Their stories, like Stephen's, have rarely been written in bold print. Yet they are shooting stars in the universe of human progress.

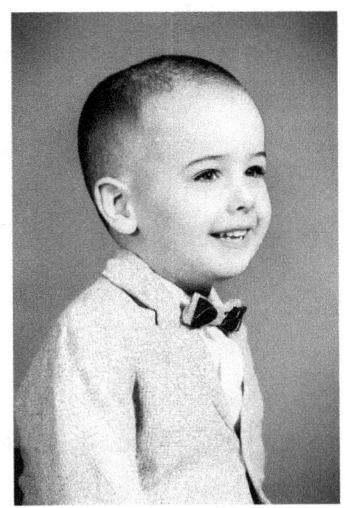

Stephen (Steve) Keith Jones

Not so long ago, society looked upon these individuals with fear and ignorance and excluded them in every way. A child who moved differently, spoke differently, or didn't speak at all might be dismissed as a burden, labeled a fool, or cast away as some sort of punishment from the heavens. Families grieved not because their children were unworthy, but because the world told them so. Educators—when they were present—had no tools, no training, and too often, no hope. Compassion was eclipsed by confusion, and the children—well, many were left in the shadows, locked behind doors both literal and figurative.

But slowly, the world began to change. A shift—stubborn and hard-won—took root. Rotatori, Obiakor, and Bakken (2011) remind us that although individuals with exceptionalities have always been part of society, they were often regarded as "burdens, worthless, demons and buffoons" (p. 3). Today, however, these same individuals are recognized as valued citizens with the ability to contribute meaningfully. The authors describe this evolving journey as "colorful, innovative, and intriguing" (p. 3).

This is the story of Stephen (Steve)—one boy among millions, yet one who quietly changed everything for those who knew him. He was not famous, not rich, not celebrated on magazine covers. But Steve's journey is a thread in the fabric of progress—stitched with struggle, and with hope. His life, marked by laughter, setbacks, trials, triumphs, and the quiet resilience of an unyielding spirit, gives human form to the abstract arc of change.

His story will not only reflect that historic evolution—it will embody it. From the dark days of segregation and silent exclusion to the hopeful march toward belonging, Steve walked, stumbled, and soared through a system still learning to see the beauty in difference. His life is both a love letter to those who never gave up and a challenge to those who still might.

So let us begin—not with pity, but with pride. For this is not a story of what was lost, but of what was found: dignity, worth, and a place in the world for every kind of mind.

ACKNOWLEDGEMENTS

Not a day goes by that I don't miss my brother, Stephen—Steve to all who knew and loved him. His absence is a quiet ache that never fully leaves me, but it's also a powerful reminder: to love more deeply, to listen more fully, and to treasure the people who walk beside us in this life.

It is because of the incredible circle of family and friends surrounding me that this book was even possible. Their encouragement and belief in both Steve's story and my ability to tell it have lifted me through every challenge and carried me forward with hope and purpose.

First and always, thank you to my parents, Keith D. Jones and Phyllis J. Jones. The courage, resilience, and fierce love they showed while raising Steve—and in sharing his story—continue to inspire me. They gave not only their time, memories, documents, and photographs, but also their hearts to this project. Their insights, their laughter through tears, and their determination to honor Steve honestly and beautifully helped shape every page.

To my beloved siblings—Susan (Sue) Jaeger-Hinz, Scott Jones, and our adopted sister, Sudabeh (Sudi) Shoja—thank you for walking this path with me. You generously offered your memories, unearthed cherished photos, provided resources, and shared your perspectives with warmth, humor, and wisdom. Your love for Steve shines through it all, making this story richer, more authentic, and more whole.

To my partner in all things, my wife, Terri L. Jones—your unwavering support is the quiet strength behind every word I wrote. You have listened with compassion, lifted me when I doubted myself, and stood beside me with patience and love. You are not only the heart of our home but the soul of this journey. I am endlessly grateful to share my life—and this story—with you.

To my extended family—my aunts, uncles, cousins, nieces, nephews, and my own children—thank you for the genuine love, laughter, and kindness you always showed Steve. You never saw him as "less than," only as more: more joyful, more spirited, more deserving of every hug, holiday, and family game. Whether it was a seat at the kids' table, a shared story, or a warm embrace at a family reunion, you gave Steve something priceless: a deep sense of belonging. Your unwavering affection helped shape the beautiful, secure person he became. I'm forever grateful.

Thank you, Jane Ann (Wallace) Jones, for uncovering photographs I thought were lost to time. The images you found brought Steve vividly to life and allowed readers not just to imagine his story, but to see it.

To my book coach, editor, marketer, audio producer, cover designer, and all those whose creative gifts and steady hands shaped this book and versions of it—I see you, and I thank you.

To my thoughtful beta readers—Dr. Kathy Martin, Dr. Andrea Hickson-Martin, Jennifer Vaughan, and Rev. Linda (Elle) Morgan—thank you for lending your time, your eyes, and your hearts to this story. Your honest feedback, thoughtful suggestions, and personal opinions gave me insight not only into the manuscript but into the way it might move through the world. I am deeply grateful for your willingness to read with both care and candor—and for helping me see the impact of this book through your eyes.

I wish to extend my deepest gratitude to Dr. Temple Grandin for graciously contributing to the Foreword of this book. Her voice, wisdom, and lifelong advocacy for individuals with disabilities lend both weight and honor to this book. Dr. Grandin's willingness to stand with me in telling Stephen's story is a gift I will always treasure, and her words set the perfect tone for the journey that follows.

My sincere gratitude is also given to Kim Dodson, CEO of *The Arc of Indiana*, for graciously contributing to the Foreword of this book. Under her leadership, *The Arc of Indiana* stands as a leading advocate for individuals with intellectual and developmental disabilities— empowering them with leadership development, community inclusion, and trusted support services throughout Indiana.

To Stephanie Schmitz, the Betsy Gordon Archivist for Psychoactive Substances Research at Purdue University Archives and Special Collections—thank you for your generosity, curiosity, and genuine enthusiasm. Your help in unearthing key materials about the Purdue Achievement Center added historical depth to Steve's journey and affirmed the importance of remembering lives like his.

To Stephanie Wolf and Teresa Pearson at the Tippecanoe County Clerk's Office—thank you for your time, your care, and your empathy in helping uncover painful but necessary truths from public court records. Your dedication reminded me that even the smallest threads of a person's life deserve to be handled with respect.

Stuart at his desk—bringing Steve's story to life, one word at a time

To the many educators, advocates, and scholars worldwide whose expertise helped inform this narrative, thank you for the work you do and the truths you preserve.

To Steve's friends and caregivers—those who laughed with him, protected him, taught him, and saw his light—thank you for loving him as he was.

To every family walking a similar journey—loving, advocating for, and learning from someone with exceptionalities—this story is for you, too.

And finally, to you, dear reader: this story was written for you, and for every person who believes that the life of someone with exceptionalities matters—that their joys, their trials, and their triumphs are worth remembering. As you walk through Steve's life in these pages, I hope you'll see not just a story from the past, but a call to compassion, advocacy, and understanding in your own life.

Let Steve's journey touch your heart. Let it challenge your thinking. Let it move you to kindness.

And if you find yourself smiling, laughing, crying, or reflecting more deeply than you expected, then Steve has done what he always did best: he made a difference.

INTRODUCTION

When Grief Whispers: The Story That Wouldn't Let Go

Why is it that thoughts of our lost loved ones can haunt us—quietly, persistently—even years later? Maybe it's unresolved feelings. Maybe it's memory's strange power to resurrect emotion without warning. Whatever the reason, these thoughts rise from the depths of the subconscious, whispering—demanding to be acknowledged. That's exactly how it's been for me. For two decades, one thought refused to let go: *Tell Steve's story.*

The author, Dr. Stuart Jones (center), with his and Steve's parents, Keith and Phyllis Jones, following a session of Steve Storytelling, June 2025

I had a choice. I could keep stuffing that thought down, denying it space, pretending the ache was gone. Or I could face it. I could grit my teeth, stop making excuses, and say to myself: *Okay, dammit. I'm doing this.* And here we are.

It took me twenty years to find the resolve—twenty years of starting, stopping, and deleting drafts as if I were erasing my own regret.

Writing this book meant facing more than memories. It meant facing grief—the kind that lingers long after the flowers, cards, and condolences are gone. I made dumb choices—like thinking I could silence grief by procrastinating. But grief is louder than denial, and far more patient.

In the summer of 1954, my brother, Stephen Keith Jones, was born with intellectual disabilities. He lived an inspiring and impactful life, as you'll witness in these pages. Steve passed away about two decades ago, at the age of 52. I've learned something profound: when someone you love dies, grief doesn't disappear. It simply changes shape. It walks beside you—softens, sharpens, shifts—but it always stays. And that's okay. What matters most is what you do with it.

Some days, grief whispers. Other days, it roars—on his birthday, the anniversary of his passing, or when I stumble across a photo, a chessboard, a Bruce Lee movie, a scripture passage. Grief has no expiration date. And neither should love.

I'm no psychologist—my sister, Susan, holds that title—but I've learned that grief needs space. Suppressing it only delays its demands. For me, writing this book has been a form of grief therapy. Not a cheap one, mind you. (Have you priced therapy lately?) But it's been healing. And healing, I've found, comes not from forgetting, but from remembering well.

So yes, this book was born of grief—but it is not *about* grief.

It's about Steve. It's about love—unyielding, unshakable love. And it's about the ones who stood by him with fierce devotion, especially when the world tried to dismiss him, label him as broken, wound him, or shut him out.

1984: Steve (left) and Stuart (right),
sharing one of many unforgettable moments on their journey together

It's about honoring a life that was, by all odds, extraordinary—not in the traditional sense, but in the ways that matter most. Steve lived a life full of quiet courage, resilience, and love. He was born into a world not ready to accept him, yet he changed that world in ways most of us could only hope to. Through the unwavering support of family, friends, and a few champions along the way, Steve carved out a life of meaning. He proved that individuals with intellectual and developmental disabilities (IDD) are not defined by what society says they lack, but by the limitless potential they possess.

Let me be clear: this isn't a story about perfection or pity. It's a story about possibility. It's the story of a young man who endured cruelty and neglect, overcame staggering odds, and lived with a kind of grace that many people spend their whole lives searching for. Steve was not a saint, but he was a teacher. Without intending to, he taught everyone around him the power of empathy, patience, persistence, unconditional love, and unwavering human dignity.

A Story of Courage, Compassion, and Change

For the Love of Stephen is a heartfelt and often humorous journey into the life of a deeply courageous boy the world tried to forget—but who refused to be erased.

Meet the Fab Four Siblings, from left to right:
Susan (sister), Steve (brother), Scott (brother), and Stuart (kneeling)

Born in the mid-1950s—decades before disability rights laws, inclusive classrooms, or national conversations about acceptance—Steve entered life too early, too fragile, and far too different for the world as it was. Persons close to the family urged his institutionalization. Society whispered shame. Our family chose something radical instead: love.

Set against the backdrop of mid-20th-century America, a time when children like Steve were routinely hidden away or dismissed, this memoir tells the story of a family that pushed back. We were no heroes—just stubborn, flawed, fiercely loyal people who chose to believe in Steve's worth when others didn't.

Steve's story is not a sanitized tale of inspiration. It doesn't flinch from the truth. He was mocked, bullied, and even abused by those entrusted with his care. Some teachers overlooked him. Peers ridiculed him. Systems failed him. Yet Steve, in his quiet, persistent way, endured. Ultimately, he triumphed—not by changing who he was, but by remaining fully, gloriously himself.

This is a story of resistance and resilience, heartbreak and humor, policy and personal transformation. It is both a searing indictment of the way our society treated people with disabilities and a loving tribute to the teachers, caregivers, and everyday allies who dared to see Steve not as a burden, but as a boy worth fighting for.

At its heart, *For the Love of Stephen* is more than a memoir. It's a call to conscience. A reminder that the smallest lives can provoke the biggest change. And an invitation to witness the grace, grit, and quiet courage of a life that, though nearly overlooked, left a mark that cannot be erased.

Through memory and history, laughter and tears, this book asks readers to look again—at disability, at difference, at dignity—and to discover, as we did, that love is not always easy, but it is always right.

This is my story, as I remember it, and as my family remembers it. While I've done my best to be accurate, memory is imperfect, and details may differ from another person's recollection. For privacy, I've changed many names and identifying details of most people outside Steve's immediate and extended family. No harm or offense is intended toward anyone mentioned or alluded to in these pages.

I miss my brother every single day. If there were any way to bring him back—even for a moment—I wouldn't think twice. But I can't. None of us can. What I *can* do is share his story, just as you may have shared the stories of those you've lost. I can honor the lessons Steve taught us by offering them to you now. I invite you to witness a life that mattered deeply.

The Fab Four Siblings on Christmas Day, 1966. Left to right: me, Steve, Susan, and Scott

His story matters—because all stories of courage, resilience, and love matter. Steve reminded us, without ever saying a word, that every person has value. That "God don't make no junk," as the saying goes (as cited in Smedes, 1993). That every human being, regardless of ability, is—as the psalmist beautifully wrote, "I praise you because I am fearfully and wonderfully made" (Psalm 139:14, New International Version).

Steve was that. Wonderfully made. And so very loved.

I hope it reminds you of someone you loved, something you lost, or maybe something you didn't know you were looking for. I hope it teaches, challenges, and comforts you. And most of all, I hope it helps ensure that people like Steve are never again left out of the story—because their stories *are* the story.

I wrote this book for the love of Stephen, the story of a boy who was never broken.

PART I

THE BEGINNING OF EVERYTHING

CHAPTER 1

THE CALL THAT CHANGED EVERYTHING

Everyone imagines how they might die someday.
No one imagines how their brother will.

— Dr. Stuart Jones

The conference center lobby was buzzing with chatter—hundreds of voices colliding like static—attendees laughing too loudly, juggling coffee cups and conference packets, completely unaware that my world was about to tilt on its axis.

That's when I felt it—a subtle vibration in my suit coat pocket.

A phone call.

I glanced at the screen. Terri.

My wife.

I hesitated.

I actually thought about ignoring it. (Shame on me—but the first workshop was about to begin.)

But something in my gut whispered: *Answer it.*

"Hello?" I said, bracing for the mundane.

Terri's voice came through, rushed and breathless, barely audible over the conference chaos in the background.

"Honey... you need to come home." The words didn't register at first—not in the way they should have. "What?" I asked, annoyed, squinting at the sea of strangers around me, still locked in their morning small talk.

"You need to come home. *As soon as possible.*"

Then, silence.

It was the type of silence that didn't feel empty. It felt... loaded. There was something she wasn't telling me.

"Why?" I snapped, frustration creeping in.

"Your brother Steve's been in an accident. He's in the hospital."

Silence again. This time, the kind that crushes your chest like a vise.

Then she said it. Not loudly. Not hysterically. Just quietly—like it took everything in her to get the words out.

"It's not good."

My heart dropped like a stone in my chest.

"What?" My voice cracked. I barely recognized it.

She steadied herself. "Steve was hit by a car while riding his bike to work."

"Is he okay?" I asked too fast because I already knew the answer. I could feel it clawing its way up my throat.

She went silent again. Then, the soft sob on the other end.

"It's not good," she said again, this time, her voice completely breaking.

I could barely breathe. "Is he… is he dead?"

"No," she whispered gently, "but you need to come home."

If you've ever received a call like that, you know the way time collapses.

Your heart stops.

You forget how to breathe.

Your stomach clenches so violently that it feels like someone just sucker-punched you from the inside out.

And then… nothing. No memory. No timeline. I couldn't tell you how I got back to the hotel, packed my bag, or checked out. I was no longer inside myself. I was watching everything from some strange, detached place.

The next thing I remember—*really* remember—was the road.

I was somewhere on Highway 30, heading south, toward the small town of North Manchester, Indiana, where Terri and I lived with my two sons, Daniel and Derek.

It was Monday, December 18, 2006. A date now burned into my memory.

The three-hour drive became a movie reel in my mind—an emotional kaleidoscope I couldn't control. Images of Steve flooded me in rapid-fire sequence:

His quirky smile.

His goofy laugh.

The times he made us laugh until we cried—and the times we just cried.

Childhood games. Family dinners. Saturday bowling. Visits to our grandparents' farm.

The memories came uninvited and unrelenting, each one stinging like salt in a fresh wound.

Fear, sorrow, disbelief, guilt, helplessness—and yes, even laughter.

God help me, I laughed out loud at one point, thinking of some ridiculous things we did as kids and adults.

But the laughter faded fast. Terri's voice echoed in my mind: *"It's not good."*

That's when it hit me.

He's dying and I'm not there.

And with that realization came a cascade of tormenting questions: When was the last time I saw him? What did we say? Did he know how much I loved him? What if I don't get to say goodbye?

As the miles rolled beneath my tires, more memories raced in my mind, tossing me into an emotional turmoil I never saw coming.

And deep down, I knew *nothing* would ever be the same again.

As I drove, my mind didn't just reel through what happened; it drifted to who Steve really was. And if you're going to understand the heartbreak of that call and the events that would follow, you need to understand Steve first.

He Was Different — But Not How You Think

Temple Grandin, author and autism advocate, said it perfectly: "Different, not less." (Grandin, 2010, p. 13). You probably think you know what "different" means. You've seen movies, read books, maybe even shared a few inspirational social media posts with soft violin music and pastel fonts about people who are "unique." But Steve… Steve redefined different. He made it impossible to look away—and not just because of his appearance. He was a walking contradiction: childlike and wise, fragile and strong, comical and tragic, inconvenient and irreplaceable.

Yes, he was different—but not in the ways most people could understand at first glance. That's the trouble with first glances—they rarely tell the whole story. Or even half.

Steve wasn't your garden-variety "different." No, he was one of a kind—beautifully, bewilderingly, unmistakably *Steve*. Physically, Steve had a presence. Not in a movie-star way—more in a "whoa, what's going on here?" way.

Picture a full-grown man, five-foot-five, with the build of a retired linebacker whose belly never quite made peace with retirement. His hair, thick and dark as espresso, defied balding with stubborn pride, often cut short as if in protest to grooming altogether. Combing? Optional. Styling? Unthinkable. Dandruff? Abundant—so much that it looked like snow. Not real snow, of course, but a constant flurry that followed

Forever our lovable Steve

him like a sad, invisible weather system. And his skin—due to an epic case of ichthyosis vulgaris—looked scaly and peeled like a sunburn that never got the memo to stop. Thoughtless kids gave him the nickname of Snowflake because of his skin. His skin simply lacked natural oil. (That may sound like a mechanical problem, but it was dermatological.)

His scent was… distinct. Let's just say the best lotions from the fanciest department stores barely made a dent. He couldn't help the sometimes "interesting" odor he carried—unless he was deliberately skipping showers, like the time Mom caught him running the water but not actually stepping in. Poor kid; showers made his skin feel tight and uncomfortable afterward, so why bother? His hands and feet resembled worn leather boots—cracked, tough, and well-traveled. If you sat on our family couch, you'd likely leave with a few of Steve's DNA flakes hitching a ride on your pants. He left his mark, literally. And trust me, you never, ever wanted to reach behind that couch—I'll tell you about that unpleasantness in just a second.

The Vision Thing—and the Nose

Steve's eyesight was another tragedy wrapped in a comedy. He was born prematurely in 1954, a time when neonatal science was more guesswork than guarantee. He spent nine weeks in an oxygen-rich incubator, which saved his life but damaged his retinas—a condition called retrolental fibroplasia. It left him with severely limited vision. He wasn't fully blind, but close. Close enough to wear glasses so thick they looked like discarded aquarium glass. When he put them on, you didn't see his eyes—you saw warps in the time-space continuum. And the glasses themselves? Often crooked, bent, cracked, or smudged with fingerprints. Even with the Coke-bottle bottom glasses, he had to lean in close just to see things.

Steve was a nose-picker of Olympic stature, unbothered by social norms, and unfazed by shame. It was almost a form of performance art. His nose was, for him, both a sensory tool and a snack bar. He didn't care about using a tissue, as my sister begged him to do. No sir. The back of the couch was right there. That poor couch became his personal art canvas, showcasing an array of smears and crusts that defied both logic and upholstery cleaner.

He mumbled when he spoke and stuttered when excited or nervous, making deciphering him part sport, part art form. He had a kind of musical cadence to his speech, like he was humming a tune only he could hear. But sometimes, the mumbling was strategic; he didn't *want* to be understood. You'd see him mutter something he probably wasn't supposed to say, then smirk, as if to say, "Good luck decoding *that*, Sherlock."

His fingernails? Long enough to qualify as multi-tools. They could have been used as emergency letter openers or box cutters if needed. We had to nag him to cut them before someone lost an eye. As kids, we feared those talons. "Steve, cut your nails!" was a weekly refrain. "You're gonna hurt somebody!" And eventually, he did. Accidentally, of course—but painfully. I received my unfair share of scrapes, as did my sister, Susan, and other brother, Scott.

Webbed Toes and Bloody Gums: A Love Story

Unless he was swimming, you'd never notice Steve's webbed toes—the same ones that, in the pool, turned him into a human torpedo. Michael Phelps had nothing on Steve once he kicked into gear. On land? Totally undetectable. Underwater? All flipper, no brakes.

Then there were his teeth—or rather, the saga of them. Steve had gingivitis—ultra-sensitive, bleeding gums, the kind that would throw a full-on protest at the mere sight of a toothbrush. A little scrubbing and suddenly it looked like a crime scene in the bathroom sink. Naturally, he wasn't keen on brushing. And let's just say that when he didn't brush, his breath could clear a room faster than a fire drill. Heck, even at night, his gums might bleed, creating a red-blotched pillowcase by morning—a horror movie prop nobody asked for. Mom, ever the hygiene enforcer for Steve, took up the noble crusade of Dental Justice. It was an uphill battle—like brushing a shark with feelings. But she kept at it, bless her heart. Poor guy. Poor toothbrush.

The Fast and the Flaky

At mealtimes, he ate like someone was going to steal his food—and let's be honest, with five other family members around, that was always a possibility. His face hovered inches above the plate, and his chewing was... assertive. A bit like a wood chipper set to "enthusiastic."

He didn't care about appearance unless an event *demanded* it, in which case he could surprise you by looking almost "shiny"—our version of a sharp-dressed man.

You know what else? We loved him with all our hearts—every bit of him—and we miss him more than words can say. Oh, what I wouldn't give to see that familiar face again, even with all its flaky charm. To wrap him in one of those big, lingering hugs he always pretended to hate but secretly loved. To hold his hand—rough and weathered as it was—just for a little while longer.

Yes, You're Judging People—Now Stop Believing Yourself

Steve was stamped early on by the system as "slow" or "mentally retarded"—terms now banished to the archives of educational malpractice. Today, we use "intellectually and developmentally disabled," or IDD. But let's be honest: if there were a genetic bad-luck tree, Steve hit every branch on the way down. But the miracle? He never complained. Not once. Not about his skin, his sight, his  gums, the cruel stares of strangers, or even the bullies who hurt him. He didn't want pity. He wanted to belong.

We've all heard the old chestnuts: *"Looks can be deceiving." "Don't judge a book by its cover."* If idioms had frequent flyer miles, those two would be seated in first class. They're classics—probably embroidered on your grandma's pillow or shoved between fridge magnets in a well-meaning therapist's office. But despite their popularity, we humans remain impressively terrible at following this advice. And by "we," I do mean all of us, including the guy writing this. Especially the guy writing this.

Because here's the irony: we know we shouldn't judge people based on how they look, but we do it anyway. Constantly. Instinctively. Like it's our evolutionary hobby.

Let's just admit it. You've probably sized someone up before they said a single word—He looks shady. She's too made up. Are those pajamas or a fashion statement? Our brains are like overcaffeinated talent scouts: quick to evaluate, relentless with commentary, and not always right. As Dr. Abbie Marono (2024) put it, "Judging by appearances, while often seen as judgmental, is a deeply ingrained human behavior with roots in evolutionary psychology and reinforced by societal norms" (para. 1). Translation: Blaming our ancestors for premature judging is totally fair game.

In other words, our brains are wired with "heuristics," those cognitive shortcuts that help us make snap decisions. Back in prehistoric days, it helped us quickly decide if someone was a threat or a potential ally—or just really, really bad at hygiene. But in modern times, it mostly means we're unfairly writing people off before they've even opened their mouths (Kahneman, 2011).

We do this with restaurants (the grimier the sign, the better the food, by the way), books (the dullest covers have the richest stories), and yes—people. Including people like my brother Steve.

If you had seen Steve before knowing him, you might've made assumptions. He didn't fit the mold of what society calls "put-together." And if you judged him too early, I forgive you—because I've done the same thing to countless others. But here's the twist: everyone who took the time to know Steve discovered someone gentle, funny, decent, loyal, and full of pure-hearted mischief. Basically, the kind of guy Hallmark would write movies about if they had the guts.

The real lesson isn't to stop making snap judgments—you *literally can't*. That's biology. But you *can* stop treating those first impressions as gospel. You can listen to that little voice in your head—the one that says, *Seriously? You don't even know this person yet. Stop it.*

Because while your brain might jump to conclusions faster than a cat in a dog pound, your heart has the final say. And those who let their hearts guide them quickly saw that Steve's exterior was just that—exterior. Inside, he was all gold.

So yes, we're stuck with judgmental brains. But thankfully, we're also blessed with the ability to outsmart them—if we try. Maybe if we all practiced just a little more humility (and listened to Grandma's needlepoint wisdom), we'd see the Steves of the world for who they really are: rare, radiant souls in less-than-flashy wrapping.

And if you're still skeptical, I know a winery in an old dilapidated barn in Massachusetts making wine good enough to convert you. Just don't judge it by the peeling paint.

The Scrappy Saint

Mentally and emotionally, Steve hovered around age 13 forever. That meant you got the sweet parts of adolescence without the smugness. He could be annoying—who isn't?—but he loved, laughed, and lived with a kind of earnestness most of us lose by middle school. He was a soft-hearted tough guy, obsessed with Bruce Lee and Dick the Bruiser, convinced he too was a force of nature in our bedroom wrestling matches. When he teasingly called me a "sissy boy," it was the beginning of our WWF-style smackdown… until Dad's voice thundered from another room: "HEY! STOP PLAYING GRAB ASS!" (Still don't know what that meant. Neither did Steve or Scott.)

The Judgment of Strangers

Steve's emotional intelligence far exceeded his cognitive assessment scores. He could read a room. He knew who liked him, who pitied him, who feared him, and who underestimated him. And he carried all of that quietly. He just didn't let it define him. He was too busy watching *Enter the Dragon* and making sure everyone knew that *he* was Bruce Lee's true spiritual twin.

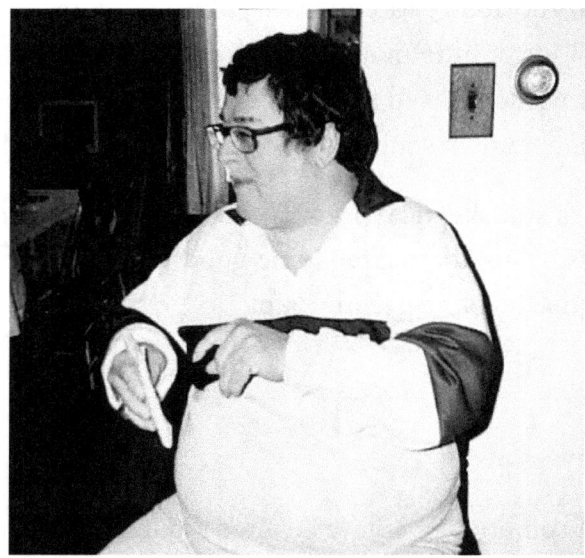

People stared. Of course they did. And it's okay—we expected it. Steve's appearance was not subtle. Strangers would double-take, children would ask awkward questions, and adults would mumble apologies after making snap judgments. You probably would have stared too. But if you looked past the dandruff, the mumbling, the glasses, and the skin flakes, you'd find a heart as pure as gold and a humor sharper than those fingernails.

What's the old saying? "Don't judge a book by its cover." Well, Steve was a masterclass in that lesson. He was proof that some of life's best stories are hidden inside the books with cracked spines and faded covers.

Steve vs. the Church Ladies

One Sunday, Steve went to church with Mom and Dad in their small Indiana town. Two older ladies behind them—blessed with bad hearing and worse manners—whispered loudly, "I didn't know they had a retarded boy. What's wrong with his skin?" Steve heard them. So did Dad. Dad turned, furious, ready to strike down the wicked with righteous Midwestern justice. Steve gently placed a hand on Dad's leg. "It's okay," he said quietly. And he meant it. He had learned the world didn't always see him kindly. But he still offered it kindness in return.

It wasn't okay to my Father, but to Steve it was. Grace under fire. Later, Dad made a point of introducing Steve to the church ladies, knowing full well it would make them uncomfortable. Steve, ever the gentleman, offered his hand. They shook it—reluctantly, uncomfortably, and probably with a generous helping of guilt. The next time Steve was invited to church, he declined. He remembered. Because people with IDD *do* have feelings—don't ever forget that. If those ladies had gotten to know him, they'd have met a Christ-like person in a flannel shirt. He'd already forgiven them. He always did. Because people like Steve don't carry grudges. They carry grace. And a moisturizer, if someone packed it for them.

Judgment Free Zone

People like Steve typically don't judge. It's just not in their wiring. I've met many people with ID and IDD, and I've found them to be the least prejudiced or judgmental humans on Earth. They don't care how you dress, how much you weigh, or whether you have some missing teeth. They care if you smile. They care if you're kind. They care if you'll talk to them or play a game. They especially care if you'd hug them; how they love to hug!

Let me tell you something: people with intellectual and developmental disabilities may be born with differences, but they are never born with prejudice. Steve accepted everyone. He didn't care about your job title, where you live, your skin color, your religion, or your flaws. If you were kind to him, he adored you. If you made him laugh, he loved you. If you hugged him, you'd get one each time he saw you. If you treated him like a

Steve's first ride in a motorcycle sidecar— getting in was a challenge and half the adventure

person instead of a problem, you earned a loyalty that could outlast time itself.

Steve's whole life was about believing in people. That belief would later lead him into two marriages—one that drained him, and one that reminded him love was worth the risk and the wait.

People often said he had "the mind of a child," but that's too simple. He had the *heart* of a saint. And the observational skills of a comedian. He noticed everything. You just had to listen closely to catch it. Steve accepted people with zero hesitation and absolute trust. He was "special," all right—special in the ways we all should be: loving, genuine, non-judgmental, and unafraid to be exactly who he was.

The Athlete Nobody Expected

Despite being labeled as someone who "would never be able to participate in regular physical activities," Steve bowled like a man on a mission. His aim was questionable, his form was unconventional, but his spirit? Unmatched. He played backyard wiffleball, church softball, and outdoor volleyball with gusto, and flailed his way through golf—cussing like a sailor while the rest of us tried not to laugh out loud. He even threw Jarts (you know, those now-outlawed, child-endangering lawn darts) with the kind of joyful recklessness that only the '70s could endorse.

Steve sometimes got frustrated with himself because his coordination and eyesight made it hard to do as well as others. But he never got mad or frustrated with anyone but himself. We were always there, patting him on the back, pumping up his self-esteem like coaches with a never-ending supply of pep talks.

Golfing with Dad, my other brother, Scott, and me at Swan Lake in Indiana was a highlight for Steve. Sometimes he'd crush a shot, other times, well… let's just say it was more "unique" than precise. I remember one time when Scott and I teased him for muttering "Goddammit" after every bad shot. Then, after he nailed a great one, Scott joked, "Why aren't you talking to God now?" He just laughed it off and kept playing like nothing happened. Classic Steve.

One legendary family fail: we gave him cigars during the golf outings, because, hey, cigars and golf are practically a package deal. Mom later found cigars hidden in his apartment and quickly put a stop to that little habit. But somehow, cigars still managed to sneak their way into our golf trips—old habits die hard.

Dad also took Steve to a small golf course near where he lived in rural Indiana, where the owner, fully aware of Steve's situation, always let him play for free. No scorecards, no pressure—just good times and lots of laughs. Those acts of kindness meant the world to us.

Steve loved games, competition, and any chance to prove he was just as capable as the rest of us—even if he wasn't. But honestly, that didn't matter to him. He measured success in fun, laughter, effort, and whether someone gave him that all-important pat on the back.

The Real Steve

If you met him, he'd confuse you, charm you, and maybe make you feel awkward. But he'd also teach you—about kindness, happiness, and what it means to truly accept someone with no caveats, no disclaimers, no "but" at the end of the sentence.

You never got to shake his coarse hand or lose to him in a chess match. But through this book, you'll meet Steve. Not the diagnosis. Not the label. Not the cautionary tale. You'll meet the real Steve. The messy, magnificent, misunderstood man who changed our lives—one flake, one laugh, one hug at a time. You'll walk with him through trials, tribulations, and more triumphs than anyone thought possible. You'll laugh, get mad, and probably cry once or twice. And you'll definitely feel something real, because it's all for the love of Stephen.

So buckle up. Grab a snack and your favorite beverage. This is the story of Steve—the flakiest, funniest, fiercest-hearted man I've ever known.

CHAPTER 2

WHAT IF HE CAN? HOW LOVE TOOK THE ROAD LESS TRAVELED

Children with disabilities are visible reminders
that life is not always fair, but it's good.

— Anonymous

Born for Love: The Story That Changed Everything

It all began on a warm spring Sunday in 1951, when fate—and a collection plate—delivered a love story for the ages. Sixteen-year-old Keith Dillen Jones, all tall and tidy in his church usher's suit, looked down from the aisle of a Baptist Church to pass the offering plate—and there she was. Sitting in the back pew like a true Baptist escape artist was a pretty girl with spark in her eyes and a friend by her side. That girl was Phyllis Joann Fife, just visiting for

The early days of young love—
Keith and Phyllis (Dad and Mom)
at age 16, spring 1951

the weekend from Delphi, ten miles and one fateful glance away.

"I looked down to hand the collection plate," Dad would recall, "and looking back at me was the prettiest girl I had ever seen."

Cue the collective *awww*.

Mom wasn't immune to the magic either. She'd later confess that the slender, handsome farm boy caught her attention just as surely as she caught his. Whether it was his smile or his suit, she didn't say, but something about him stood out in the way that people remember forever.

After church, young Keith put his teenage sleuthing skills to work, tracked her down (without texting, mind you), and asked her out. And just like that, a courtship blossomed—innocent, hopeful, and bathed in the glow of small-town Sundays and soda fountain dates.

They dated all through their junior and senior years—he at Camden High, she at Delphi High—bonded by love letters, weekend visits, and maybe a little bit of stolen time in the backseats of Buicks. By the time they graduated in 1953, they were smitten beyond repair. Two young hearts—not even old enough to vote, but sure enough to promise forever.

Now, the timeline here takes a gentle skip forward. The romantic bubble of their early love was soon joined by a reality check of the bouncing baby variety. Mom, all of eighteen, was the first to know. After several mornings spent racing to the toilet and missing a couple of lady cycles, she connected the dots. A baby was on the way.

With a mixture of nerves and excitement, she shared the news with Dad, whose reaction was one part stunned silence, one part hopeful denial: "You sure?"

Oh, she was sure. Between the upchucking and the skipped cycles, there wasn't much left to doubt.

So, like many couples of that era—nervous, a little green, but determined—they did the sensible thing and got married. Not because they had to, but because they were already planning to. The timing just got a nudge from the universe (and probably a little of something else).

And when did they tie the knot? On Valentine's Day, of course. February 14, 1954—a warmer-than-usual day that felt more like April than February. They married in the same small Baptist Church where they first locked eyes. Romantic, right? Nicholas Sparks couldn't have scripted it better.

Five months later—yes, just five—Stephen Keith Jones made his grand entrance into the world on Thursday, July 22, 1954, at St. Elizabeth Hospital in Lafayette, Indiana (the same birth

Mom and Dad on their wedding day, 1954—the beginning of a lifelong journey

date as his Grandpa John Fife). Steve, as he would be known, was tiny, born about two months early, but full of fight and fire. Much like his parents' whirlwind love story, he arrived ahead of schedule, but not a moment too soon.

The young couple started their life together in a humble little rental house on the edge of Flora, Indiana—a town as quaint as its name. It was nestled between Camden and Delphi, their two hometowns, which made it the perfect middle ground for a new beginning.

Now, here's where the romance turns inspirational. When they said, "You're too young!"—and *everyone* said it, from relatives to neighbors to passing farmhands—Mom and Dad didn't flinch. In fact, Nat King Cole's hit song "Too Young" (1961) became Mom's personal anthem. Every time it played, she smiled like a woman who knew the secret.

"They tried to tell us we're too young…" Yeah, well, over seventy years of marriage later, who got the last laugh? That's right—Mom did.

Mom and Dad

Keith Dillen Jones

Keith Dillen Jones—his middle name taken from his mother's maiden name—was born on a Wednesday, July 31, 1935, in a modest farmhouse near Camden that would eventually become the bunkhouse for his father's farmhands. He was the second of three sons born to Harold and Thelma (Dillen) Jones. The oldest was Gordon, and the youngest, Phil. Tall, strong, and handsome, Dad grew up learning the sacred rituals of rural life: feed the cows, milk the cows, fix the thing that broke while feeding or milking the cows. Life was hard but honest. He graduated in 1953 from Camden High School in a class of just 26. For a short time, he attended evening classes at Indiana Business College in Logansport before the Army Reveille blew its horn.

Phyllis Joann (Fife) Jones

Phyllis Joann Fife entered the world a few months later on Sunday, October 27, 1935, in Monticello, Indiana, but grew up in Delphi. She was the firstborn of John and Eva Marie (Bose) Fife, but she was mostly raised by her grandparents, Fred and Ethel Bose, who lived just around the corner. Her childhood was shaped by post–Great Depression hardship; shared bedrooms, hand-me-down dreams, and a deep well of grit. When her younger siblings, Jimmy and Betty, arrived—both with fragile health—money became even tighter. Her grandparents stepped in, paying for school lunches and other essentials, while young Phyllis started working as soon as she could just to earn a dollar or two. She paid for her own clothes and shoes, proving that independence isn't something you learn—it's something you live. She was small in stature, barely a wisp on the scale, but she was a force of nature who graduated from Delphi High in a class of 70.

Dad: The Stoic Commander Who Found His Mission

Dad was a man carved from tough, stubborn wood—a product of his time, his upbringing, and the hard lessons learned on the dusty farms and battlefields of his youth. During our early childhood years, he was serious, often grumpy, and could shoot a wrinkle-free scowl that could curdle milk from across the room. His adult job in a factory was a grind he hated. He was a man who held his feelings tight, like secrets too dangerous to share. Affection was a currency rarely spent, and love was something you simply assumed, not voiced.

He ran the family like an Army drill sergeant commanding his platoon: orders given, discipline enforced without question, and obedience and respect expected without hesitation. Discipline—his word, his definition—didn't mean calm conversations or gentle timeouts because you had big feelings to work through. It meant

the belt, delivered with precision and absolute authority. Dad's occasional quick temper wasn't a mystery; it was a legacy handed down from his father, Grandpa Harold, who himself was as tough and unyielding as the Indiana farmland they called home.

But that was only the first tour of duty.

Behind the stern gaze and clipped commands lay a man wrestling with his own battles and heartbreak. The bottle had its grip on him for several years, making storms in our home that tested all of us. Yet, like a soldier fighting through a grueling campaign, Dad fought back. He found his way to sobriety, and with it, a remarkable transformation unfolded that changed our world for the better.

Faith became his command post, the church his rallying point. Christ became not just a Sunday ritual but the foundation of our family's new life. The man who once barked orders with the sharpness of a drill sergeant softened into a father who was more loving, compassionate, and—dare I say it—funny at times. His laughter, when it came, was a surprise, like a sudden ceasefire after a long battle.

He became a well-studied Christian and a devoted Bible teacher, known for his insight and quiet wisdom. In every church he served, he earned the respect of pastors and congregants alike, not as a loud voice in the pulpit, but as a steady, thoughtful lay minister who walked the walk.

His patience? That never improved. I inherited mine from him, so my sons paid the price, too.

Dad was fiercely loyal—whether to his wife, his children, or his vision of what our family could be. He defended us with the fierce protectiveness of a platoon leader guarding his squad. He pushed us hard because he believed failure wasn't an option, and mediocrity was the enemy. "Don't do anything half-assed," and "Always give it your best" weren't just advice—it was a mission order etched into the fabric of his character and ours.

But Dad wasn't all discipline and duty. He was the organizer of family morale—planning yard games, coordinating trips to Indiana's parks, and never missing a chance to rally the troops with hot dogs at Wrigley Field to cheer the Cubs. He had ambitions—not just for himself but for all of us—a better life, a good education, a better world where Steve could have more  than pity or resignation. He was determined to buck the system, fight the low expectations placed on his intellectually disabled child, and provide Steve with both opportunity and hope.

Dad was always learning, always striving, reading, never settling. His intelligence was sharp, and if he didn't know something, he found a way to read about it. He was the family's tough, no-nonsense strategist, forever pushing boundaries while demanding we stand tall behind him. He was sometimes gruff and intimidating, and at other times a beacon of love and redemption. Always our dad—steadfast, proud, and ardently committed to the family he built from the ground up.

For a long time—especially during my childhood, teen, and young adult years—I just didn't get him. But today, I absolutely adore, respect, and love him.

Mom: The Quiet Backbone, the Loud Laugh, the Steady Flame

If there was ever a woman who could simultaneously run a household, soothe a crying child, nurse a preemie, and bake a casserole without breaking a sweat, it was my mother. She didn't wear a cape—though if she had, it would've been handmade, pressed, and starched within an inch of its life. She wasn't flashy, and she wasn't loud. But her presence? It filled a room. Her love? It could rebuild you.

She was also the kind of woman who could change the entire atmosphere of a room with a single belly laugh—and if you were lucky enough to be on the receiving end of one of her smiles, you'd find yourself grinning like an idiot without quite knowing why.

At just over five feet tall (and that's being generous), Mom somehow commanded authority in the gentlest of ways. She believed, with near-religious conviction, that a woman's highest calling was to be the domestic glue of the family. Not because anyone told her to, but because it was what she had seen modeled by her own mother and grandmother, what she'd been taught in high school Home Economics classes, and what she believed in her bones. Cooking, cleaning, mending, polishing—you name it, she did it with skill, grace, and just enough vinegar to keep everyone in line.

She never needed a spotlight. She worked best behind the scenes, quietly keeping the wheels on the wagon while Dad handled the steering. She let him do the punishing—including Steve—but she was always right behind him, arms outstretched, ready to hold whoever needed holding, whispering that things would be alright, even if they weren't at the moment.

Mom was the nurturer-in-chief. If one of us needed emotional repair, she was already there with a hug, a hot meal, or a hand on the shoulder that somehow made the world feel less cruel. She told us often—without irony—that we were all special, all loved equally. Of course, the siblings still like to claim I was the favorite, but let the record show, she denied it every time. (Which, now that I think about it, is exactly what someone *with* a favorite would say.)

She adored Steve—not just with gentle affection, but with a fierce, maternal loyalty that could melt a glacier or eviscerate a school administrator who underestimated him, or her. She was the classic Mama Bear: soft and cuddly when things were peaceful, but if someone messed with her son, those claws came out faster than you could say "Individualized Education Plan."

And it made perfect sense that her favorite animal was the bunny rabbit. She adored all things soft, sweet, and innocent. In fact, she often saw herself as Thumper's mother in *Bambi*—a calm, moral compass in a chaotic world, urging her little ones to choose kindness and keep their mouths shut when necessary. "If you can't say anything nice, don't say anything at all," she'd recite like scripture. It wasn't just a motto—it was law. Violators could expect a guilt trip, a disapproving look, getting their mouth washed out with soap, or, in extreme cases, a celery stalk to the backside.

Yes, a celery stalk. When my sister Susan slipped into full teenage diva mode one day—complete with sighs, eye rolls, and the kind of whining that could peel paint—Mom, in an uncharacteristic display of kitchen-to-combat improvisation, grabbed the nearest stalk of celery and let her have it. Not hard, mind you. Just enough to say, "I see you. And I am not above turning vegetables into disciplinary tools."

Mom battled waves of depression at various times. Life threw more than a few gut punches her way. But she never gave up. She grieved quietly, stayed strong publicly, and loved all of us with a tenacity that defied logic and ignored exhaustion. Even on her worst days, she managed to feed, clothe, hug, guide, and gently shape us into people who knew—no matter what—that we were deeply loved.

She was the grace in our struggle. The calm in our storm. The miracle in a kitchen apron.

When the Two Became Three

Together, Keith and Phyllis were a classic American love story: boy meets girl, girl bats lashes, boy offers collection plate, girl says yes to the future, and baby makes three. Their story wasn't picture-perfect, but it was real, raw, and rooted in the values that actually matter: commitment, resilience, love, and laughter.

And Steve—tiny, early, and strong—was the first symbol of that union. He would grow to be one of the most memorable, cherished souls in their lives and in this story. But for now, he was just a newborn, swaddled in love, nestled in a humble home, born from two people who dared to love too young—and proved the world wrong in more ways than one.

A Fragile Start, A Fierce Love

Stephen Keith Jones—Steve to everyone who truly knew him—came into this world the way he lived in it: unexpectedly, with a fight in his bones, and a purpose no one could yet see.

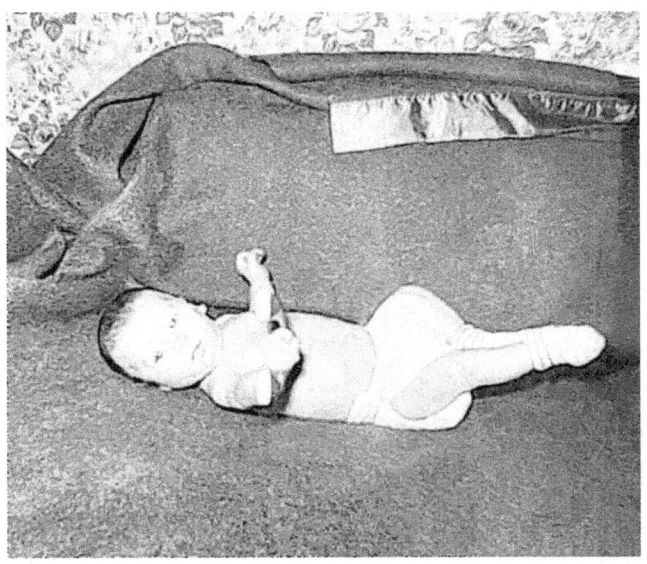

A very fragile start for preemie, Steve

Born in July 1954, Steve arrived prematurely, small enough to cradle in one hand, weighing less than five pounds. In a time before neonatal intensive care units as we know them, this was not a reassuring number. His newborn cries were faint, his limbs underdeveloped, and his very breath fragile. Doctors whisked him away without ceremony, placing him in a Plexiglas incubator that looked more like a science experiment than a cradle for human life.

To his young parents, just 18 and newly married, the joy of childbirth was immediately replaced by paralyzing fear. They hadn't even picked out his name yet. The hospital nurses wrote simply "Baby Boy Jones" on his chart. It would be a day or two more before his name would be decided. What mattered first was survival.

The nurses moved efficiently, but—as my Mom recalled—the air in the hospital nursery hung heavy with tension. This wasn't just another baby, and they all seemed to know it. Something about him was different. Fragile, yes, but also determined. His chest moved with shallow, shaky breaths under the steady hum of the oxygen machine. He was fighting. But would it be enough?

Then, a week into his neonatal journey, my parents recalled the bottom falling out.

At 2:00 a.m., the hospital called the pediatrician, Dr. Miller. He woke to the shrill ring of the rotary phone, its chime slicing through the silence like a warning bell. He barely heard the nurse's words: "You need to come. Now. It's the newborn baby, Stephen." The caretakers didn't expect Steve to make it through the night. Dr. Miller—a good man with a quiet intensity—rushed to the hospital, scrubbed in, and took over. He didn't call in favors. He didn't ask for backup. He worked with what he had, what he knew, and who he was.

And somehow, by sunrise, Steve had stabilized. Just barely. The emergency passed, but the shadow remained. That moment marked the beginning of a pattern that would define Steve's life: brush up against the impossible, refuse to surrender, and pull through—again and again.

Yet it wasn't only Steve who fought. My parents, still teenagers, suddenly found themselves navigating a world of uncertainty, exhaustion, and grief wrapped in baby-blue hospital blankets. There was no instruction manual for raising a child like Steve. What they had were instincts, faith, and something deeper: an unshakable, unconditional love for their first child.

Mom remembered driving the 25 miles every day from their little home to Lafayette to sit by her baby boy's incubator. She couldn't afford an overnight motel. She couldn't even hold Steve for very long—not yet. But she could speak to him. Pray for him. Watch for the rise and fall of his tiny chest. Sometimes she just sat there in silence, feeling helpless and scared and very, very young.

Phyllis and Keith with their firstborn, Steve—beginning a journey of courage, love, and resilience

Dad reminisced about working full shifts at the Flora Grain Elevator during that time, shoveling feed and loading bags until his muscles ached. He didn't complain. He couldn't. One day in the hospital cost the same amount of money as he made in a week. And there were nine weeks of that. Nine weeks of bills and worry and wondering if they would bring Steve home at all. Dad joined Mom at the hospital on most evenings after physically exhausting work hours.

Steve's condition was made more complicated by the very thing meant to save him. Like most premature infants at the time, he was placed in an incubator rich in oxygen. But too much oxygen, it turned out, could be toxic. Since 1942, doctors had known that high doses could rupture the delicate blood vessels in a baby's eyes, leading to a condition called retrolental fibroplasia, now known as retinopathy of prematurity (Terry, 1942). Dr. Miller knew this and tried to be cautious—taking Steve in and out of the incubator in shifts—but nine weeks of exposure was still enough to leave permanent eye damage.

Steve would grow up with very poor vision, almost legally blind. But no one could know that yet—not fully. There were still more pressing questions: Would he grow? Would he walk? Would he ever speak?

And if so, would anyone listen?

Finally, after 63 excruciatingly long days, the glorious day came: It was time to bring Steve home. My parents recalled he still weighed just five pounds—half the size of a Thanksgiving turkey. My mom held him like porcelain, careful not to jostle his head or disturb the medical advice echoing in her mind. The formula he'd been given in the hospital for milk allergies, Nutramigen, wasn't working. It was expensive, hard to find, and Steve hated it. He hated drinking it, no matter how many lullabies or coaxing bottles came near him.

Then, one day, a local neighbor, a mother of six with more experience than credentials, suggested something else: "Give that boy cow's milk with Karo syrup." It sounded more like pie filling than baby formula. But Mom was desperate, and the hospital had no better ideas.

They tried it. Steve loved it. He sucked down that sweet homemade concoction like it was liquid gold. And wouldn't you know? He started gaining weight. Getting stronger. That chubby baby glow finally showed up, months late, but oh so welcome.

Dr. Miller wasn't thrilled. "That could be dangerous," he warned. "He's allergic to milk." But Mom had found her rhythm. She listened politely, then went home and kept pouring the syrup.

Yet even as Steve's body filled out, the developmental milestones remained elusive. At nine months, he hadn't rolled over. Didn't sit up. No babbling, no crawling, no reaching. Something wasn't right.

Dr. Miller sat my parents down. "Your son is slow," he said, choosing words that felt delicate but clinical, even then. "He will never be like normal children."

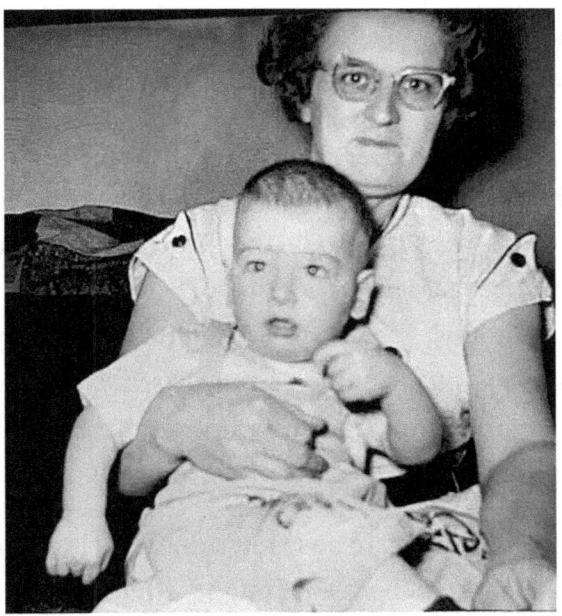

Steve with his beloved grandmother, Thelma Jones

That was it. No roadmap. No plan. Just a vague diagnosis and a gaping chasm of fear.

In today's terms, Steve had an intellectual and developmental disability (IDD). But in 1955, terms were harsher. "Mentally retarded," most called it—words that carried weight and stigma, slamming doors before they were even opened.

And yet, my parents didn't walk out of that office and give up. They walked out holding hands, holding hope, holding the belief that Steve could be more than what the doctors saw on a progress chart.

But the voices around them weren't so sure. Friends and even a few relatives began whispering suggestions about Longcliff State Hospital—a state institution known for warehousing "defectives," the mentally ill, the disabled, the unwanted. One doctor my parents knew well even praised the place. "I put my wife there," he said, as though that were the gold standard of care. (One can only hope she got better living conditions than his golf clubs.)

They said it as if it were kindness. As if handing Steve over to become a ward of the state would be "best for everyone." A mercy. A relief. A way out.

And Grandma Thelma? She responded to Steve's diagnosis the way some folks react to an IRS audit—with denial, indignation, and a sudden bout of genealogical amnesia. "There's nothing like that on *our* side of the family," she insisted, straightening her apron like she was preparing to slap a lawsuit on science itself. Never mind that she had not one, but *two* first cousins who were institutionalized with severe intellectual disabilities. Details, schmetails.

It turns out that when you're busy rewriting the family tree to prune the inconvenient branches, you might forget which limbs were already growing wild.

My parents said they never saw Steve as a burden. They saw him as their son. Their flesh and blood. A human being with a soul and a future—even if no one else could yet imagine what that future would be.

They made their decision quickly and with conviction: No institution. No matter what it cost. No matter what it would take.

And take, it did. It took courage. Perseverance. Faith that sometimes wavered but never broke. There were hard days. Lonely days. Uncertain days. Days when the bills stacked high and the milestones never came. But there were also moments of quiet joy.

My parents vividly remembered one of those that came in the summer of 1958. Steve was three years old, and Aunt Betty Lou (Mom's sister) had taken it upon herself to try to teach him how to ride a bike (with training wheels, of course). She was convinced he could. She worked with him day after day, balancing his little body on the seat, guiding his hands to the handlebars, and encouraging every hesitant push of the pedals.

And then one day—just like that—he did it. He rode. Wobbly, slow, unsure, but he rode.

You'd have thought he'd won the Tour de France, judging by my parents' tears.

That moment changed everything. If he could ride a bike, what else could he do?

The world had told my parents all the things Steve probably couldn't do. But they started asking a different question: What if he can?

They never stopped asking it.

For me, Alan Turing's words come to mind: "Sometimes it is the people no one imagines anything of who do the things that no one can imagine" (Tyldum, 2014).

That was my brother. That was my parents. That's what love made possible.

Disability is real. But so is love. So is family. So is faith in the face of fear.

Let's not overcomplicate things: when a parent learns they'll be raising a child with IDD, they typically go down one of two roads. On one side, there's the road marked *Hope, Determination, and an Industrial-Strength Coffee Maker.* On the other hand, a darker path lined with *Fear, Resignation, and too many brochures for long-term care facilities.*

Of course, it's more nuanced than that—but let's face it, attitude is everything. And parents generally lean toward one of two emotional drivers: hope or fear. These aren't just sentimental buzzwords either; they're backed by science. According to Bujnowska, Rodríguez, García, Areces, and Marsh (2019), the emotions of hope and anxiety are often deeply intertwined, and how a parent balances them can have long-term consequences. When one emotion dominates the other, it tends to push a person toward either optimism or pessimism.

And let's be honest—pessimism never built a future for anyone except the guy who invented padded walls.

Thankfully, my parents weren't wired for surrender. Keith and Phyllis— just a pair of small-town Hoosiers with strong faith and stronger wills—chose the path of *hopeful rebellion*. They embraced what researchers call the motivational model of hope (Bujnowska et al., 2019), which basically means they saw challenges not as stop signs but as detours worth navigating.

And they did it with a fierce conviction: Steve would learn. Steve would grow. Steve would develop to the best of his abilities. That wasn't negotiable. They didn't frame it as some Norman Rockwell inspirational painting—it was simply their job, and they intended to do it well. They learned that in disability lies ability: the ability to change, overcome, and empower.

That's why the idea of institutionalizing Steve—a common and even recommended practice at the time—was never seriously on the table. Not even on a bad day. The kind of "hospital" available for children like Steve in the 1950s and 60s wasn't what you'd call a nurturing environment. More like a human warehouse for the "infirmed, disabled, and insane," where development was less of a goal and more of an afterthought.

Instead, my parents envisioned a different future. A classroom, not a ward. Goals, not limits. Dignity, not dismissal. As the Bujnowska study notes, when hope takes the driver's seat, people tend to zero in on actions that actually move the needle forward. My parents weren't just hopeful—they were strategic. Their belief in Steve's potential became the fuel that drove every decision, every battle, and every uncharted step on the road ahead. And that road turned out to be what Robert Frost described as "the one less traveled by, and that has made all the difference" (Frost, 1916/1993).

Grace in the Struggle

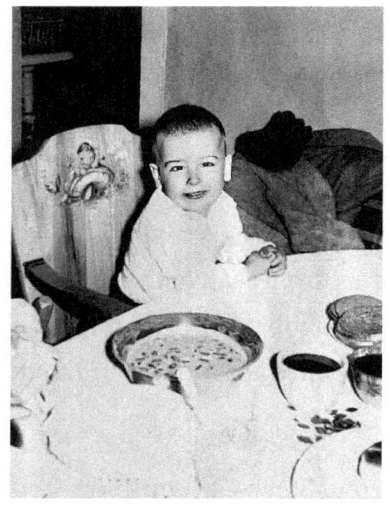

There are many theories about children like Steve. Some say they're sent to special families for a reason. Some believe they choose their families before birth. Others call it fate. Or luck. Or bad luck. Or divine mystery.

All I know is this: My parents never asked why.

They only asked how.

How to love him. How to teach him. How to protect him.

How to help him live a full, joyful, dignified life in a world that too often says, "He doesn't belong."

But he did belong. He belonged in our family. In our home. In our hearts. And not for a moment did they ever regret it.

Parenting a child with special needs is often described as a journey—sometimes uphill, sometimes sideways, and occasionally upside-down. But for those who've walked that path, it's more than a poetic metaphor; it's a lived experience that brings with it both profound joy and bone-deep exhaustion.

Haley Goleniowska, a mother and advocate, captures this emotional complexity beautifully in her writing. On her blog, *Downs Side Up*, she reflects:

> Perhaps some of us are lucky enough to have learnt such a lot from our children, sat back and allowed them to teach us, that they have made us a tiny bit wiser and stronger, more resilient than we were before they were born... It's not always the case; many of us feel overwhelmed and under-supported. We often feel we are doing our best and still feel guilty that it might not be enough. Or we are exhausted from the battles we face, or we despair as we try to erase the struggles in our children's paths (Goleniowska, 2012).

That's not just poetic—it's painfully accurate. I know my parents could relate to every word of that quote. Depending on the day, the moment, or even the hour, they felt inspired, overwhelmed, proud, disheartened, determined, victorious, and flat-out worn down. Sometimes all at once. And who wouldn't? There was no instruction manual for parenting a child with disabilities in 1954. Even if there were, it would likely self-destruct after chapter one.

When Love Leads the Way

For my parents, raising Steve was never about overcoming a burden—it was about embracing a blessing wrapped in unexpected challenges. Their story wasn't one of denial or defeat, but of fierce hope and unyielding love. Every laugh shared, every tear shed, every sleepless night was a thread woven into the fabric of a family that refused to let fear write their story.

Steve taught them—and all of us—that the measure of a life isn't in how easy the path is, but in how boldly you walk it. That love, in its purest form, isn't just a feeling; it's a daily choice, a stubborn refusal to give up, and a promise whispered in the quiet hours: "I am here. I will fight for you. You are not alone."

As I look back on those early days—the laughter, the fears, the small victories—I see a family not defined by diagnosis or struggle, but by an unbreakable bond. That bond carried us through every trial, every unknown, and every "it can't be done" whispered by the world.

This is the love story that began with a church collection plate, survived a premature baby's fragile breaths, and grew into a legacy of hope. It is the story of Stephen Keith Jones—a boy who arrived early, but on time. The story of a boy who was not broken. And of parents who overcame various obstacles and chose love, laughter, and a little surprise, above all else.

Because in the end, that's what mattered the most: the love of Stephen.

Four generations of Jones men: Harold Jones (grandfather, left, holding baby Steve),
Keith Jones (father, standing), Howard Jones (great-grandfather, right)

Four generations: Phyllis Jones (mother, left, holding baby Steve), Thelma Jones
(grandmother, standing), Maude Jones (great-grandmother, right)

CHAPTER 3

CALL HIM STEVE: A REQUIEM FOR THE WORDS THAT TRIED TO DEFINE HIM

Words wield power, so let's choose them with care and compassion. A world of empathy begins with our voices.

— Anonymous

Let's be honest: words can hurt—hell, they can eviscerate. And for people with intellectual and developmental disabilities—and the families who love them—the English language has historically been about as gentle as a sledgehammer to the face. Labels weren't just words; they were tiny social death sentences, dressed up in academic robes and inked in bureaucratic cruelty.

Take Steve, for example. He collected more labels than a thrift-store clearance bin. Not because he asked for them, but because society decided early on that compassion is optional when your IQ doesn't fit on their scale. So, prepare yourself for a little snark along the way—I've earned it.

A Short History of Long-Lasting Damage

Back in the not-so-good old days—when bloodletting was considered medicine and leeches were practically prescription staples—respected professionals classified people with terms like *"idiots," "morons,"* and *"imbeciles."* These weren't playground taunts; they were official diagnostic categories. Imagine being told, "Congratulations, your child has been given the diagnosis of 'imbecile,'" and then receiving the bill for the privilege (Global Down Syndrome Foundation, 2025).

Over time, the medical establishment shifted—though often it seemed less like progress and more like a search for new labels. Out came *"handicapped"* and, later, the infamous *"mentally retarded."* Cruel slang followed quickly: *"retard," "tard," "reject," "mutant."* Steve heard them all. So did I, and so did our family.

As his brother, I developed a kind of radar for this kind of language—a built-in sensitivity that alerted me whenever words were used carelessly or cruelly.

If you are the type who enjoys a historical backstory with occasional head-shakes, then buckle up.

Ancient Wisdom, Modern Cringe

We're going back a long way. Ancient Egypt—yes, the land of pyramids and pharaohs—mentions conditions resembling intellectual and developmental disabilities (IDDs) in the *Papyrus of Thebes*, written around 1500 BCE (Smith, 2020). They didn't use today's terminology, but they clearly recognized differences.

Fast forward to the Greeks and Romans, who often explained disabilities as the result of displeased gods. A child who didn't speak by age three? Clearly, the goddess Hera wasn't in a generous mood.

By the early Christian era, disabilities were framed in complex theological terms—sometimes viewed as the result of sin, sometimes as part of humanity's shared brokenness. It was, in a sense, a theological balancing act: blame, absolution, and shame often woven into the same sermon (Eiesland, 1994; Stiker, 1999).

Even today, remnants of those ideas remain. Some people still turn to spiritual explanations, suggesting prayer as the first—and sometimes only—response. While faith can be a source of comfort, it also reflects how deeply historical perspectives continue to shape modern conversations about disability.

Enlightened Pity and Eugenic Pride

By the 19th and early 20th centuries, things got more... sophisticated, if that's the word we're using for it. Samuel Gridley Howe—the abolitionist and advocate for the blind—tried to classify people with intellectual disabilities in his 1848 report *On the Causes of Idiocy*. Sounds noble. Until you read the actual labels: "idiots," "simpletons," and "fools." These weren't just descriptions—they were verdicts. Once labeled, people like Steve were often shipped off to institutions and forgotten (Howe, 1848/1976; Trent, 1994).

And then came Henry Goddard, who in the early 1900s blessed us with the term *moron*. He wasn't trying to be cruel—just efficient. Goddard genuinely believed society would collapse under the weight of so-called "feeble-minded" citizens, so he championed intelligence testing, institutionalization, and—wait for it—forced sterilization. His work helped inspire eugenic policies around the world. It's one thing to be wrong; it's another to be dangerously persuasive (Goddard, 1912; Trent, 1994).

From Institutions to Integration (Sort Of)

The mid-20th century offered some hope, but also a ton of hypocrisy. Institutions like the infamous Willowbrook State School housed people with disabilities under the guise of care, but investigative journalists like Geraldo Rivera exposed the truth: abuse, neglect, overcrowding, and humiliation (Rivera, 1972). Steve never lived in an institution, thank God—but that was a miracle of family persistence, not societal mercy.

By 1975, the U.S. passed Public Law 94-142, requiring public schools to educate children with disabilities. This was a tectonic shift—but like most tectonic shifts, it came slowly and with plenty of friction (U.S. Congress, 1975; Education for All Handicapped Children, 1975).

Steve was among the first wave of children with IDDs to enter public schools without this law to help him. A pioneer, whether he wanted to be or not.

At his first evaluation meeting, a specialist remarked, "Well, he's *not uneducable*, at least." That was meant to be encouraging.

And yet, Steve thrived. Not because of the system, but in spite of it. He learned to read, do math in his head, and make friends. He held jobs. He sang, loudly and out of tune, and insisted on hugs. He outloved most of the people who tried to measure his worth in IQ points.

The Psychology of Labels: A Hidden Bruise

Psychologists like Erving Goffman (1963) described how labeling creates "spoiled identity"—when a single characteristic (like an intellectual disability) becomes the entire lens through which others see a person. Labels become scripts. People live down to them—or fight every day to disprove them.

Steve knew when people were talking about him, even if they were using "technical" terms. He could feel the chill behind the smile, the pause after "retarded." He once asked my Mom, after overhearing a staff member say he was "low functioning,"

"Am I broken?" he asked.

That must have gutted my Mother.

Modern Words, Modern Problems

In 2010, President Barack Obama signed Rosa's Law, replacing "mental retardation" with "intellectual disability" in federal documents (Rosa's Law, 2010). Named after Rosa Marcellino, a girl with Down syndrome, the law marked progress. But in 2025, seven U.S. states still haven't updated their language. Because apparently, it takes longer to delete a word from a file than to send a rover to Mars.

Rosa (front center) with the Marcellino family and President Barack Obama at the White House, 2011. Official White House Photo, Public Domain

And let's not pretend that replacing a slur with a more politically correct phrase automatically erases the mindset behind it. Today, we hear "special needs," "challenged," or "differently-abled"—terms that sound polite but still feel like side doors out of the human race.

Some folks wrap their prejudice in velvet: "Well, bless his heart, he tries hard." Others weaponize pity as judgment: "It must be so hard for your family." Meanwhile, kids like Steve are in the kitchen making spaghetti and telling knock-knock jokes. Who's disabled *now*?

So What About Steve?

Here's the truth: none of these terms ever came close to describing Steve.

He wasn't "feeble-minded" or "defective." He was Steve. That was his diagnosis. That was his label.

His defining traits weren't "slow processing speed" or "adaptive limitations." They were love, humor, loyalty, and warmth. Try fitting that on a clinical mental disorders checklist.

The adorable duo—
Steve and his sister Susan, 1957

We've spent centuries trying to fit people like Steve into diagnostic boxes, only to discover that humanity doesn't come in standard packaging. The most accurate label? Person. Or, if you're lucky enough to know someone like Steve, teacher.

Final Diagnosis

So, what should we call people with intellectual disabilities?

Start with their name. Then maybe call them a friend, a coworker, or a teammate. Terms like "intellectual disability," "cognitive disability," or "neurodiverse" are appropriate—but they still fall short of the one word that truly matters: *human*.

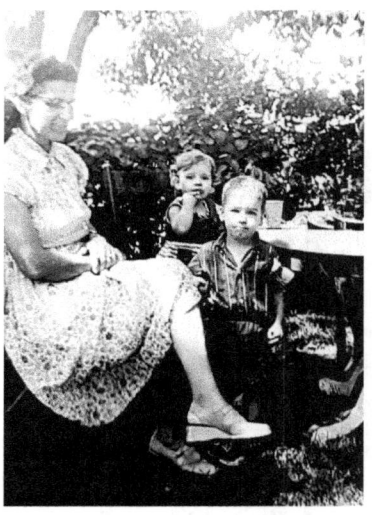

Steve (center, standing) always loved a good picnic—family, food, and fun

Here's to Steve. He endured the name-calling, outlived the ignorance, and stayed kinder than those who tried to label him. He made peace where others made policies. He made friends where others saw problems. He made us better—just by being.

Yes, here's to Steve: fiercely unlabelable, gloriously unscientific, and unmistakably, unapologetically loved.

Yes, it's all for the love of Stephen, a boy who was never broken.

CHAPTER 4

DIFFERENT, NOT DEFECTIVE: UNDERSTANDING STEVE'S WORLD

Children with disabilities are like butterflies; they may require a little extra nurturing, but on the inside, they are all beautiful.

— Anonymous

L et's face it—nobody wakes up thinking, "I really hope to read about intellectual and developmental disabilities today!"

This isn't a light and breezy topic to read. It's definitely not light and breezy to write. But this story is about Steve. As you get to know him, you'll continue to see that, no matter how hard it is for you to read or for me to write, it's a story worth telling. And telling that story comes with a sprinkle of science and a dash of history. (The final exam will be open book.)

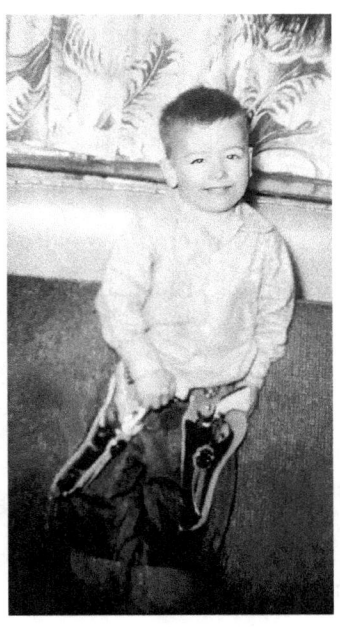

Because our mom idolized John Wayne, we grew up watching his movies and dreaming of becoming cowboys. Here's our cowboy, Steve

What Is IDD?

Intellectual and developmental disabilities (IDD) are lifelong conditions that begin early in life, affecting intellectual functioning, such as reasoning and learning, and adaptive behavior, such as communication, self-care, and social skills (American Association on Intellectual and Developmental Disabilities [AAIDD], 2023).

Put simply:

1. **Cognitive functioning:** learning, problem-solving, judgment—think, the reason tax forms make your eyes cross.
2. **Adaptive functioning:** managing daily life, reading social cues, communicating—basically, not microwaving a Hot Pocket in foil.

You might recall the outdated, offensive term, "mental retardation." Thankfully, the DSM-5-TR replaced that term with "intellectual developmental disorder," reflecting a shift toward respect and dignity (American Psychiatric Association, 2022). Words matter; people like Steve deserve kindness and precision.

IDD is a neurodevelopmental difference, like running a different operating system: some people run Windows, others run Mac. Steve? Pure analog in a digital world—making it work with style.

About Steve

Steve's IQ hovered around 65—not high by standardized test standards—but IQ alone doesn't capture worth or ability. It's been criticized as biased and incomplete for years (Gould, 1996; Schalock et al., 2010). So let's not pretend it tells the whole story.

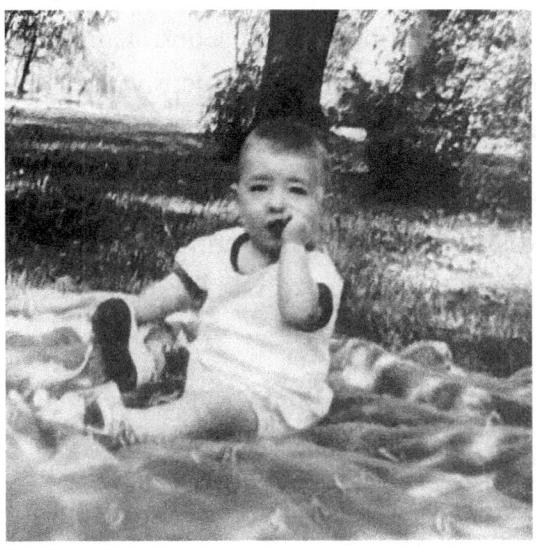

Where Steve truly shone was in adaptive behavior. He needed help, but who doesn't? I know adults who panic reading directions for microwaving a frozen Lean Cuisine. With patience and support from family, neighbors, and teachers, Steve lived with remarkable independence.

He had routines, rhythms, and relationships. A favorite seat at the dinner table. A TV-watching system rivaling any programming algorithm. Steve thrived with consistency.

Why Was Steve Born With IDD?

Genetics? A fluke? Cosmic bingo night? We asked—quietly, repeatedly—but never got a satisfying answer. Eventually, we stopped needing one. As siblings, we didn't even realize he had "issues" until we were middle-school age.

IDD can arise from many causes: genetic syndromes like Down syndrome or fragile X; prenatal exposures to things like alcohol, drugs, smoking, or infections; birth complications; environmental toxins; or unknown factors (Centers for Disease Control and Prevention [CDC], 2024). For Steve, prematurity, oxygen deprivation, and early trauma were in the mix—no definitive cause, just a constellation of possibilities.

As Kramer said on *Seinfeld* (David & Seinfeld, 1992), "Mother Nature's a mad scientist, Jerry!" Sometimes, the answer is simply: we don't know—mother nature is a mad scientist—and learning to sit with that is part of the journey.

Steve didn't waste time wondering why. He was too busy living.

The Science-y Bits

IDDs affect multiple aspects of development—physical, emotional, intellectual—and various body systems (Eunice Kennedy Shriver National Institute of Child Health and Human Development, 2023). Experts group IDDs broadly into:

1. **Nervous system disorders** (brain and spinal cord), like cerebral palsy, epilepsy, and learning disabilities. Steve had learning challenges and a speech disorder likely rooted neurologically.
2. **Sensory system disorders**, affecting sight, sound, and touch. Steve had visual and auditory impairments—enough to need adaptations like sitting closer to the TV or amusingly mistaking "You want a taco?" for "Let's go to the store."
3. **Metabolic disorders**, impacting nutrient and energy processing. Steve had some metabolic challenges influencing weight and energy. But hey, who doesn't crave cinnamon Pop-Tarts and avoid cardio?

4. **Degenerative disorders**, which worsen over time. Steve plateaued developmentally in young adulthood but didn't lose skills—he just pitched his tent on a different mountain.

So, What Is IDD, Exactly?

It depends on who you ask. Schools, the Social Security Administration, clinicians, and advocates each define IDD slightly differently (U.S. Department of Education, 2017). Most agree it means significant limitations in intellectual functioning and adaptive behavior beginning before age 18 (AAIDD, 2023).

Steve checked those boxes:

1. Sat up, crawled, and walked later than peers.
2. Spoke late, with a unique speech style.
3. Struggled with abstract concepts and memory.
4. Didn't quite grasp money's logic.
5. Had trouble reading unspoken social rules and consequences.
6. Found structured problem-solving challenging.

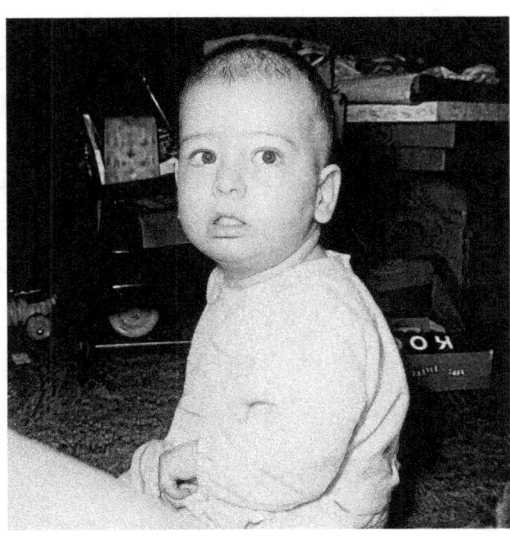

Yet he sensed moods, remembered your favorite snack, and made people laugh without trying. His logic might not fill textbooks, but it worked in his world.

Steve had an IDD. But he also had an infectious laugh, a talent for chess (knights especially), doing math in his head, and an ability to curse under his breath with poetic precision. He was a full human being, not a diagnosis.

You've made it through dense material—research, definitions, and enough acronyms to cause fatigue. I boiled thousands of pages down to a few. You're welcome.

Through Steve's Eyes

If you really want to know what the world was like for Steve, imagine stepping off a plane in a country where you only know a handful of words. You can tell when people are happy or mad. You can see the way their eyes light up or narrow. You can feel the energy in the room. But the conversations around you? They move too fast, twist in directions you didn't expect, and sometimes you only catch the edges of the meaning before the moment is gone. It's hard to keep up.

That's not to say Steve didn't understand things—he understood a lot. But he understood them best when they were clear, concrete, and offered up one at a time. If life came at him in a rush of details, it was like pouring a gallon of water into a funnel—you had to pour slowly and give it a minute to get through. And if the plan changed without warning, well, it felt like someone had tried to fit the whole gallon into a pint glass.

Steve saw the world in bold strokes. Loud rooms felt louder. Bright lights felt brighter. A sharp word could cut deeper, and a kind one could light up his whole day. He noticed little things most of us miss—a bird hopping across the driveway, the exact way someone's laugh changed when they were genuinely happy versus just being polite.

Social rules, though? Those were trickier. He didn't always catch the unspoken stuff—sarcasm, hints, the delicate dance of small talk. But he could spot genuine kindness a mile away, and once he trusted you, that trust was complete and unshakable.

Steve's emotions were worn right on his sleeve. Joy came out big and unfiltered. Hurt sometimes lingered longer than it should. And in a world that often moved too fast, too loud, or too unkind, he still found his bright spots: family, familiar routines, moments when someone took the time to slow down and meet him where he was.

He might not have seen or processed the world exactly the way you or I do—but that's part of what made him remarkable. He noticed the beauty we'd walk right past, laughed at things we'd casually overlook, listened intently to understand, and lived in the moment in a way most of us only wish we could.

Why All This Matters

Steve was one of an estimated 7.4 million Americans—and up to 200 million people worldwide—living with IDD (World Health Organization [WHO], 2023). Each experience is unique, but understanding these basics helps us move beyond labels toward empathy.

We don't learn this to "fix" anyone, but to respect, support, and fully include them.

This isn't about memorizing terms. It's about walking a mile in someone else's shoes, to understand how their mind works and their world feels. It's empathy—the kind that makes us better family members, neighbors, and citizens.

We have reached the end of Part I, so you now know more about IDD than most—and you did it with humor, compassion, and maybe a chuckle or two. Congratulations on making it this far!

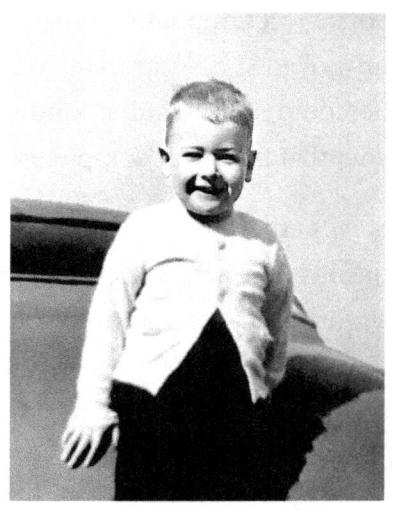

In the preceding chapter, we walked through the historical labels slapped on people with IDD— some laughable, some downright infuriating. In the next section, we'll take a closer look at what life was like growing up in the Jones family, but for now, I just want to say thanks for caring enough to get this far. Because all of this is for the love of Stephen, a boy who was never broken.

As my brother, Scott, says, "He was one of the good ones." Understanding him means understanding a little more about what it means to be human.

PART II

BUILDING A LIFE
THAT MATTERS

CHAPTER 5

JOY COMES IN THE MORNING

It's not what happens to you, but how you react to it that matters.

— Epictetus

Private First Class, Public Lessons

It was just after the guns went silent in Korea in July 1953 that President Dwight D. Eisenhower and his brass hats began to sweat—not because of war, but because peace had a problem: no one was volunteering for the military. Americans were relieved the war was over, understandably uninterested in signing up for the next one. In response, Eisenhower urged Congress to renew the Selective Service Act. The sanitized term was "conscription," but regular folks called it what it was: "the draft."

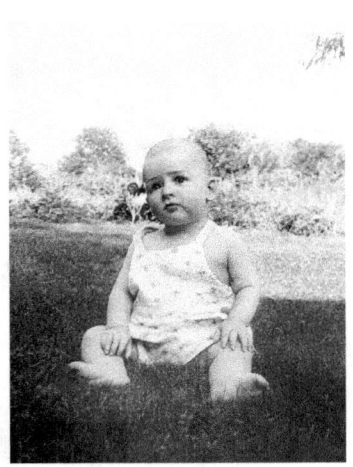

1955: Steve, just over a year old— and already beginning to write his own story

"For the foreseeable future," Eisenhower declared in his 1955 State of the Union Address, "our standing forces must remain much larger than voluntary methods can sustain. We must, therefore, extend the statutory authority to induct men for two years of military service" (Annual Message to Congress on the State of the Union, 1955, January 6).

That "statutory authority" came knocking at our door in the form of a letter for my dad. He met all the criteria: male, over 18, not in college, married with only one child. Uncle Sam didn't say please. Six months later, however, that damn policy changed—men with one child were exempt. But by then, Dad was already lacing up his government-issued boots. Timing is everything.

So off went my father to serve in the U.S. Army for two years, full-time. He and my mother had barely celebrated their first anniversary. Steve, their firstborn son, was just seven months old when Dad shipped out for basic training at Fort Leonard Wood, Missouri, in February 1955. But before he left, Dad gave Mom a little parting gift—another baby in the belly. Classic Dad move: knock her up, then ship out. Poor Mom.

Off to basic training—because nothing says "welcome to adulthood" like a five-mile run at 5 a.m.

Back in Delphi, Mom moved in with family, who provided emotional and practical support, especially her Grandpa Fred, who was more like a second father. Sadly, Fred passed away just a few months after Mom returned home. One loss would follow another, as if sorrow had just started scribbling its early drafts.

At Fort Leonard Wood, Dad endured the grueling rites of basic training. The base, deeply involved in preparation to send young men like my dad off to another possible war, was still on edge. They were training men for conflicts that hadn't yet arrived. It was during this time that Dad got a letter from Mom with joyous news: another child was due in October. When he wasn't firing rifles or running drills, he was reading letters with trembling hands.

After surviving basic (which many claim as their only real war story), Dad was transferred to Fort Sill, Oklahoma, for Advanced Individual Training. He was a farm boy who could already shoot straighter than most, and the Army turned him into a sharpshooter. At Fort Sill, he became one of the best in his brigade. Even the Army knew not to underestimate a kid raised around hogs and hay bales.

Specialist 4 Keith Jones,
U.S. Army, 1955

From there, he received his P.C.S.—Permanent Change of Station—to Fort Bragg, North Carolina, where he joined the 285th Forward Observation Battalion. Thankfully, peace held, and Dad remained stateside. Still, Mom and Steve were stuck in Indiana for months before they could reunite.

When October's winds blew in, Mom gave birth to John (Johnny) Howard Jones at St. Elizabeth Hospital in Lafayette, just 15 months after Steve had made his own debut. Johnny was healthy—a relief, given the unspoken anxiety that followed Steve's early health scares. The Army didn't grant Dad leave for Johnny's birth, but by Christmas, Mom, toddler Steve, and baby Johnny loaded up a rusted-out Chevrolet and braved the winter roads to finally reunite with Dad in a rented trailer near Fort Bragg.

It was the happiest Christmas they ever had—or so my parents always said. Reunited, however humble the circumstances, they were a family again.

Johnny (left) and big brother Steve—sharing a special
Christmas moment frozen in time in Fort Bragg, North Carolina

But as joy often walks beside sorrow, something else was stirring. Dad quickly noticed that Steve—almost two years old—wasn't quite keeping pace with the other kids on base. Dr. Miller was right about the "slow" diagnosis. Steve wasn't running, wasn't talking like the others. Still, Steve didn't throw tantrums. He wasn't a "terrible two." He was gentle, joyful, and perhaps most memorably, utterly without guile. Steve didn't throw things; he offered them. He didn't scream; he laughed. The Army base toddlers had nothing on this little guy.

By military pay standards, our family was below broke. Dad made $110 a month—pay was $83.20 if you were single. Trailer rent ran $40. That left seventy bucks to feed four mouths. They could afford meat only when Spam was on sale, and some dinners were just peanut butter on white bread. Mom, already seasoned by poverty growing up, knew how to stretch a dollar. For Dad, it was a new low.

His father had been a successful farmer—no one at their table ever went hungry. This was uncharted terrain.

And yet, the family grew.

In 1956, Mom discovered she was pregnant yet again. Dad's "urges" didn't exactly come with an off switch, and Mom—despite raising two little boys on next to nothing—couldn't say no. Looking back, I chuckle. Years later, Dad sat me down for the awkward "birds and bees" talk and cautioned me to control my urges. Really, Dad? You, the man whose urges filled half a church nursery?

A Winter of Separation and Sorrow

By the winter of 1957, the young military family had already endured much. They had made it through two pregnancies and the constant upheaval of military life, anchored only by the unwavering love between a devoted young couple and the two little boys who had made their home feel full, even in the most modest of Army housing.

You can never have too many toys for Christmas

But this third pregnancy was different. Difficult. Demanding in ways no one had quite expected.

Mom, usually steady and strong even under pressure, was frequently nauseated and deeply fatigued, far beyond the first trimester. This wasn't just morning sickness; this was a daily battle with exhaustion that stole her strength and dimmed her usual spark. And yet, even while pregnant and unwell, she still had two little boys—Steve and Johnny—to care for. She was expected to cook, clean, grocery shop, wash laundry, and manage all the duties of a mother, all while carrying a third child and battling illness. It was too much. Something had to give.

And so, in January 1957—just two months before Dad was due to be discharged from the Army—help arrived in the form of two deeply devoted sets of grandparents. Harold and Thelma, along with John and Eva, offered to make the long winter drive from rural Indiana to Fort Bragg, North Carolina, to pick up the boys. Their mission: bring Steve and Johnny back home to Camden for a couple of months to give their kids time to prepare for the birth of another child and transition out of the Army and back home.

It was a lifeline, and one Mom and Dad gratefully accepted. The drive was over 700 miles, made through cold, wintry roads and small-town back highways. But love drove the grandparents forward. When they arrived, they scooped up their grandsons—curious Steve with his big brown eyes, and baby Johnny with his blonde hair and gentle spirit—and began the journey back to Indiana.

The plan worked—at least at first. Back near Camden, the grandparents shared in the joy and work of caring for the boys. Mom stayed behind in Fort Bragg, finally able to rest with Dad by her side, as they prepared for the arrival of their third child. For a brief, hopeful window of time, everything felt under control.

But life—especially life with children—is never predictable.

My parents recall that soon after returning to Indiana, Harold and Thelma began to notice something odd about Steve. He didn't seem to track things well with his eyes. He'd fumble when reaching for toys, and occasionally seemed disoriented in bright light. Thelma, ever the observant former schoolteacher, recognized the signs. She had learned to spot learning and sensory challenges in children, and she knew what she was seeing.

She took Steve to the family optometrist in nearby Logansport—a compassionate and capable woman named Dr. Kirlin. The diagnosis was swift and sobering: Steve had severe vision impairment, caused by the long, oxygen-rich incubator care he'd received as a premature infant. It was an ironic twist of medical necessity; the same oxygen that had saved his fragile life quietly damaged his sight. If his vision had been any worse, he would have been declared legally blind.

Dr. Kirlin fitted Steve with his very first pair of glasses, one of the strongest prescriptions available for a child his age. When he slid them on, the world, once blurred and murky, suddenly bloomed into focus. The change was immediate and wondrous. Steve, just a toddler, could finally see people's faces, the shapes of leaves, the outlines of his toys. A whole new world had opened up for him. He hadn't known he couldn't see. Now he could. The cost of the glasses was covered by his grandparents without hesitation. For them, giving Steve the gift of vision was simply what love required.

But not all was well. While Steve's world was brightening, Johnny's was beginning to fade.

Little Johnny—just 15 months old—fell ill. At first, it seemed like an ordinary childhood sickness: a fever, a cough, a little fatigue. But it didn't go away. In fact, it worsened quickly. He grew weaker by the day, his tiny body struggling to fight what turned out to be a severe case of pneumonia.

Harold and Thelma rushed him to their trusted country doctor, affectionately called "Doc Wise." One look was all it took. Doc sent them immediately to St. Elizabeth Hospital.

The doctors and nurses there did everything they could: antibiotics, oxygen, supportive care. But this was 1957, and even though penicillin had brought hope in the fight against pneumonia, it was not enough in the face of a rising storm.

That year, a new and dangerous strain of influenza—H2N2—began sweeping across the country. It triggered a pandemic that disproportionately affected young children and caused a sharp uptick in pneumonia-related deaths, even in otherwise healthy toddlers. *The New England Journal of Medicine* would later document the deadly surge in childhood mortality during that year, linking it to the influenza pandemic that overwhelmed the nation's hospitals and homes alike (NEJM, 2000). Johnny became part of that grim statistic.

On Sunday, January 20, 1957, Johnny died.

Just like that—swept away in the arms of a virus no one could have seen coming. His little lungs, still growing, simply couldn't fight any longer. He was gone.

The call came to Fort Bragg on a cold winter morning. My grandparents, voices shaking, reached out through the military's lifeline—the American Red Cross. They needed to speak to their son, my father. It was urgent. Tragic.

My father was in the middle of drills, surrounded by the rhythm and rigor of Army life, when he saw them approaching—three solemn figures cutting across the parade ground: the base chaplain, Commanding Officer Davis, and a Red Cross representative. No one needed to say a word. The gravity on their faces told him of tragedy before they even spoke.

When they finally did, they were direct but kind, as if trying to soften a blow that could not be softened. Johnny—his baby boy—was gone. Just a toddler, still so new to the world. And now, just... gone.

The officers drove my father back to his trailer home. That drive must have felt like an eternity—every turn of the wheels pulling him closer to a moment he wished he could postpone forever. When he walked through the trailer home door, my mother took one look at his face and knew something was wrong. The same three men who had stood with my father in his anguish now stood with both of them, gently delivering the news that would break my mother wide open.

Her body seemed to fold in on itself, as if the enormous weight of the news was too much to bear. No words could soothe her, no embrace from my Father could steady her—her wailing filled the room with a rawness that silence could not contain. Grief consumed them both. The air in that little trailer turned heavy with sobs and disbelief.

For days, they were lost in sorrow—too surreal to comprehend, too shocked to speak, too devastated to sleep. Word spread quickly through the trailer park, a tight-knit Army community of young soldiers and their wives. And like a makeshift family, neighbors came with casseroles, prayers, and tearful hugs, trying to fill the unspeakable void, if only for a moment.

But the heartbreak didn't end there.

Mom, already struggling with a difficult pregnancy, began to spiral. The news of Johnny's death struck her body as cruelly as it struck her heart. Her condition quickly turned serious. The Army doctor issued an uncompromising order: she was absolutely forbidden to travel the 700 miles back to Indiana for the funeral. The risks were too great for her and for the baby she still carried.

And so, they stayed. My parents—grieving, broken, and stranded—were forced to miss their own child's funeral. It was a kind of sorrow no parent should ever endure: to bury a child from afar, unable to kiss his forehead one last time, unable to whisper goodbye.

The arrangements fell to my grandparents, who carried the unbearable weight on their behalf. Johnny's funeral took place a few days later at the Baptist Church—the very place where Mom and Dad had met, fallen in love, and exchanged vows with dreams of a bright and happy future. That same church now echoed with the quiet sobs of family and friends mourning a life that barely had a chance to begin.

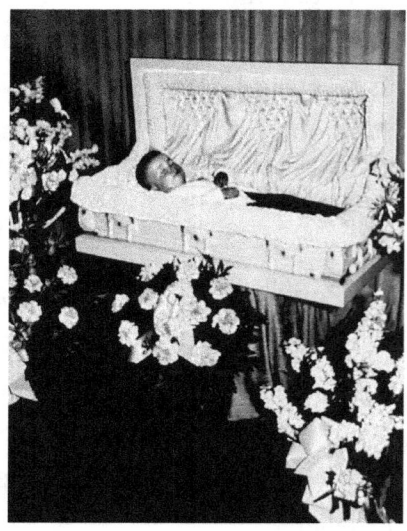

Johnny's funeral—photos to remember the child and brother who left too soon

Photos were taken—not out of vanity, but necessity. Nine black-and-white images: a tiny casket, sprays of flowers, and the small frame of a boy, now only the quiet echo of who he was. My grandparents knew that someday, those pictures would be the only way my parents could be part of their son's final moments. Those nine photos now rest in an album that no one ever really wants to open—what may be the saddest little collection of images in our family.

Johnny was laid to rest among other Jones and Dillen family members in the Camden Cemetery. And even now, decades later, my parents can't stand at his gravesite without tears. I've stood there with them. The ache never went away; it simply folded itself into their souls.

What haunted them the most was the unbearable irony: Mom and Dad had said goodbye to Johnny for what they believed would be just a short time. A couple of months at most. A temporary arrangement. They had no way of knowing it would be forever. No one ever expects that the last hug is the last.

There are moments in life that split time in two—before, and after. For our family, January 20, 1957, was one of those moments.

In the days that followed, my mother's health declined. She was hospitalized in early February, physically depleted, emotionally shattered, and nine months pregnant. No one knew what would come next. But life, in its cruel but mysterious way, continued.

In the shadow of tragedy, Steve's journey—fragile and full of hurdles—was just beginning. A child who had once struggled to see had been given the tools to explore his world. But the cost of that new beginning came with unimaginable loss. A brother he would never grow up beside. A grief he could not name, but that would follow him quietly.

Love Never Ends

For my parents—so young, so brave, and already worn thin—the road ahead was steep. For months, they stumbled through their sorrow, often holding each other up with trembling arms. Grief seeped into their marriage like water through cracked plaster: the self-blaming, the unspoken *what ifs,* the silences heavy with absence. Yet even in their weakness, they kept walking. For Steve. For the new baby coming.

In ways only heaven can explain, God extended to them over the years the quiet gift of grace—just enough strength at needed times for their next steps, just enough comfort to remind them that Johnny was not lost, but safely in the care of angels. That promise of reunion—that one day the whole family would be together again in a place where death and sorrow cannot enter—was the thread that stitched their hearts back together.

Fifty years later, they would be called to walk that road again. This time, they laid Steve to rest. In his grief, my father returned to the little grave where Johnny had been buried so long ago. Beside him stood Mom and her mother, my grandma Eva. The weight of both losses pressed hard upon him, and through tears, he whispered what he had carried in silence about Johnny for decades: "I thought it would get easier over time." Gently, with the wisdom of her own broken heart, Grandma replied, "Honey, it never gets any easier." She would know. She had buried four children of her own.

Johnny's short life carved a permanent place in my parents' hearts, as did Steve's. Their absence was real, but so was their presence—in memory, in love, in the hope of eternity.

As I wrote at the beginning of this book, "When someone you love dies, grief doesn't disappear. It simply changes shape. It walks beside you—softens, sharpens, shifts—but it always stays. And that's okay. What matters most is what you do with it."

My parents knew that truth all too well. They carried their grief, yes—but they also carried faith. And through that faith, they discovered that even in sorrow, love never ends.

Joy Comes in the Morning

On February 7, 1957, after everything she had endured—after every sob and sleepless night in that Army hospital grieving the loss of her baby boy, Johnny—my mother gave birth to a baby girl. They named her Susan Diana. And in that moment, Psalm 30:5 became flesh and blood: "Weeping may endure for a night, but joy comes in the morning" (New International Bible).

For my mother, it was literal. Her arms, once empty, were filled again. Not in replacement, never that—but in redemption. In grace.

And so, through agony and awe, a new chapter began.

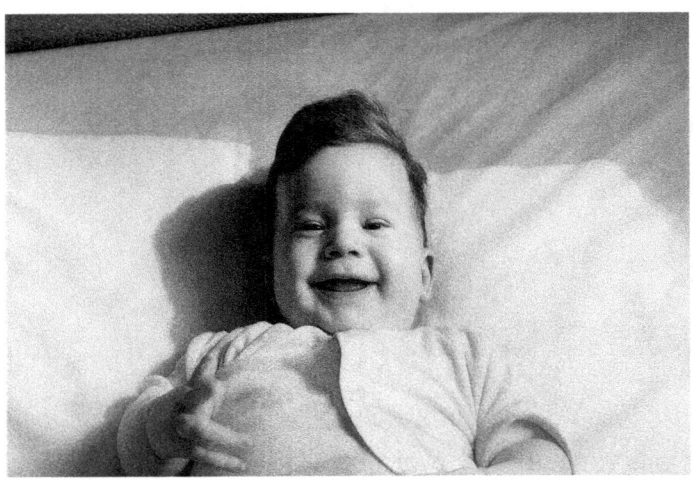

Baby Stuart—making an entrance big and loud enough to be remembered by Steve

Steve, at two and a half, didn't remember Johnny. He also wouldn't remember Susan's arrival, nor the birth of another sibling, Scott, eleven months later, on January 4, 1958. He didn't remember that Mom experienced another heartbreaking loss—a miscarriage after Scott. But Steve wouldn't forget—who among us could—March 28, 1961, the day I arrived. (Well, my siblings may have tried.)

Years later, I asked Steve if he remembered when Susan and Scott were brought home to the family. He didn't. I asked if he remembered when Mom and Dad brought me home, given that he was almost seven years old at the time. He said, "Yeah... yuyuyu, you were fffat and loud." Thanks, Steve. I was indeed; nine pounds of screeching baby boy—the heavyweight champion of family entrances. Ta-dah!

At this point, Mom emphatically declared the family complete. No more babies. No more "urges." Dad had to keep his hands to himself.

It was eighteen years later—but the family grew again—despite no more pregnancies!

It was 1979, and our family chose to grow once again—not by biology this time, but by heart. That year, we met Sudabeh (Sudi) Shoja, born in 1956 in Tehran, Iran, who had just arrived at Purdue

University as a graduate student in civil engineering. Our connection to her came through the international student ministry of First Baptist Church in Lafayette, Indiana—a place where students far from home often found community, friendship, and, in Sudi's case, an American family connection.

The timing of her arrival was anything but simple. Relations between the United States and Iran had reached a breaking point under Ayatollah Khomeini's new Islamic Republic. In 1979, 66 Americans were taken hostage in Tehran, and those Iranians living in America were suddenly viewed with suspicion by both nations—suspect here for their nationality, and suspect there for being too close to "the West" (Encyclopedia Britannica, 2025). For Sudi, the danger was real and terrifying. Returning to Iran after graduation meant imprisonment, or worse. Staying in the United States required legal protection, and my parents stepped in to ensure her student visa would not expire.

By 1982, Sudi and her little daughter, Salma, were formally adopted into our family. Though she never shared a childhood with Steve—he was twenty-five when they met, and she was twenty-three—Sudi quickly became his sister in every way that mattered. She came to know him not as a diagnosis or a set of limitations, but as a brother

Sudi and Salma—adding new chapters to our family story

to love. And Steve, true to form, welcomed her and Salma with the uncomplicated acceptance that was his gift to us all.

When I told her I was writing about Steve's life, Sudi said, "I am so happy you've embarked on writing his story. I think it is so important! It was definitely a learning experience for me to watch him, along with Mom and Dad, and all of you wanting to take care of him. I always thought how happy he must have been inside because of his sense of humor and the fact that he never complained. He always had a positive outlook."

She knew him pretty well.

Quiet Strength, Radiant Smile

Steve's early childhood was anything but stable. He bounced between Army bases, trailer homes, and family houses. By the time he was seven, he had already lost one brother, then gained a sister and two more brothers.. Yet through it all, he remained uniquely Steve. Quiet. Sweet. Resilient. He didn't tantrum. He didn't demand. And when he finally got his first pair of thick, coke-bottle glasses, his whole world opened up.

That's the story of Steve's early years in a nutshell: he didn't know what he was lacking—until someone gave him the tools to thrive. And then he smiled. He smiled a lot.

That smile would accompany him through a lifetime of challenges, yet also through moments of radiant joy, infectious humor, and flashes of unexpected brilliance. Long before his own schooling had officially begun, he was already teaching—quietly, joyfully, and in ways no one could forget. And always, everything we did was for the love of Stephen.

CHAPTER 6

JUST SIBLINGS, FOREVER CHANGED

Every child is a different kind of flower, and all together,
they make this world a beautiful garden.

— *Anonymous*

No Manual, Just Mom and Dad

In the background—and oftentimes the foreground—Steve's differences demanded something more from us, his siblings. Not in a burdened, obligatory way. Rather, in a quiet, natural, this-is-just-how-it-is kind of way. We didn't make a family plan or form a sibling strategy committee. We just... showed up. Like kids do. Like family does.

The Fab Four: Steve, Susan, Scott, and Stuart—looking angelic, but really co-conspirators and partners in crime from time to time

"The role of a sibling in the life of a person with an intellectual and developmental disability is as complex as it is meaningful. Siblings can be friends, confidants, and caregivers. Whatever their role, a sibling is a unique person in the life of someone with IDD" (The Arc, 2025).

When I came across that quote, I had to pause and reread it. Not because it was profound—though it is—but because it made me realize the entire time we were going up, we were doing something profound without even realizing it. Growing up, my sister Susan, my brother Scott, and I didn't call ourselves Steve's caregivers, advocates, educators, or allies. We were just siblings. We played together, argued over who got the front seat, blamed each other when things broke, and occasionally tried to drown each other at the local pool (the usual sibling stuff).

Our adopted sister, Sudi, hadn't grown up alongside Steve, but you wouldn't have known it. She quickly became one of his champions, too, jumping into the current of our lives as though she'd always been there. She had a heart tuned to the same frequency, and Steve knew it.

My father once told me, "Steve had a big advantage growing up because he had brothers and a sister. He learned many

Susan and Steve—siblings and lifelong buddies

things because you kids taught him." At the time, I didn't think of myself as a teacher. None of us did. But in hindsight, he was right. We were the ones there in the quiet moments—in the in-between times, the transitions, the ordinary routines. And in those moments, we became Steve's unofficial classroom. We taught him how to be silly, how to take a joke, how to endure a sibling prank, and how to give one right back. And he taught us patience, perspective, and how to laugh at ourselves when life didn't go as planned.

Back in those days, there were no support groups for siblings. No Zoom therapy. No handouts from the school counselor titled *So You Have a Brother with a Disability*. We had no concept of "sibling burden" or "coping tools." We had each other. And we had two parents who, to their immense credit, didn't just support Steve—

they supported all of us. They didn't let Steve's needs eclipse ours, and they didn't let us get lost in his shadow.

Guess who's not in this picture? Yep—me, likely staging a one-person rebellion [sigh]

Looking back now, I realize how much our understanding of Steve and his disability was shaped by our parents' approach. They never pitied him. They never limited him. They never apologized for him. They loved him exactly as he was and expected the world to follow suit. And so we did, too.

That kind of modeling is powerful. When you grow up in a home that sees disability not as a tragedy but as a difference to be respected, you don't need to be convinced to love your sibling. You just do. You don't view him as "special" in the condescending, whisper-it-in-a-hallway kind of way. He's just your brother. Sometimes annoying. Sometimes hilarious. Always there.

Santa's got some convincing to do—Susan and Steve are unimpressed, but Scott's making sure his name stays on the Good List

There's a fancy psychological word for what happens to siblings like us: parentification. It means that kids often take on grown-up responsibilities when there's a sibling who needs more care. We didn't know the word, but we knew the feeling. We carried the responsibility without calling it by name. And yes, it had ripple effects.

"As young adults," psychologist Rachel Landman (2020) noted, "siblings may struggle to understand how much caretaking is normal in a relationship or a marriage after taking on so much caregiving as children." If you ask me, that's spot on. Each of us—Susan, Scott, and I— took that caretaking mindset into our adult lives, whether we realized it or not. Into our friendships, our parenting, and even our marriages.

But we weren't just caretakers. We were kids, too. We asked questions—not aloud, but internally, when the house was quiet and nobody else was looking: Why did Steve have to be born this way? Could I have a child like him? Who will take care of him when Mom and Dad are gone? Those questions aged us. They changed the way we saw the world. They made us more mature and more vulnerable. We had to think about things our peers never considered.

And yet, we also swam. A lot.

Wrinkled, over-chlorinated, and slightly disoriented—again, where the hell was I? As kids, Susan and Scott tried to convince me I was adopted, which made me cry—maybe they were right after all

We swam at the over-chlorinated Edgelea pool, just a few blocks from our house on Fairwood Drive. Sometimes we would swim at Columbian Park. Four quarters bought all four of us an afternoon of glorious, water-logged chaos, with a hundred other kids all screaming like they were auditioning for a sitcom. Sometimes we had no adult supervision—can you imagine? And most of the time, it was pure fun.

Until it wasn't.

One day, when we were older, two boys took an interest in Steve— not the good kind. They followed him around in the water, snickering and scheming. Their plan? Dunk him. Hold him under. Harass the different kid for sport. It was almost like a reflex—Steve was vulnerable, so they encircled him, preparing to pounce.

Thankfully, Susan saw it before it happened. She marched over to Scott and me and ordered a retreat. We grumbled. We had just started to wrinkle. But we obeyed. We left. Steve was safe—because Susan saw what could've happened, and acted.

This was classic Susan.

Susan Diana: Sister, Shield, and Softie (with a Side of Sass)

Of all of us, Susan was the closest to Steve in age—just two and a half years behind— and, in many ways, the closest in soul. She was the only girl in a house full of brothers, which meant two things: (1) she never got a moment's peace, and (2) she developed a sixth sense for incoming nonsense. She had to. It was self-preservation. Living in a boy-brained world where conversations involved sound effects, injuries, and too much testosterone, Susan stood her ground with a clarinet in one hand and a deadpan truth in the other.

As you recall, she was born in North Carolina while Dad was stationed at Fort Bragg for Army duty, making her the only non-Hoosier among us—proof that irony runs in the family. Even as a kid, she had Mom's loud, contagious laugh—one of those unstoppable belly laughs that could change the chemical makeup of a room. It was the kind of laugh that made you feel like whatever dumb thing you said was actually hilarious, which worked out nicely for those of us who lived to push buttons.

She was a pretty girl—and I mean that in the objective sense. Boys noticed her, and Susan noticed that they noticed. But she wasn't the type to be impressed by shallow charm. She could spot a phony from across the street and was not above calling him out with surgical precision. More than once, I saw some poor, unfortunate soul try to impress her, only to be mentally dismantled and sent packing with his self-esteem in a paper bag.

Despite that steely radar, Susan had the softest heart in the house. She felt everything deeply. She couldn't understand cruelty—not when it was aimed at Steve, not when it was aimed at me (which, okay, was occasionally warranted), and not when it bubbled up in everyday life. She was compassionate, caring, and attentive. The kind of person who remembered your pain even after you'd forgotten it, and then asked you about it three months later just to make sure you were okay.

Susan was always tuned in to what was going on—emotionally, socially, even spiritually. She could read people like novels, and she didn't mind skipping to the last chapter if it meant calling out your bad behavior before you acted on it. She was the family's official truth-teller, whether you asked for the truth or especially when you didn't.

Susan and Jon—still smiling, still standing strong, side by side

She was also Steve's fiercest protector. Sure, he was technically her big brother, but when it came to looking out for him, Susan was the one with the instinct to circle, growl, and pounce. She could see the setup coming before anyone else did—the mockery, the marginalizing, the petty slights—and she was already moving into position. She had a black belt in "Oh no you don't," and Steve knew it. So did the kids who dared pick on him.

And me? I found trouble like it was buy one, get one free. But Susan still had my back, even when I'd clearly earned whatever beating or consequence was on the horizon. Scott didn't get picked on. Steve didn't deserve it. I, however, was a walking cautionary tale. Still, Susan defended me like I was innocent until proven mouthy.

In the end, Susan was more than just our sister. She was a one-woman support team: part lioness, part therapist, part FBI profiler, part judge and jury. She could laugh, cry, call you out, and lift you up all in the same afternoon—and still have energy to belt out a Carpenters song with everything she had. She wasn't just the glue that held things together. She was the safety pin, double-sided tape, and industrial-strength thread all rolled into one.

And in our family growing up, that made her something close to sacred.

That was the rhythm of our sibling lives with Steve: see the threat, intervene early, keep him safe. Over and over again. In between those times, it was play, have fun, and avoid internal fights. We did everything we could, but protecting Steve wasn't always possible. We couldn't be there 24/7. Those were the times when cowards attacked an unarmed man.

What really got under our skin was also seeing other special needs kids get picked on or bullied, because to us, those kids were just as special as Steve. Like Susan and me, Scott didn't hesitate to jump in when he saw injustice. Once, he gave two boys a serious dressing down for teasing a kid named Steve Sanders—another Steve, quiet and kind-hearted, just like our Steve. Steve Sanders was in Scott's class, but the two Steves would eventually meet as employees at Home Hospital and become friends.

Life has a strange way of weaving connections. Scott didn't cross paths with Steve Sanders again after graduation—until more than thirty years later, at our brother Steve's funeral. It turned out that the two Steves had actually worked side by side in housekeeping at Home Hospital and St. Elizabeth. They'd built a friendship at work without ever realizing they both knew Scott. The dots just never quite connected.

At the funeral, Steve Sanders looked at Scott with a quiet understanding, like the pieces finally clicked. Sometimes, life's overlaps don't reveal themselves until the moment they matter most—two Steves, one hospital, one unexpected bond.

Scott Joseph: The Quiet Force

If Susan was the pretty one and I was the mouthy one, Scott was the golden child—literally. Tall, slender, movie-star handsome, with sun-bleached blonde hair, a voice like an FM radio DJ, and teeth so straight they should've paid him to be in dental brochures. If a Hollywood talent scout had ever gotten lost in Lafayette, Indiana, they would've stumbled upon Scott and thought they'd discovered the next Robert Redford. Meanwhile, I 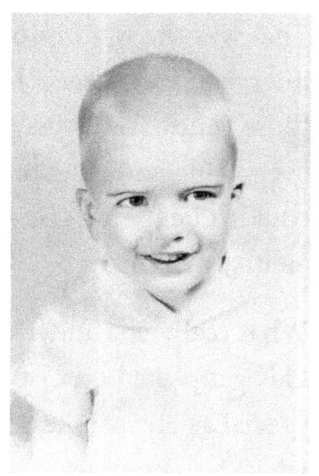 was just trying to keep up, armed with crazy crooked teeth and an unfortunate haircut that Dad kept giving me with those damn Army clippers.

But behind that leading-man exterior was someone more complex and far more grounded. Scott was the quiet one, which in our family was no small feat. Between my theatrical flair and Susan's social sparkle and teenage drama, someone had to choose silence just to get a word in. He wasn't shy, just selective—a discerning introvert who still enjoyed people, but had no interest in being the center of anything. Unless it involved wiring something, fixing something, or making sure someone (usually Steve) didn't get left behind.

He was Dad's son in all the best ways: strategic, practical, and a fixer. He watched, listened, and filed everything away like an internal hard drive you didn't even know was running. He worked side by side with Dad, fixing cars and solving household mysteries, not because he had to, but because he genuinely wanted to understand how the world worked—how things fit together. He played with Tinkertoys and Lincoln Logs because you could build things with them. He was a builder, not just of things, but of trust, consistency, and quiet loyalty.

Scott had more patience than the rest of us combined. He could endure nearly anything—until he couldn't. And when the fuse finally reached the dynamite, it was best to take cover. Loyalty to him wasn't optional; it was currency. Once betrayed, there was no coming back from it. That was part of his code—unspoken but unwavering.

He had a moral compass so finely tuned you could've used it to write a new gospel of decency. Honesty, ethics, integrity—these weren't vague virtues to Scott; they were the non-negotiables. And while partying was never his scene, he'd light up around a small circle of trusted friends, preferably while spinning Queen or Eagles records with perfect pitch and a full drum solo on the kitchen counter.

And then there was Steve. Scott was more than a brother—he was Steve's steady wingman. At church, in Boy Scouts, at school, on the golf course, on the sidelines—he was there, scanning the perimeter, making sure Steve wasn't forgotten, left out, or slighted. He didn't make a fuss about it; he just handled it. Inclusion wasn't a campaign to Scott—it was the baseline.

Scott and Donna—partners in love and life

He played in the backyard universe we all shared—where our backyard was a baseball diamond, the giant tree a lookout post, and our bedroom a race track, jungle gym, and Army battleground all in one. He joined us for church league volleyball and basketball, shared the laughs and bruises, and tried to keep our wild energy tethered to the earth, gently reminding us of our language and behavior.

I was the dreamer, and Scott the realist. Scott was the calm in the storm, the quiet leader, the principled brother who could fix your brakes, out-sing your tenor section, and pull you back to the moral center with nothing more than a raised eyebrow. He was a steadying force in Steve's life—and in mine. And if he didn't always speak first, you'd be wise to listen when he finally did.

Questions Without Answers

As we got older, so did our questions. They evolved from childhood worries—*Will Steve embarrass me in front of my friends?*—to teenage uncertainty—*Will people stop coming around if they meet him?*—to adult concerns—*Who will help Steve when Mom and Dad are gone? Will I have to be the one to step in? Can I handle it?*

When you have a sibling with a disability, your life unfolds with one foot in the present and one in the future. You're always scanning the horizon, wondering when the next big

The Fab Four (family edition) with our all-star cousins—Gaye and Jo Lynn standing proud in the center, Howard stealing the spotlight from the middle seat

responsibility will land in your lap. You learn to smile at parties and carry heavy thoughts at the same time. You become an expert in duality.

And you also become acutely aware of how cruel the world can be.

Steve was mocked. Stared at. Picked on. Tripped. Hit. Called names. Laughed at. Sometimes, we witnessed it. Sometimes we heard about it later. Sometimes the school called home—not because Steve had started anything, but because he'd been targeted again. I imagine Mom and Dad hated those calls.

Even at home, the discrimination seeped in. I remember kids asking me, "What's wrong with your brother?" as if I had a quick and easy answer tucked in my back pocket. I didn't know what to say. I was embarrassed—not by Steve, but by my lack of words. I'd sometimes mutter, "Oh, he was born retarded and has a skin problem," just to shut them up. It was a crude answer, and I wince now thinking about it—but I was a kid. I was flailing. No one had ever prepared me for that question. Unkind kids would then mock me, "Yah, well you're retarded too!"

Eventually, I outgrew the embarrassment, and the shame turned into strength. The stares didn't faze me. I stood taller next to Steve in public. But not every sibling gets there at the same pace. Some take longer to be proud. Some never fully do. That doesn't make them bad siblings—it just makes them human.

Disability invites judgment. It always has. But it also reveals character. Some people see a person like Steve and walk away. Others stay—and when they do, they become part of a sacred circle. A rare group who learns to value people not for what they can do, but for who they are.

Steve was different. He looked different. He sounded different. He moved different. But he also loved different—bigger, more openly, without condition. He didn't care what people thought. Maybe he didn't notice. Or maybe, heroically, he just didn't let it bother him.

A friend of mine once described siblings of kids with disabilities as "emotional co-pilots." That feels about right. We were never the ones steering the ship, but we were always in the cockpit, keeping an eye on things, ready to help land safely. That was true in childhood, and it has stayed with all of us as we grew up and started our own families.

Us rocking Christmas Day, 1966—no autographs, please

And though Steve is no longer with us, his life shaped ours. In the way we raised our kids. In the way we react when we see someone being mistreated. In the way we carry both pride and pain in the same breath.

Our brother taught us what courage looks like. What perseverance feels like. What love acts like when it's completely unfiltered.

We weren't perfect siblings. But we were present. We were consistent. And we were his.

That, in the end, was everything.

The Bank of Big Brother

A couple of years after Scott got his driver's license—and after he'd logged what felt like a few thousand miles chauffeuring himself around in Mom's and Dad's hand-me-down VW Beetle—he decided it was time to declare automotive independence. He wanted his own car. Something with a little more personality and a little less "smells like leaking gasoline." There was just one tiny problem: Scott's bank account had the financial strength of a wet tissue.

Enter Steve. Big brother. Quiet hero. Secret financier.

Caution: extreme fluff levels detected—may cause uncontrollable squealing

Steve knew what was up. He could smell that mix of desperation and Armor All from a mile away. So, one day, out of nowhere, Steve just said, "I'll loan you the money." Just like that—$400 straight from the Bank of Steve. No questions asked, no paperwork, no co-signer, not even a single, "Are you sure you're responsible enough to own a car and not end up in a ditch?" Just faith and brotherly love.

Now, Scott—being the ever-honest type (and slightly terrified of karmic retribution)—insisted on paying Steve back, with interest, no less. This was bold for a teenager making $1.90 an hour at whatever part-time job he could find. At that rate, he basically paid Steve back one quarter at a time. But true to his word, he did it.

Wowzers—who knew we had this level of fashion game in us?

There was no payment plan. No monthly statements. No menacing glances from Steve, wearing sunglasses and brass knuckles. Just trust. Steve never brought it up. Never reminded him. Just smiled and took whatever cash Scott scrounged together.

And Steve? He was proud. Proud to help his little brother get his first car. Proud to be the guy Scott came to for help. And probably too proud—because honestly, with interest rates at the time, he could've made out like a bandit if he'd charged 17.2 percent.

Then again, Steve wasn't in it for the profit. He was in it for the joy of watching Scott drive off into the sunset… in a car that may or may not have needed jumper cables every other day.

Just Siblings—But Forever Changed

All siblings of children with disabilities must find their own way of coping—and no, there's no "how-to" manual for that. Some dive into perfectionism. Others build thick skins. Many—like us—do both, and then some.

Ellen Braaten, Ph.D., who had a brother with Down syndrome, summed it up honestly, writing, "Sometimes it can lead to negative consequences, like feeling isolated or a need to be perfect to make up for the sibling's challenges. But there are also positive consequences... an increased capacity for empathy, greater tolerance for individual differences, and resiliency" (Braaten, 2025).

Left to right: Scott, Susan, Mom, Dad, Sudi, and me.
This is us—almost, wishing Steve were still here to make it whole

Forgive me if it sounds like I'm trying to make our family into a Disney movie—or a tragedy. We were neither. Scott, Susan, and I weren't victims, and we sure weren't saints. We were just born into a uniquely complicated and ultimately beautiful situation. And we were gifted—yes, truly gifted—with a brother who taught us more than any teacher, therapist, or textbook ever could.

Steve had intellectual and developmental disabilities. He also had a built-in radar for family tension and a relentless desire for peace. He was, perhaps surprisingly and hilariously, the peacemaker in our house.

You haven't lived until you've crammed four squirrely kids and two mildly desperate parents into a 1960s station wagon with no air conditioning on a July afternoon. Tempers flared. Elbows flew. Susan would screech, "Mom, he's looking at me," (referring to me, of course). And at least once per trip, Dad's voice would ring out from the front seat like a thunderclap:

"If I have to pull this car over, one of you is going to get it!"

That was no idle threat. But interestingly, it was never directed at Steve. He wasn't a pot-stirrer. He rolled his eyes, tuned out the chaos, and looked out the window like a Zen monk on a pilgrimage. It's not that he didn't get disciplined—Dad's belt didn't discriminate—but Steve rarely provoked.

We were typical siblings—we picked on each other, fought, made up, and fought again. Occasionally, I channeled my inner spider monkey and launched myself at Susan for some unknown crime like stealing my cereal toy. And there Steve would be, dragging us apart—not out of frustration, but a sincere desire for harmony. He was non-aggressive, non-confrontational, and, to our surprise, incredibly effective at conflict resolution for someone who didn't speak in paragraphs.

The Fence-Hopping Pacifist: Steve to the Rescue

Steve wasn't the kind of guy who went looking for trouble, but if trouble came knocking on his little brother's door, Steve answered with gusto. He was, as we liked to call him, a pacifist protector. Think Gandhi... if Gandhi could hurdle a backyard fence and scare the pants off a couple of bullies.

Let's be honest—when I was a kid, I had a mouth that could talk its way into a headlock in 30 seconds flat. I had a talent for flipping switches and lighting fuses. So it wasn't all that surprising when one day, after I'd been running my mouth like a broken fire hydrant, a couple of neighborhood boys decided it was time to teach me the ancient art of silence—via shoves and a flying tackle.

Turkey Run State Park never knew what hit it—enter the Fab Four

Down I went, right on the side of our house, limbs flailing, dignity crumpled.

Steve, who'd been peacefully hanging out in the backyard playing catch with Dad—probably minding his own business and contemplating the mysteries of the universe—saw me get leveled.

And something in him clicked. Before Dad could even process what was happening, Steve shot off like a linebacker on a mission from heaven.

He jumped the fence. Not climbed. Jumped. Like an Olympic hurdler fueled by justice and big-brotherly instinct.

The bullies looked up from their prize (me, in the dirt) and saw an indignant freight train of fury coming right at them. Steve didn't throw a punch. He didn't yell. He just stood there, tall, quiet, and built like a refrigerator with feelings. That was enough.

Those kids ran like they'd seen a ghost—or at least a very determined older brother who wasn't having it today.

Dad was stunned. I was dusty. Steve went right back to the backyard like nothing happened. Just another day being Steve: peace-loving protector, fence-hopping superhero, and the guy who always had your back—even when you kind of deserved what you got.

The Sibling Effect: What Steve Taught Us That Research Missed

Our memories aren't made up of diagnoses or therapy appointments. They're made up of pear tree climbing (Susan stopped after biting into a wormy one—so gross), skateboarding down steep driveways, and neighborhood bike rides where Steve, being built like a linebacker, would hoist Susan over his shoulder like she was a grain sack headed to market. We fought, sure. But mostly, we played.

And we cared. For each other, yes—but especially for Steve. Watching the world's intolerance, ignorance, and casual cruelty toward him made us see everything differently. We learned to love deeply, to advocate fiercely, and to protect those who couldn't protect themselves.

Is it just me, or do I (far right) look like a young Austin Powers?

Back in the 1960s and '70s, researchers classified siblings of children with disabilities as a "disadvantaged population." That's a strange label. We never felt disadvantaged because of Steve— maybe misunderstood by a few clueless adults and classmates, but not disadvantaged. More recent research has thankfully caught up, suggesting that when siblings participate in caregiving or education, it leads to growth for both the sibling and the child with disabilities (Shivers & Plavnick, 2014).

Our parents, of course, didn't need a journal article to tell them that. They just did it based on what their parents did to them. They included us in Steve's life, trusted us, and showed us how to raise each other up. There wasn't much guidance back then. No podcasts, blogs, YouTube, or support groups—just phone calls to teachers, letters from specialists, and the slow grind of learning through trial and error.

Later research adopted a more positive tone, highlighting how siblings often grow up to be more adaptable, empathetic, and tolerant (Dykens, 2006). Check. Check. Check. And yes, there are darker shades too—some studies suggest we're more prone to anxiety, depression, or peer struggles (Goudie et al., 2013). Those challenges haven't been strangers in our lives, but they haven't been dictators either.

Want more research? (Of course you do—who doesn't love a literature review in the middle of a memoir?) Turns out, most siblings of individuals with disabilities don't end up in helping professions (Taylor & Shivers, 2011). Funny—we missed that memo. Susan became a psychologist. Helping profession. I went into Christian ministry and later, higher education. Helping professions. And Scott? Well, he did what research told him to do. He became a construction manager. You could argue he just preferred complex building projects over complex personal issues. Still counts.

Ah, the 1970s—a kaleidoscope of groovy vibes, bold styles, leisure suits, and endless good times. Groovy, man

What research often doesn't highlight enough is what we feel: that our lives are richer, deeper, and more meaningful because of Steve. He didn't "inspire" us in a corny, made-for-TV way. He shaped us— flaws and all—into people who understand what it means to love without condition, to respect without exceptions, and to find purpose in imperfection. As Braaten wrote, it's about "an appreciation for the diversity of humanity. A deep sense of loyalty. An opportunity to learn to love someone because of their imperfections" (Braaten, 2025).

We didn't treat Steve like he was "special" in that euphemistic, patronizing sense. We just treated him like our brother. Sometimes we were kind, sometimes we were brats. We shared snacks, secrets, and the occasional headlock. But we always expected others to treat him with respect—and woe to the playground punk who didn't.

Sadly, it's now just the Fab Three. Left to right: Scott, Susan, and me— still keeping the spirit alive

To us, Steve wasn't defined by his disabilities. He was defined by his difference, and that difference made him unforgettable.

The Guilt That Shouldn't Be There (But Sometimes Still Is)

Some people are born to be saints. Others are drafted. I, for one, wasn't handed a halo at birth or a clipboard by a nonprofit recruiter in the hospital nursery. But growing up as Steve's sibling, I've often asked myself: *Should I have done more? Should I be doing more?*

Not because anyone in my family told me to. Not even Steve, who would've preferred I become a Kung Fu master, Cubs ballplayer, or chess aficionado—preferably all three. But because society sometimes sneaks a silent script into your backpack as a sibling of someone with

126

special needs: *You, dear sibling, are now an auxiliary member of the caregiving corps. Report to duty—preferably unpaid, and with a good attitude.*

The truth? I didn't make disability support my full-time career. I've helped. I've volunteered. I've filled out enough paperwork to wallpaper a small bathroom and stepped in during more than a few quiet, behind-the-scenes meltdowns. But sometimes, I still feel like the sibling credential comes with a punch card of guilt. *Did I show up enough? Speak up enough? Fight the good fight often enough?*

Making Christmas memories with Mom and Dad—Terri and I love this annual Yuletide tradition

And yet, experts would gently (and firmly) remind me—and maybe you too, fellow siblings—that this guilt is not only unnecessary, it's unhelpful.

Researchers like Jürgens and Heston (2018) explain that siblings of people with intellectual and developmental disabilities navigate a lifelong balance of love, responsibility, and self-definition. They say that some *are* drawn into careers in special education or advocacy; others support in quieter, more personal ways. Both paths are valid. One isn't more noble than the other. What matters most, they argue, is whether the sibling relationship is rooted in empathy, respect, and shared humanity.

And if that isn't enough to release us from the quest for sainthood, Stoneman (2005) offers a helping hand. Her research reminds us that there is no one-size-fits-all sibling experience. The ways siblings cope, contribute, or find meaning are as diverse as families themselves. To paraphrase her gently: Not every sibling is meant to wear a cape—or a staff badge at a disability agency.

Some of us help in loud, visible ways. Others show up in the quiet hours, behind the scenes, with food, car rides, heartfelt belly laughs, and big hugs. That matters. That *counts*.

So yes, I've had pangs of guilt—those "I could've done more" moments that drift through the heart like unwanted pop-up ads. But when I catch myself in that spiral, I try to remember something important: Steve never asked me to be an angel with a name tag. He just needed a friend.

And I'd like to think I was that. Still am. Even on the days when I didn't show up with a clipboard.

Popcorn, Potatoes, and Pixie Dust

Time didn't weaken our bond with Steve—it deepened it. As adults, we intentionally showed up—each carved out our own "Steve time," precious little pockets of connection that reminded us of what really mattered.

We came to treasure those rare one-on-one moments with Steve like gold—or maybe more like a tub of buttered popcorn at the movies: warm, nostalgic, and gone way too soon. I got to live with him for a year during college, and let me tell you, nothing

Steve (middle left) at Disney World, bracing for a plunge with his sister Susan (front left) and nephews David and Ben close by

128

says roommate "bonding" like chowing down on a Domino's pizza while watching an Arnold Schwarzenegger action flick on a tiny TV with questionable reception.

Scott had his time, too—culinary time. He taught Steve the sacred art of microwaving a baked potato and dousing it in so much butter and sour cream it crossed the line from snack to full-blown dairy delivery system. Steve was hooked for life.

And Susan? She went all out—sweeping Steve into the magical chaos of Disney World with her boys, Matt, David, and Ben, where Steve powered his way through roller coasters, mouse ears, and possibly a mild case of whiplash just to keep up with his nephews.

Each of us had our "Steve time"—not often enough, but always unforgettable. These were the moments that stitched us together as young siblings and older adults, deepened our love, and reminded us just how lucky we were to call him ours.

How we all wish we could have those times again.

Adventures with Steve: Hold Onto Your Hat!

Steve was the kind of guy who packed joy like luggage and brought it to every family gathering—especially the epic ones. Sure, he was always there for the holidays, but when it came to real-deal, memory-making, map-worthy adventures, Steve wasn't just invited—he was essential gear. Not because anyone felt sorry for the "poor disabled kid," but because we knew a secret: Steve turned every trip into something more. More laughter. More magic. More unexpected memories.

Stuart (left) and Steve—serious fishermen, serious sunglasses and hat, questionable bait

He was the undefeated champion of the annual Jones Farm Picnic—our own Hoosier Olympics. The croquet and softball games were fierce, the food was bottomless, and the homemade ice cream was churned with the same dedication people reserve for sacred rituals. Steve? He brought the joy and full belly laughs, playing with grit and determination like this was the seventh game of the World Series.

State parks like Turkey Run and Spring Mill became our family's wild frontiers. We weren't just hiking—we were explorers! Lewis and Clark had nothing on us. (He was a Boy Scout after all.) With Steve in the lead, we'd trek up hills, through ravines, ride bikes like daredevils, and occasionally saddle up for a horseback adventure that was one part *Bonanza* and one part *Blazing Saddles*.

Green Lake, Wisconsin, was where spiritual retreat met outdoor mayhem. We'd go to the American Baptist Assembly almost every year. Steve had a knack for balancing quiet moments of prayer and outdoor vesper services with rowdy fishing expeditions and unmarked hiking trails that felt one prayer away from poison ivy. He could commune with God and catch a smallmouth bass in the same afternoon.

Then there was that one epic week in Arkansas—a legendary Jones family getaway that practically needed its own soundtrack and travel documentary. Swimming, fishing, campfires, boating on the lake—and yes, letting Steve steer the pontoon boat. Dad nearly had a heart palpitation watching him take the wheel, but Uncle Gordon just waved him off and said, "Relax! There's nothing to hit in open water!" And there wasn't… unless you count Steve's ego inflating as he sailed us across the lake like a sea captain born of Midwestern soil.

Wrigley Field? Oh, Steve was there with the rest of us, Cubs cap on, hot dogs and shelled peanuts in hand. That is, until one year, when we scored front-row seats in the upper deck, directly above the abyss of the lower level. Turns out, Steve had a fear of heights no one knew about, not even Mom or Dad. He held onto that railing in front of him like it was the only thing keeping him from plummeting into Lake Michigan. He didn't let go until the 7th-inning

Singing a solo at an outdoor vespers service at Green Lake—as for whether I could actually sing, only the brave worshippers in attendance could answer that

stretch—and even then, he sang "Take Me Out to the Ball Game" with white knuckles.

If you invited Steve to a dramatic live reading of the county sewer ordinances at the town hall, he'd go—probably bring snacks and applaud at the end. All you had to say was, "Hey Steve, want to go?" and you could barely finish the sentence before he was in the car. He didn't care where—we could've been headed to Indiana Beach, the church rummage sale, or a backyard bonfire with s'mores and mosquito bites. If there was something to do, Steve was doing it.

Especially those Kings Island and Bunker Hill airshow trips organized by the hospital crew where he worked for many years— Steve was first in line. Roller coasters, giant swings, air shows, funnel cakes, you name it. He was in. Hands up. Hair blowing in the wind. Laughing later like the death-defying rides didn't really scare him, even though his face was white and he was trying to hold down his lunch. He'd do it again, however, in a heartbeat, if you asked him.

Adventure? Hell, yes.

And none of us had any idea Steve would walk down the marriage aisle—twice, in fact. But looking back, the seeds of his longing for companionship were already there.

The Gift We Never Asked For

Marla Murasko, a mother of a child with disabilities, wrote a poem that says what I've perhaps struggled to put into words. It's called "*Special,*" and it goes like this (Murasko, n.d.):

Although my needs may be special,

    I may not walk and run so fast.

Although my needs may be special,

    I may talk a little funny.

Although my needs may be special,

    I love and want just like you.

Although my needs may be special,

    I may look a little different.

Although my needs may be special,

    I'm just as curious and scared.

Although my needs may be special,

    I may learn and read a little slower.

Although my needs may be special,

    I AM SPECIAL, I'm a child of God.
    like you.

Steve was special. Not because he had needs, but because he met our needs, too. He made us better. Not perfect. Just… better. More patient. More open. More human.

And that's a gift we never asked for—but would never trade.

It was because of the love of Stephen.

Steve (left) and his trusty wingman Scott (right)—
holding down the fort at a family gathering

The shield and the softie—Susan (right) at another family gathering
(I told you Steve attacked his food)

CHAPTER 7

WHERE THE ROAD WASN'T PAVED: EDUCATING STEVE

Every child deserves a champion—an adult who will never give up on them, who understands the power of connection and insists that they become the best they can possibly be.

— Rita Pierson

Steve's Early Educational Years — Pioneering the Path for Possibility

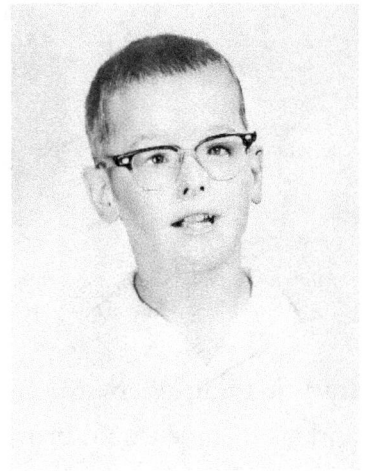

While most kids were worrying about losing their #2 pencils, spilling Elmer's glue, or choosing the right Crayola crayons, Steve was quietly preparing to do something far more revolutionary: he was about to attend school—despite a system that, for all its chalkboards and cheerleading, was absolutely not built for him.

You see, for many years, students with disabilities weren't just overlooked by public education—they were locked out. Literally. Homeschooled children with disabilities were considered lucky. Others were institutionalized, hidden from the world in facilities more focused on containment than learning, where "education" meant being clothed and occasionally not yelled at (Access Press Staff, 2025). The education system offered about as much for children with intellectual and developmental disabilities as a snow globe offers directions—pretty, maybe, but ultimately going nowhere.

In Indiana, things were... complicated. In 1931, the state passed a law requiring special education, decades before it was a national priority (Indiana Disability History Project, 2025). Progressive, right? Well, kind of. Having a law on the books is one thing. Acting on it is another. Indiana dutifully filed that law somewhere between "Prohibition repeal" and "Things We'll Get to Eventually."

Mom holds baby Susan, Steve stands proudly in the center, and Dad cradles little Scott—
I wasn't born yet, which is why I'm missing this time

Into this murky environment was born Steve—premature in body and, as history would prove, far too early for the world to be ready for someone like him. By the late 1950s, Steve was attending school before "special education" had become the structured, legally backed, resource-supported field we recognize today. Back then, it was more like educational alchemy: mix one part hope, two parts untrained enthusiasm, and a dash of trial-and-error, and maybe—just maybe—a child would learn something. Steve was among the first test subjects in this well-meaning, underfunded experiment.

In 1959, five-year-old Steve was ready for kindergarten in Camden, Indiana. Unfortunately, Camden wasn't ready for Steve. The concept of individualized education plans (IEPs), adaptive curricula, or accessible classrooms hadn't arrived yet—not in Camden, not in Indiana, not even in Washington, D.C. Most children like Steve were either shuffled into state hospitals ("custodial at best," said historians with grim understatement) or ignored altogether (2025).

But Steve had an edge: parents who weren't ready to accept the unacceptable.

Mrs. Kendall's 1960–61 kindergarten class—Steve sits in the top row, second from the left, ready to take on the world with a shy smile and sturdy glasses

They enrolled him in Camden Elementary, where Mrs. Malinda Kendall—armed with kindness, patience, and exactly zero training in special education—welcomed Steve into her kindergarten class of 24 neurotypical children. She was told he was "slow," which, at the time, was the best anyone could come up with. Labels were vague, and the resources were vaguer. While the other kids painted with their fingers and sang the days of the week, Steve struggled to understand what a week was. And Mrs. Kendall, despite her good heart, couldn't transform herself into a full-time special educator on the fly.

At year's end, she gently suggested Steve repeat kindergarten. My parents, swallowing a dose of disappointment, agreed. But when, after a second year, Mrs. Kendall recommended a third round of kindergarten, my parents decided to pivot—because even in 1961, they knew that kindergarten wasn't meant to be a lifelong commitment.

Then fate tossed them a headline.

In nearby Lafayette, they read about new educational efforts for children with intellectual and developmental disabilities. Imagine their hope as they discovered the 1931 law requiring special classes for students "retarded in mental development"— language that today feels barbaric, but at the time was considered clinical. For once, Indiana had been ahead of the curve, acknowledging that these children had a right to instruction tailored to their needs (2025).

Of course, just because something's written into law doesn't mean it's followed. And schools across Indiana—from the cornfields of Carroll County to the steel of South Bend—mostly did what people do best when faced with inconvenient mandates: nothing.

Why? Well, for starters, no one had the training. Colleges weren't offering special education degrees in the '30s or even the '50s except for Indiana State Normal Teachers College (now known as Indiana State University). It would take institutions like Ball State and Purdue years to build special education into their curriculum. Secondly—and let's be blunt here—there was bigotry. The idea of spending public funds on "defective" children didn't sit well with certain gatekeepers of public education. So instead of support, most children with IDD received rejection, pity, or institutionalization.

But 1961 marked a turning point for Steve. That same year, Purdue University's Department of Education began experimenting with new approaches to teaching children with intellectual and developmental disabilities, led by psychology professor Dr. Newell C. Kephart. His research center—eventually called the Purdue Achievement Center for Children—was born out of a grant, a house donated by the Purdue Foundation, and a belief that these children could learn. His work wasn't just academic—it was revolutionary.

Dr. Newell C. Kephart—pioneer in special education and child development. Photo credit: The Achievement Center for Children and Purdue University Archives and Special Collections

Kephart's team of professors, therapists, and graduate students worked with around 170 students annually, all with varying degrees of intellectual disability. His methods were experimental, hopeful, and wildly optimistic by 1960s standards. Kephart believed that 60–80 percent of his students could eventually live semi-independent lives (Purdue Alumnus, 1964, November 1). He'd already written *The Slow Learner in the Classroom* (1960), a seminal work in the field. In a world still referring to these kids as "retarded," Kephart was saying: they are teachable. They have potential. They matter.

My parents, moved by this possibility and driven by the kind of stubborn love that defines parenthood, packed up our family and relocated from Camden to Lafayette—26 miles southwest, and 50 years into the future.

We squeezed into a small townhouse on 26th Street. Dad landed a job at Fairfield Manufacturing thanks to his father-in-law, my Grandpa John. Mom took charge of the household. I had just arrived that March—too young to remember it, but old enough now to appreciate its significance.

Purdue promised Steve a spot—but not right away. Their program was full, so they pointed my parents to another option: the Wabash Center. Founded in 1953 in the basement of an unfinished United Pentecostal Church, this grassroots institution was formed by parents who simply refused to accept the fate society assigned to their children.

It started with a newspaper ad from two local families. Eleven students. One rented teacher. And a dream.

Over time, the Wabash Center grew, moved, expanded, and became a beacon of hope in a world that still largely ignored children like Steve. While it lacked trained special education professionals, it made up for it with fierce commitment. Volunteers and parents pooled resources, time, and wisdom—often with nothing more than a chalkboard, a folding chair, and a prayer.

James R. Tilton, Wabash Center's long-serving executive director, recalled that physicians back then routinely advised parents to institutionalize their children and "not to hope for much" (Long, 2023). But hope, as it turns out, is not so easily extinguished.

The cost of enrollment was $90 a month—a financial strain, but my parents didn't flinch. Because Steve deserved a chance. He wasn't just receiving an education. He was quietly helping to build the very system that would later become his legacy: IDEA, IEPs, inclusion, dignity.

Steve was never given the advantages we now consider essential for children with special needs. But his journey—from Camden's kindergarten rooms to Lafayette's pioneering programs—mirrors the broader arc of America's conscience finally waking up. He was a forerunner, a pathfinder, a quiet rebel in a world that once called him "retarded" but could never call him defeated.

And so, with a glue stick in hand and crayons at the ready, Steve began walking a road that hadn't yet been paved—so that someday, other children wouldn't have to walk it alone.

Steve, the System, and the Spark of Something Better

In 1961, the concept of "special education" was about as advanced as a caveman's toolkit—primitive, limited, and mostly improvised with whatever was lying around. The Wabash Center had something far more valuable than sophisticated pedagogy. It had heart. Big-hearted, hope-fueled, and bravely underprepared, they welcomed eight-year-old Steve into their "school"—a term we'll use generously here.

At Wabash, there were no grade levels, no individualized education plans, no speech therapy sessions tucked into tidy pull-out schedules. Instead, all children, regardless of age, diagnosis, or previous education, were folded into one large classroom. It was less of a school and more of an educational petri dish—everyone learning together, often by trial and error.

Still, even this was more than most kids with disabilities had. According to the U.S. Department of Education, only one in six children with disabilities in the U.S. received any public education in 1961 (U.S. Department of Education, 2020). The others were often hidden away in institutions, deemed "untrainable," or politely (or not-so-politely) excluded from classrooms under state laws that barred access to those who were blind, deaf, mentally ill, or severely developmentally delayed.

While Steve faced cognitive challenges, he was not considered severely impaired. Instead, he was one of the "lucky" few labeled with that mid-century euphemism: "trainable mentally handicapped." You'll forgive us if we don't embroider that one on a pillow. But in those days, this label meant something powerful—it meant Steve was allowed in.

Still, after a year at Wabash Center, Mom and Dad sensed the limits of what the Center could offer. Despite their immense heart, Wabash couldn't yet provide the educational structure Steve needed to blossom. So began a desperate search—part parent-led IEP planning, part real estate scavenger hunt.

They'd heard whispers among other Wabash parents that James Murdock Elementary School had launched new special education classes for students with intellectual and developmental disabilities (IDD). And wouldn't you know it, their rental lease was almost up. Fate, or maybe divine bureaucracy, intervened. My parents found a rental listed next to Peerless Wire Company on Ferry Street—a house big enough for their growing family and just over a mile from their current place. They pounced on it. One might say it was the best thing to ever happen next to a wire factory. That's where I started my wild and wacky journey into this life.

By the fall of 1962, Steve was enrolled at Murdock Elementary in a bona fide special education classroom, surrounded by peers with similar challenges. He was now in a structured, consistent environment, thanks to his new teacher, Mrs. Taylor—a beacon of compassion and professionalism in a field still emerging from the educational Stone Age.

Mrs. Taylor knew what many did not: that while Steve struggled to match the academic pace of a typical third grader, he excelled in citizenship, kindness, and eagerness to please. She celebrated these traits, and for Steve, they became seeds of confidence. The whole tone of his education shifted—from chaotic to consistent, from ambiguous to intentional.

CERTIFICATE OF *Merit*

THIS CERTIFIES _STEPHEN JONES_

has been awarded this certificate for

CITIZENSHIP and _GOOD MANNERS_

Given at _MURDOCK_ *School*

Date _Dec. 4, 1962_

James French _Mrs. Taylor_
teacher

BECKLEY-CARDY COMPANY, CHICAGO.

Steve proudly received school recognition for his good manners and outstanding citizenship—a quiet moment that spoke volumes

As Murdock provided structure, Purdue University's Achievement Center for Children stepped in with a strategy. The Center, an experimental hub for both teaching and research, agreed to begin assessments and developmental support for Steve. Twice a week, my mother drove him the 10-mile round trip from Ferry Street so Purdue's specialists could work with him and—equally important— teach my folks how to support his learning at home.

It was a heady time. The Achievement Center was building the academic architecture for what would become special education as we know it. They weren't just helping children—they were training teachers, conducting research, and blazing trails. According to Dr. Kephart, one of the Center's guiding lights, the Center offered a "three-fold service: training teachers in this specialized educational field, providing services for retarded children and their parents, and conducting a research program to discover what more can be done for the handicapped child" (Achievement Center for Children, n.d.).

Now, a quick note on language: yes, "retarded" was the term of the time. It has since, quite appropriately, been retired. Words matter, as we learned in an earlier chapter, and we've evolved. Thank goodness.

As for Steve, my parents saw progress. He was still academically behind— by 1963, he had only achieved a first- grade level in reading and math— but he was moving forward. More importantly, the educational system was finally moving with him.

There was, however, a catch. The Achievement Center's strategies, while innovative, occasionally wandered into the realm of the questionable. For instance, Kephart insisted that "the first thing we do with all these children is to establish control. You get rapport much faster if you control the child than if you cajole him" (Achievement Center for Children, n.d.). In less scholarly terms: don't bother with connection—just bark orders. Control was king.

Parents, including mine, were trained to praise good behavior (a solid start), be stern (fair), yell as needed (questionable), and, if necessary, dole out punishments to "correct" non-compliance. These techniques were categorized under "a repertoire of techniques for presenting information in a myriad of ways" (Kephart, 1960). It sounds like a euphemism for "do what you must to get results," doesn't it?

Steve, gentle soul that he was, did not respond well to yelling or harsh treatment. Instead of motivating him, it shut him down. The more punitive the approach, the more Steve retreated emotionally and cognitively. Eventually, my parents had had enough. With no formal degrees, they marched into Purdue and told the experts (politely, I imagine, but firmly) to cut it out. Steve didn't need to be "controlled"—he needed to be understood.

Meanwhile, another philosophical rift emerged. The Achievement Center advised my Mom and Dad to focus all their efforts on him. After all, their other three children—Susan, Scott, and I—were "normal" and would presumably develop just fine on their own.

This idea didn't sit right with our folks. They loved Steve deeply, but they weren't about to sacrifice the growth and emotional well-being of their other three children on the altar of developmental theory. They decided to support all of us—and they did.

By this time, Steve's educational support team included teachers, professors, researchers, health professionals, and student teachers—

all committed to his growth. Most importantly, however, he had parents who trusted their instincts, questioned authority when necessary, and refused to let theoretical models dim the light of their son's potential.

Image credit: The Achievement Center for Children and Purdue University Archives and Special Collections. Used with permission

Steve's journey didn't follow a conventional path—but then again, conventions hadn't yet caught up to kids like Steve. He wasn't broken. He wasn't defective. He was differently wired—like the wire factory we lived next to—and deeply worthy of a world willing to meet him where he was.

Steve's Ascent – The Slow, Stubborn March Toward Inclusion

From the 1960s through the 1990s, the American education system underwent what one might generously call an "evolution" in how it treated students with IDD. And like most evolutions, it was slow, awkward, and often resistant to change—kind of like your grandparents finally figuring out how to use email or television streaming services.

The federal government had finally decided that children with disabilities deserved more than dusty corners and institutional walls. Programmatic winds began to shift away from separate, isolated facilities toward what educators began calling "mainstreaming." The goal? To integrate children with special needs into regular classrooms with their non-disabled peers, at least "whenever feasible"—a phrase that conveniently  left a lot of wiggle room for inaction (Encyclopedia of Indianapolis, 2025).

The Achievement Center for Children took this federal push to heart. Its lofty aim was to transition children like Steve out of segregated settings and into public schools. The idea was bold, progressive, and, at the time, about as welcome as a fire drill in winter.

Behind the scenes, Purdue University's visionary Dr. Kephart was already hatching plans with local public school superintendents, including the long-serving and influential Dr. J.R. Hiatt, who helmed the Lafayette School Corporation from 1952 to 1977. Dr. Hiatt, though not known for reckless innovation, was at least willing to listen. That, in itself, was a small miracle.

At the time, Indiana's special education landscape—much like the rest of the country's—resembled a patchwork quilt stitched together by hope, bureaucracy, and a whole lot of trial and error. Many states had only begun addressing special education after closing down large state institutions that had warehoused the "mentally retarded" and physically disabled, sometimes with all the compassion of an IRS agent at audit. These institutions, let's be honest, weren't known for their academic rigor—unless you count Bingo as a core subject.

Fortunately for Steve, his path never led through the gates of such institutions. Thanks to my parents' relentless advocacy and refusal to accept the state's "best" offer of exclusion, Steve remained in the community, where education— albeit in its primitive form—was at least an option.

Still, Dr. Hiatt wasn't exactly rolling out the red carpet. His hesitation wasn't rooted in cruelty but in a deeply entrenched educational orthodoxy: that "normal" students should not be "distracted" by those deemed different. Heaven forbid an intellectually disabled student share a classroom lest someone catch the learning disability by osmosis. Yet Kephart and his team believed quite the opposite: that positive behavior could be contagious. Thus began the years-long polite chess match between Kephart's optimism and Hiatt's caution.

By 1964, Steve was enrolled in Lafayette's Special Education Program. I use the word "enrolled" lightly—he was still in a separate facility, and calling it "fourth grade" was more aspirational than factual. Special education classes weren't arranged by grade level but by ability, which meant Steve's learning environment was more like a one-room schoolhouse with lesson plans made on the fly.

That same year, my family faced yet another move. Our home, sitting innocently next to the expanding Peerless Wire Company, was unceremoniously declared collateral damage. With bulldozers on the horizon, our parents found us a new home on Lafayette's far south side: on humble Fairwood Drive, a 1,025-square-foot kingdom for six. Three brothers—Steve, Scott, and I—shared one small room, our three twin beds arranged in a U-shape like some low-budget naval fleet. And in that room, amid battles between G.I. Joe and Cobra, Matchbox car racetracks, and countless games of Mouse Trap and Operation, we carved out a playland. My sister, Susan, had her own room. Must have been nice! And of course, my parents had their couple's suite.

While my siblings and I attended Southside public schools, Steve's educational experience was a daily experiment in what society would—and wouldn't—accept. Sometimes he was placed with other special education students; other times, he found himself in general education classrooms, navigating unfamiliar terrain. And always, Dr. Kephart and Dr. Hiatt continued their cautious dance, discussing, negotiating, and testing the limits of what "inclusion" could mean.

Our small childhood home on Fairwood Drive—where countless memories were made

To his credit, Hiatt eventually softened. With enough persuasion and what I assume were some animated meetings over lukewarm coffee, he agreed to begin mainstreaming select IDD students into public schools—on a trial basis, of course. Teachers were asked to volunteer for this "experimental" integration. Many did. Others clutched their lesson plans like holy relics and muttered, "Not in my classroom."

Mainstreaming kids like Steve, while far more humane than locking them in an institution and throwing away the educational key, was not without its own brand of cruelty.

One afternoon, my sister Susan was sitting in high school choir class when her teacher, in a stunning display of unprofessional indiscretion, told a mocking story about a "weird retarded boy" who had auditioned for choir. She referred to him as "Snowflake" and said he was the worst singer she had ever heard. The teacher laughed. The class laughed. Susan didn't. Sadly, some kids at school had a nickname  for Steve: Snowflake. He was labeled a snowflake because of both his flaky skin and his childlike mind. She knew immediately that the teacher was talking about her brother, Steve. As tears welled in her eyes, a brave friend took Susan by the hand after class, marched her to the teacher, and declared, "The boy you're making fun of is her brother." The teacher awkwardly waved it off as a harmless joke. Susan wasn't laughing. She would eventually leave the choir. That was her first painful lesson in the callousness of some professional educators who should have known better.

In 1968, Dr. Kephart retired. The following year, in 1969, the Achievement Center proposed its first wave of mainstreaming students into Jefferson High School. Steve, who by then had shown promising academic progress, was included on the list. But when the roster was finalized, his name was mysteriously absent. The newly retired Dr. Kephart was furious. After a single phone call to Dr. Hiatt—oh, to have been a fly on the wall—Steve was reinstated for the following year, becoming the first student on the list for the upcoming 1970 school year.

Victory, at last!

Stephen's proud and handsome senior portrait—a powerful culmination of a long, challenging, but successful journey

That fall, Steve entered Jefferson High School as a sophomore. He was in the first IDD class of students integrated into the general student body. It was not easy. Parents of "normal" students railed at school board meetings, warning of the dangers of exposing their children to "retarded kids," as though IDD was contagious. Letters flew. Administrators braced themselves. And Steve? He endured daily bullying from other students who took cruel delight in taunting "Snowflake."

My sister Susan continued to see it firsthand. Walking home, she saw Steve ahead of her, flanked by a pack of teenage boys yelling insults. She quickened her pace and caught up with him. The boys, now with two targets, turned up the volume. "Is that your boyfriend?" "Why don't you kiss him?" Susan ignored them. Steve kept walking. And eventually, the boys, starved of reaction, gave up. Sometimes the bravest thing you can do is say nothing at all.

To their credit, school administrators did what they could. They talked with angry parents. They tried to educate the educators. They kept working the system—even when the system resisted. Their goal: give students like Steve a real shot at a diploma. Not a participation ribbon, but the real thing. A high school diploma that said, "You did this. You earned it."

And Steve did.

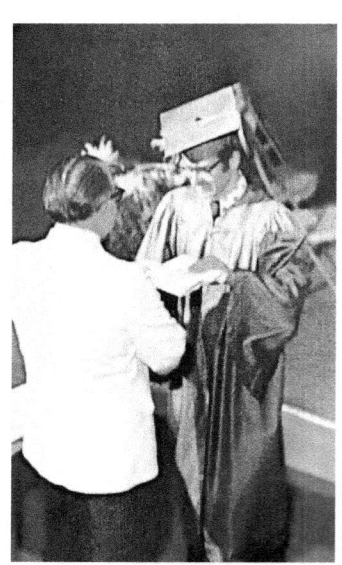

In May 1973, after years of persistence, evaluations, tutoring, sheer grit, blood, sweat, and sometimes tears, Steve walked across the stage and received his diploma. He was one of the first IDD students in Lafayette's history to do so.

It wasn't smooth. It wasn't easy. But it was a victory—one that still echoes through the halls of Jefferson High and the hearts of our family.

A glorious day of celebration— graduation smiles and an educational dream coming to fruition

Because sometimes, a "Snowflake" doesn't melt. Sometimes, he shines.

Steve—The First Through the Wall

Long before terms like IEP and IDEA became fixtures of our educational vocabulary—before government mandates, federal dollars, and reform-minded superintendents—there was Steve. Steve, who could neither spell bureaucracy nor benefit from it, was already navigating the wild, untamed frontier of special education in the 1950s, '60s, and early '70s. And while others waited for permission, Steve—God bless him—showed up at the door of public education, hand in hand with my parents, and knocked anyway.

Let's be honest: special education back then was less a system and more a patchwork of good intentions, occasional miracles, and far too many locked doors. It wasn't until the mid-1970s—two full years after Steve's high school graduation—that the nation decided that maybe, just maybe, children with disabilities deserved a place in public schools.

As Rotatori, Obiakor, and Bakken (2011) noted, special education's journey from isolation to inclusion has been one of "significant growth and changes," particularly as the field transitioned from a separate, often overlooked system into an integrated and essential part of the broader educational landscape. With the passage of the Education for All Handicapped Children Act, the United States finally got the memo: exclusion was no longer an option. Every child—yes, even the ones some schools would rather forget or avoid funding—was entitled to a free and appropriate public education.

That same year, Lafayette, Indiana—encouraged by early grassroots efforts like the Wabash School, the Purdue Achievement Center for Children, and Murdock Elementary—began to move beyond improvisation and toward meaningful education. The result? A local revolution in educational equity.

The Greater Lafayette Area Special Services (GLASS) cooperative was formed—a collaborative effort spanning Lafayette, West Lafayette, and Tippecanoe County. GLASS began providing a full continuum of services for students aged 3 to 21, from preschool programming to speech therapy to classroom inclusion, all guided by Indiana's Article 7 special education regulations. What began as a fragile patchwork became, at long last, a system—one that recognized that students with disabilities deserved not just a desk in the classroom, but dignity and opportunity, too.

Sadly, as of December 2024, the Tippecanoe, West Lafayette, and Lafayette school corporations decided to withdraw from the GLASS special services cooperative. Their decision reflects a belief that they can provide services more effectively on their own, outside the cooperative model. It's a significant shift—one aimed at decentralizing special education efforts. I sincerely hope this change serves students well, because these children matter far too much to become casualties of bureaucratic missteps.

But Steve? He never got special services or an IEP—the now-standard Individualized Education Program introduced in 1977 that promised tailored instruction and support. By then, Steve had already weathered the storm. His education wasn't shaped by mandates or multidisciplinary teams. It was forged in the crucible of trial, error, and love. And while we now celebrate those with IEPs, we must never forget the pioneers like Steve, who charged headfirst into public high school with no legal safety net.

Let's be blunt: being "the first through the wall" is not for the faint of heart. "The first guy through the wall always gets bloodied," as the saying goes—and Steve certainly did. During his three years in public high school, he faced bullying, ridicule, and ignorance—from peers, yes, but tragically, even from a few educators who should've known better. Other stories, in Steve's adult years—some heartbreaking, others infuriating—will be told in an upcoming chapter. For now, it's enough to say that Steve's courage during his school years paved the way for others to walk through that same wall with less injury and far more support. Thank God!

From Exclusion to Inclusion: A National Awakening

The numbers alone are sobering. According to *Access Press* (2025), by the mid-20th century, nearly 3 million children with disabilities were receiving inadequate education, and 1 million more weren't receiving any education at all. Let that sink in. One million children were not allowed to go to school simply because of who they were.

When Steve was born, it was still considered progressive—perhaps even radical—to suggest that children with intellectual and developmental disabilities belonged in the classroom. The idea that everyone deserved to learn was, at best, a whispered dream among the few visionaries willing to challenge the system.

Change finally came with the 1975 passage of Public Law 94-142, the Education for All Handicapped Children Act. This law laid the groundwork to ensure that children with disabilities had the right to an actual education. It provided:

1. Free, appropriate public education (FAPE) for students with disabilities ages 3 to 21,
2. Due process protections for families,
3. Education in the least restrictive environment,
4. Federal funding to support the inclusion of children with disabilities, and
5. The creation of IEPs—individualized learning roadmaps for each student.

Still, Steve missed it all by a whisker. The protections came two years too late. But he became living proof that children with disabilities could learn, should be included, and must be respected.

The IDEA of Progress

The momentum didn't stop in 1975. In the 1980s, pressure mounted to move beyond segregation and toward integrated educational experiences. The new philosophy was clear: students with disabilities should learn alongside their non-disabled peers whenever possible. And yes, it turns out that's better for everyone.

In 1986, Congress amended the law to include a focus on early intervention, requiring states to create systems to serve infants and toddlers with developmental delays (U.S. Department of Education, 2020). Then, in 1990, the law got a much-needed facelift—and a more dignified name: IDEA, the Individuals with Disabilities Education Act (U.S. Department of Education, 2020). Updates included:

1. New eligibility categories like autism and traumatic brain injury,
2. Requirements for assistive technology devices and services.

The 1997 reauthorization was another landmark moment. It emphasized transition services—plans to help students move from school to post-school life—and mandated that IEPs be more measurable, transparent, and collaborative. General education teachers were now required to help design IEPs. No more "not my job" excuses.

Finally, ADD (Attention Deficit Disorder) and ADHD (Attention Deficit Hyperactivity Disorder)—once dismissed as "behavior problems"—were included under the law as "other health impairments." Another overdue but welcome evolution.

Steve's Legacy: Busting Down the Wall So Others Could Walk Through

Thanks to IDEA, children with disabilities today attend their neighborhood schools. Many graduate from high school. Some go on to college. But it wasn't always this way—or this easy.

Steve didn't have federal law on his side. What he did have were two extraordinary parents and siblings who refused to accept the notion that their son and brother didn't belong. They made sure Steve was given a chance—not because the law demanded it, but because love did. It was all for the love of Stephen.

Of course, Steve had limits. But he also had abilities—often revealed when someone had the patience to teach him with consistency, encouragement, and a touch of fun. He could learn. He did learn. And most importantly, Steve proved that children like him belonged in school well before the government agreed.

His life is a reminder: real change often starts with one family, one child, one act of faith. And sometimes, before the policies and protections arrive, someone has to be the first to walk through the wall.

Steve was that someone.

Wanted Ads and Work Ethic – Steve's Lifelong Education

Thanks to the formal high school education he received—one that was occasionally sprinkled with job and life skills—Steve achieved something once thought improbable for people like him in earlier generations: lifelong employment. From graduation until the day he died, Steve never stopped working. Not once. That may sound ordinary, but for a man with IDD navigating a society still waking up to the concept of inclusion, it was nothing short of brave and historic.

Back then, special education didn't exactly roll out the red carpet to help students find a job after school. Nor were employers jumping up and down to hire them. No career fairs. No transition planning. No charming LinkedIn profiles. Once a student like Steve graduated, the responsibility to secure employment typically fell to caregivers or, more often, family members armed with determination and a pocket full of hope. My parents had both those attributes.

Enter my father—the original LinkedIn algorithm—who, in 1973, spotted a promising job posting in the Wanted Ads section of the local newspaper. (For those born after disco died, this was the analog ancestor of Indeed.com—minus the search filters and spam emails.) Purdue's Animal Clinic needed a helper to care for the clinic animals: cage cleaning, feeding duties, and the occasional pat on the head. Dad helped Steve apply, drove him to the interview, and beamed with pride when Steve landed his very first job.

But fate, as always, had a twisted sense of humor.

Steve's animal-care career came to a screeching halt shortly after it began—courtesy of a dog bite. A real one. Right on the arm. After a trip to the doctor, some medicine, and a bandage over a wound, Steve's enthusiasm for cage-cleaning and dog-feeding had understandably gone the way of the dinosaurs. And who could blame him? I was bitten on the face by a rather surly canine at age six, and I still walk wide circles around large dogs. Some traumas just hang around.

Home Hospital, Lafayette, Indiana. Photograph by Derek Jensen (Tysto), 2007
Licensed under CC BY-SA 3.0 via Wikimedia Commons.

So it was back to the drawing board—or more accurately, the Wanted Ads.

Once again, my father—part-time career counselor and full-time believer in Steve—came across a listing for a full-time housekeeper at Lafayette's Home Hospital. No email. No online application portals. You had to physically show up in real time, fill out a paper application in your best penmanship, and hand it to a real human. Medieval, right?

Dad helped Steve complete the application, drove him to submit it, and later returned with him for the interview. The hospital staff liked what they saw—Steve's kind demeanor, his eagerness to work, and probably his ironclad punctuality—and hired him on the spot. Just like that, Steve became a hospital custodian.

And there he stayed—for 33 years—until the day he died, in that same hospital.

Let that sink in. Thirty-three years of service. In today's world of three-month job stints and "career pivots," Steve was a model of old-school loyalty. He took immense pride in his uniform, in his job, and in the reputation he built among the doctors, nurses, and administrators who came to adore him. Ask him what he did, and he'd gladly tell you about his work in the housekeeping department. For a time, he was assigned to operating room clean-up—yes, mop in hand, scrubbing up after surgeries like a backstage janitor at a horror show. Blood, guts, and who-knows-what. Egads! Not exactly the dream job, unless your dream involves bodily fluids and bleach. Eventually, he ended up in laundry services. That had to smell a bit better—but still, those bodily fluid–stained sheets. Oh my! My father once tried to correct the way he was folding his sheets and towels at home, and Steve rebuked him: "Dad, d-d-do you know what I do for a living?" *Mic drop.*

His sunny attitude made him a hospital favorite. His commitment to showing up—sick or not—was legendary. In Steve's mind, missing work was simply wrong.

So, how did Steve defy a world that so often tried to count him out? He had champions.

Rita F. Pierson, a beloved educator with more than 40 years in the field, once said: "Every child deserves a champion—an adult who will never

A glorious day of celebration—graduation smiles and an educational dream coming to fruition

give up on them, who understands the power of connection and insists that they become the best they can possibly be" (TED Staff, 2013, June 28).

Steve had many champions—starting with his parents and siblings, and extending to the countless educators and mentors who saw his potential instead of his limitations: his elementary teachers, the teachers at the Wabash Center, the team at Purdue University's Achievement Center for Children, the Lafayette School Corporation, and yes, his employer at Home Hospital.

Through their support—and his own determination—Steve never stopped learning. He couldn't afford to. Life isn't easy when you're expected to function in a world built for those with adult intellect while having the mind of a child. But Steve adapted, endured, and even flourished.

Let's be honest: education doesn't stop at graduation. For some, it barely begins there. Steve was the embodiment of lifelong learning— not the kind where you collect degrees, but the kind where you collect life lessons. Through setbacks, breakthroughs, and the everyday grind, he kept learning and growing. His "classroom" was the world, and his "homework" was life itself.

Whether you're reading this as a teacher, parent, student, or casual reader, Steve's story offers something we all need: perspective. He challenges us to remember that learning isn't just about books, grades, or schools. It's about becoming better human beings. As long as we're breathing, we're still learning.

Steve was always eager to learn if someone took the time to teach. That's all it really takes. A little patience. A little kindness. And a lot of belief.

In the end, education isn't just a school building. It's not a degree in a fancy frame on your wall (and this is coming from a guy with several). It's not a line on a résumé. It's a way of seeing the world. And Steve, in his quiet, consistent way, saw it clearly—with heart, humility, and an openness that many of us would do well to imitate.

If his story adds even a sliver of knowledge, compassion, or hope to your life, then mission accomplished.

Isn't that why we read stories like this?

And this story, as you know, is for the love of Stephen.

Empathy is about finding echoes of another person in yourself.

— Mohsin Hamid

CHAPTER 8

GOD DON'T MAKE NO JUNK!

There's a lot of diversity in the human condition,
and we need to respect that.

— William K. Rasko

The Sunday Sermon That Changed Everything

In the 1970s, First Baptist Church of Lafayette, Indiana, was a lot of things—dignified, musically gifted, educationally high-brow, socially influential, and very active. It was also, to our surprise and gratitude, quietly revolutionary and surprisingly down-to-earth. Somewhere between the soaring chords of a Mozart cantata and the potluck line in the fellowship hall, something sacred was stirring. This is where our family went to church after Dad's revival. I was 10 years old. My brother Scott was 13, our sister Susan was 14, and Steve—our oldest—was 17 when we were first introduced to Jesus and the rhythms of church life.

First Baptist Church, Lafayette, Indiana. Photograph by Derek Jensen (Tysto), 2007.
Licensed under CC BY-SA 3.0 via Wikimedia Commons

At the heart of that sacred work was Rev. Bruce Morgan, our senior pastor.

Before we knew it, all four of us Jones kids were corralled into Rev. Morgan's confirmation class to learn the basics of Christian living—specifically the Baptist variety—complete with its own user manual and full-immersion lifetime warranty. We spent several weeks learning about Jesus, the Bible, and why real Baptists don't just sprinkle—they dunk.

Eventually, Rev. Morgan decided we were spiritually seasoned enough to graduate from classroom Christianity to full-blown baptism. This meant that at the end of a Sunday morning service, while the congregation belted out the final hymn with gusto, the entire Jones clan made the holy hike down the center aisle to publicly profess our faith. It was a full-family affair: my parents rededicated their lives to Christ, we kids stood there like little disciples-in-training, and Rev. Morgan declared that the whole blessed Jones bunch would officially join the church. And then came the part we'd been both anticipating and slightly dreading: the dunking.

It all went down on Sunday, June 25, 1972. Mark the date: four grubby little sinners were ceremoniously scrubbed clean in the steamy baptismal waters of First Baptist Church. According to Baptist bylaws (written somewhere between the Book of Acts and the church newsletter), this act granted us automatic lifetime membership—as though we'd been given a heavenly punch card and had just earned our free salvation smoothie.

Now, we had rehearsed the procedure beforehand. Rev. Morgan walked us through every step: walk down the baptismal steps calmly, don't trip, fold your arms just right, bend your knees, and for heaven's sake—hold your breath. But like many sacred rituals, things didn't go exactly as planned.

First, someone had clearly left the water heater running on Pentecostal power overnight. That water was hotter than a fire-and-brimstone sermon in July. Rev. Morgan warned us, but nothing could prepare us for the sensation of being baptized in what felt like spiritual chicken soup.

Second, despite all instructions, when it was my turn to be lowered into the water, I—holy novice that I was—completely forgot to hold my breath. I came up flailing, sputtering, coughing, and looking less like a redeemed child of God and more like a cat tossed into a bathtub. Not exactly the serene image of rebirth I was going for.

Steve, on the other hand, stepped forward with the quiet seriousness of a saint. He had listened intently in every confirmation class, nodding earnestly at Rev. Morgan's words as if he were already halfway to seminary. On the day of our baptism, he walked into that water like he was stepping into the Jordan River itself. No flailing.

No sputtering. Just complete, childlike faith and calm obedience. It meant something deep to him. This wasn't just a ritual—it was real. He believed wholeheartedly in what he was doing and who he was doing it for. Of course, I did too.

And Steve lived his faith. He would go on to be one of the most faithful churchgoers you could ever meet. Rain or shine, winter or summer, Steve was in the pew—usually early—ready to worship, pray, sing off-key with all his heart, and shake hands with everyone within a five-row radius. His love for Christ was simple, sincere, and deeply rooted. And his faith, like everything else with Steve, wasn't just about belief—it was about action. He'd spend the rest of his life helping others, showing up for people in quiet, steady ways that looked an awful lot like Jesus with a lunchbox.

So while I came up sputtering and coughing like a soggy convert in need of a towel, Steve came up glowing—and maybe even glowing before he went under.

A Joyful Noise (Even If Considerably Off-Key)

At the time we attended First Baptist Church—FBC, to the insiders— it was a thriving hub of holy activity. On any given Sunday, the sanctuary was packed, with latecomers hustling up to the balcony like it was opening night on Broadway. It wasn't just a church; it was a spiritual ecosystem, bustling with church events, potlucks, Sounds of Truth youth choir, and enough Bible studies to make your head spin (in Jesus' name, of course).

Sunday evenings belonged to Dad. He led a Bible study for youth and young adults, often held in our small living room. And yes, Steve came too. He didn't like to read aloud—reading and public speaking weren't exactly his favorite sports—but that didn't matter. No one pushed, no one judged. He belonged. People leaned in when he spoke, not just out of kindness, but because they wanted to hear what he had to say (plus he was a little hard to understand if you weren't used to his unique cadence).

Steve also gave the youth singing group, Sounds of Truth, a good old college try. He'd rehearse with his headphones on at home, belting along with cassette tapes like a rock star in the privacy of his own world. Unfortunately, the musical gifts had skipped right over him like a divine game of duck-duck-goose. He couldn't read music, and as for staying on pitch—well, let's just say the Lord might've been the only one who could decipher his joyful noise—and He seemed just fine with it. The saintly choral director, Mrs. Luann Spencer, welcomed him into the choir unconditionally (but secretly prayed he would sing a little quieter). Eventually, Dad had a gentle heart-to-heart with him. No shaming, no drama—just a redirection. "Let's find a better fit," Dad probably said. And they did.

First Baptist Church's "Sounds of Truth" in 1973—a one-of-a-kind youth choir that hit the road every summer. Let's play Where's Waldo—can you spot me, Susan, and Scott in this sea of harmonies and hairspray

Steve found other ways to serve. He passed the offering plate like his Father before him with the solemn dignity of a deacon-in-training. He helped clean up after church dinners in the Fellowship Hall, moving chairs and wiping tables like it was his ministry—because, in a way, it was. There was no task beneath him, and no person beneath his notice. Everyone knew Steve. Everyone loved Steve. Church was his community, his stage, his sanctuary.

God Don't Make No Junk

Sometime after our baptism, Rev. Morgan delivered a sermon I'll never forget. He was young for a senior pastor, kind-eyed, well-spoken, and a bit of a firebrand when necessary. That Sunday, he took to the pulpit and delivered a sermon that, even now, decades later, has lost none of its impact for me. It was titled "God Don't Make No Junk!"—a grammatically flawed, theologically rich phrase that gripped the hearts of many and got under the skin of a few others.

FBC had a remarkable ministry for individuals with intellectual and physical disabilities. It was called BYKOTA—"Be Ye Kind One To Another"—which, in our family, was less a slogan and more of a lifestyle. Mom, always up for a bit of holy mischief, threw herself into the ministry. I sat in as a volunteer from time to time; I loved those kids! My Mom taught in the program and served as a summer camp counselor at Camp Reyoad in North Webster, Indiana. Later, my brother Scott would join the ranks as a BYKOTA teacher. For us, disability wasn't a project. It wasn't a label. It was kinship. It was Steve.

Steve was a joyful, brave, quietly funny soul. He faced a mountain of challenges that most folks couldn't see past—but those who did were better for it. Though BYKOTA offered a nurturing, welcoming place, Steve attended a different Sunday School class—thanks to Dr. Jim Yakel, a Purdue University professor and holy troublemaker in his own right, who told my parents, "Steve belongs in my Sunday School class." It was for regular kids. It was bold. It was integrative. It was wise. It was inclusion before inclusion was a buzzword. And it worked. Steve did belong there, too.

And That's Where Things Got... Complicated.

Not everyone shared our family's sense of joy. And that's where things, indeed, got complicated.

First Baptist Church sanctuary, Lafayette, Indiana. Photograph by Derek Jensen (Tysto), 2007. Licensed under CC BY-SA 3.0 via Wikimedia Commons

Some folks of the church, polished in posture and pocketbook, weren't always endeared to the presence of kids with disabilities. They whispered concerns: "Too many," they said; "Too loud." "Too unpredictable in worship service." In other words, "not good for the image." After all, this was a church where the choir sang Beethoven. Not exactly Jesus Loves Me territory.

But Rev. Morgan had heard enough (as he told me years later). That Sunday, with Psalm 139:14 as his anchor—"I praise you because I am fearfully and wonderfully made…"—he declared from the pulpit what should've already been obvious: God doesn't make mistakes. And more to the point, "God don't make no junk."

He said it plainly, like a prophet with a Midwest accent. He told us that every person—disabled, disfigured, misunderstood—was made in God's image. "You are a masterpiece," he said. "Not a mistake. Not an embarrassment. A masterpiece." He reminded us that if we believe God is the Creator, then we must believe that every part of that creation (including Steve) was intentional.

A divine original.

Seeing Steve with New Eyes

I was a preteen. Insecure. A few pimples and raging hormones starting to kick in. A little embarrassed by my brother sometimes, not out of cruelty, just out of that achy, awkward self-consciousness adolescence gives you. But something shifted that Sunday. I saw Steve through a new lens: not as someone to manage or explain, but as someone to behold.

He *really was* fearfully and wonderfully made. I'd always known it in theory. But now I knew it like you know a sunrise: full in your face, impossible to ignore.

But what also stuck with me was what happened after the sermon. The BYKOTA volunteers started repeating the phrase "God don't make no junk!" to their students like it was scripture—and to those kids, it was. They recited it proudly, their heads high, their voices strong. And my parents, God bless them, made sure Steve never forgot it.

One day, after another round of bullying at school (we lost count), Mom and Dad sat Steve down. My mother, always tender, was emotional. Dad spoke. "Do you know why you're not those things they call you?" he asked Steve. Silence. "Do you know why you're special?" he asked again. Steve looked up through his thick glasses and grinned that familiar, mischievous grin. "C-Cause…God don't make no junk."

More Than a Catchphrase—A Theology

I know—it's not in the King James Bible. And sure, it offends the grammar police. But the theology? Rock solid.

"God don't make no junk," affirms a radical, ancient truth: human beings have intrinsic worth. Not because of what they can do. Not because of how they appear. But because of who made them.

This isn't just spiritual sentimentality—it's grounded in real theology. Nancy Eiesland, a pioneer in disability theology, challenged the Christian world with her book *The Disabled God* (1994). In it, she insists that the image of God must include the experience of disability. In other words, if we can't see God in someone like Steve, we're not really seeing God at all.

Psychologist Martin Seligman (2006) also reminds us that human flourishing depends on a deep sense of meaning, identity, and purpose. People who believe they are valuable tend to live fuller, more resilient lives. When you tell someone—especially a child with a disability—that they are not broken, you're not just being nice. You're saving their life.

The phrase "God don't make no junk" has been attributed to jazz legend Ethel Waters, who once said, "I know I'm somebody, 'cause God made me, and God don't make no junk." Since then, it's appeared in books (MacTaggart, Jaye, & Swanger, 1984), rock albums (*The Halo Benders*, 1994), DIY art, Pinterest boards, and even T-shirts on Amazon. But for me, it isn't a slogan. It's Steve's legacy.

From the Pulpit to the People

The sermon didn't just affect our family. It had ripple effects. The "more fortunate" among the congregation—those with advanced degrees and country club memberships—began to rethink things. Some even got involved in BYKOTA. You could see it in how they greeted the kids, how they spoke to them. There was less pity. More pride.

And those kids? They rose up. Not physically, perhaps, but spiritually. They began to see themselves as part of God's tapestry. I remember one girl in BYKOTA who clutched a handmade sign she made that said, in bright marker, "GOD DON'T MAKE NO JUNK!" She carried it like armor.

These kinds of affirmations matter. As the Catholic Church's Respect Life campaign teaches, all human beings have inherent dignity "from womb to tomb" (United States Conference of Catholic Bishops, n.d.). That includes people like Steve. Especially people like Steve. It is a moral imperative to see and protect the value of those who struggle to speak it for themselves.

In our culture of performance and perfectionism, it's easy to reduce people to their "usefulness." But disability challenges that economy.

It dares to ask: What if being made in God's image has nothing to do with achievement, and everything to do with being?

*Steve, bravely unwrapping yet another shirt from Mom on Christmas morning—
our family's not-so-subtle attempt to upgrade his wardrobe
(I'm in the foreground, recognizing his admirable effort to be grateful)*

Steve never had an austere job title. Never went to college. Never had children. And certainly didn't become a professional singer. But he taught a church how to see. He taught a brother how to love better. He taught a pastor how to preach like a prophet.

He taught us all that God's artwork doesn't need our approval to be considered a masterpiece.

It was because of the love of Stephen.

CHAPTER 9

RUN, STEVE, RUN! — THE UNSTOPPABLE JOURNEY OF A QUIET HERO

The greatest gifts we can give our children are the roots of responsibility and the wings of independence.

— *Johann Wolfgang von Goethe*

Finding Forrest in Steve: A Tale of Unexpected Parallels

If you had asked me years ago why *Forrest Gump* (Zemeckis, 1994) is my all-time favorite movie, I might have shrugged or muttered something about nostalgia or Tom Hanks' performance and charming smile. But after watching it for the hundredth time, a revelation hit me head-on: Forrest Gump was Steve—at least, in spirit.

"Stupid Is as Stupid Does": Challenging Labels and Low Expectations

"Stupid is as stupid does," Forrest's mama famously said (Zemeckis, 1994). It's a line that captures the tension between society's labels and the true measure of a person. Forrest, with his gentle wisdom and simple honesty, challenged the notion that a low IQ equals low worth. Her wisdom extended beyond clever quips to deep lessons in love, patience, and respect—values Steve's parents embodied every day.

Intellectual Disability: Understanding the Facts Behind the Myths

Today, Forrest Gump's mild intellectual disability—reflected by an IQ around 75—would likely qualify him for special education services under the Individuals with Disabilities Education Act (IDEA). He'd have an Individualized Education Plan (IEP) tailored to his needs, complete with speech goals, transition plans, and maybe even a therapist-approved fidget spinner. But back when Forrest—and my brother Steve—were growing up in the 1950s, none of that existed. No IEPs, no aides, no "inclusive education" posters on classroom walls. Just grit, trial by fire, and the slim hope that someone might believe in them.

Steve (left) and his brother Scott (center) surrounded by nephews Matt and Ben and his niece Sarah—fully immersed in a spirited game of Hearts, with family, fun, and fierce competition all in one. Not fully pictured is his nephew Brian, sitting straight across

Steve's IQ was about 10 points lower than Forrest's, thus placing him in a category too often met with low expectations and even fewer opportunities. He had to navigate a world that didn't yet recognize his strengths or provide the tools to develop them. Yet neither Steve nor Forrest were ever truly defined by numbers.

As the American Association on Intellectual and Developmental Disabilities (AAIDD) explains, intellectual disability is a lifelong condition involving limitations in intellectual functioning and adaptive behavior—not a disease or a mental illness, just a different way of thinking and experiencing the world (Schalock et al., 2010). People with IDD can learn, grow, and achieve—sometimes in unexpected, extraordinary ways.

Run, Steve, run—just like Forrest, his magic legs carried him through life's challenges with steady determination

Sure, Forrest is a fictional character, but let's be honest—if he were a kid today, he'd probably have a file folder thicker than a dictionary labeled "IEP." Still, despite the lack of support, Forrest somehow managed to graduate from the University of Alabama on a football scholarship from Coach Bear Bryant, because he could "run like the wind blows" (Zemeckis, 1994). Steve didn't go to college—but oh, could he run. If Coach Bryant had ever seen him tear across the front yard chasing the ice cream truck, he might've offered him a full ride right then and there. Steve didn't have a uniform or a screenplay—but he had heart, and he had it in spades.

The Village That Raised Steve: Family, Games, and Growth

Steve was one of those people who worked hard—many times to the point of frustration—to master skills most of us take for granted. When his patience wore thin, colorful language flew out of his mouth faster than you could say "timeout." And yet, he always earned an A+ for effort and a lifetime of admiration from those who knew him. I always admired how he could string together so many expletives in one sentence.

Steve (left) and I locked in an epic Risk battle—doesn't he look like he's ready to conquer the world Watch out, global domination is in sight

Like Forrest, Steve had parents who invested time, love, and sweat equity into his development. Outside of school, they worked with him on reading, writing, math, and life skills. Dad's introduction of chess to Steve unlocked a remarkable cognitive ability: Steve's talent for strategy and calculation. While I still rely on my phone calculator, Steve could do mental arithmetic on the fly. His love of games extended beyond chess to card games like Hearts and Euchre, board games such as Risk and Monopoly, and even billiards. You really have to know the game of *Hearts* to appreciate this, but the only time I ever saw Steve turn competitively malicious was when he could stick someone with the dreaded Queen of Hearts. Man, did he relish dishing out that 13-point punishment! The gleam in his eye said it all—sweet, strategic vengeance never felt so good.

But one of his greatest passions—something he proudly shared with our Grandma Fife—was bowling. And not the casual, Saturday-night-bumper-lane kind. No, Steve was a *serious* bowler. He had his own custom ball, his own snazzy bowling shoes (not the rental kind with funky smells), and he played in a Lafayette league like it was the PBA tour. One year, his team even made him captain—which we all agreed made perfect sense. Steve had the rare ability to keep score in his head, cheer on his teammates, and trash-talk with surgical precision, all while chugging a root beer. Grandma Fife would've been proud. Or possibly jealous.

Steve's eagerness to learn made him a beloved student—not just in school, but in the "village" of family and community that supported him. An old African proverb says, "It takes a village to raise a child," and Steve's village was a determined one. His siblings, Susan and Scott, closer in age, eagerly tutored him in their studies. Their shared learning and laughter underscored the power of family.

The Rat Patrol Rises

Let's be honest—Steve's education didn't stop at books, bells, and blackboards. No, sir. His real-world schooling happened in the basement of a Methodist church in Lafayette, Indiana, where the scent of old hymnals, musty wood, and bug spray filled the air. That's where Dad found a Boy Scout troop led by two legends in their own right—Mark Ellison and Evan Carlin. These guys weren't just scoutmasters; they were like Indiana Jones with clipboards.

Steve rising with the Rat Patrol, proudly sporting his full Boy Scout apparel—ready for adventure and new challenges

Steve joined up, and of course, Scott joined as well to serve as Steve's wingman. Eventually, I graduated from Cub Scouts and Webelos (which I thought sounded like a bug infestation), and I joined them. And before long, the three Jones boys were proudly marching through the Boy Scouts together.

Now, within the troop, we had something called "patrols," which were like little mini-squads. I managed to talk our group into being called The Rat Patrol, inspired by a 1960s TV show I was obsessed with. You've never seen anything so majestic—or so proudly duct-taped together—as our hand-crafted flag: two rats with helmets riding in a makeshift Jeep. We were very intimidating.

Steve fit in seamlessly. He was one of the guys—laughing, marching, fire-building, marshmallow-burning. Whether we were roughing it in tents or lounging in cozy cabins, Steve loved every minute of camping. He loved the woods, the team spirit, and probably the endless supply of s'mores. Dad even trusted Steve with his very own Boy Scout knife—one of those multi-tools with big and little blades, a file, and enough hidden gadgets to make James Bond jealous. Scott had one too. Me? I was deemed too young—and, let's be honest, the world was probably safer that way.

Dad told my brothers to hide their knives so I couldn't get my grubby little hands on them. They followed orders. I never did find Scott's, no matter how hard I searched. Steve also tried to hide his, but he didn't have Scott's talent for concealment. Which meant, of course, I found it.

One day, there I was, proudly inspecting Steve's knife, blade out, holding it by—naturally—the sharp edge. Steve panicked when he saw it, lunged to save me from myself, and in the process, yanked the knife away and across my fingers. Cue the blood, the tears, and my dramatic portrayal of a wounded soldier. Poor Steve looked horrified. In trying to protect me, he was the one who cut me. Dad came running, and justice was swift: Steve got in trouble, and so did I. Still, I received a touch of mercy since I needed four bandages for four fingers (but, thankfully, no stitches).

Come to think of it, I never did get my own Boy Scout knife—ever. Apparently, once you spill blood, the badge of trust is permanently revoked.

Now, the Boy Scouts had this whole system of merit badges. You had to earn your way through Tenderfoot, Second Class, and First Class—kind of like leveling up in a game, but with more knot-tying and fewer explosions. I marched five miles on the Harrison Trail in the pouring rain just so I could finally have a super cool medal to wear on my shirt like Steve and Scott had.

Steve earned his Tenderfoot and Second Class badges like a champ. But First Class had one major obstacle: swimming.

And here's the thing—despite all the lessons we took at the YMCA, Steve never learned to swim well enough to keep himself afloat. It wasn't for lack of effort, mind you. Oh, he tried—boy, did he try— charging into the water with all the gusto of a Labrador puppy discovering its first bathtub. At the public pool, he'd stick to the shallow end, making absolutely certain his toes stayed firmly planted on the crusty, sun-warmed bottom. But no matter how hard he paddled, floating just wasn't in the cards. It bummed him out. He felt stuck, left behind while others moved ahead. But Scott, ever the steady wingman, reminded him that no badge could measure your worth. Especially not in the Rat Patrol, where loyalty beat swimming strokes every time.

And speaking of loyalty…

One night, our Scout troop were outside playing Capture the Flag—a game that's part strategy, part chaos, and all mosquito bites. Suddenly, someone ran up to Scott, yelling that Steve was in a fight with one of the older, bigger boys. Scott sprinted across the dark field like a linebacker ready to rescue his brother, only to find that Steve already had the "big kid" pinned to the ground like a wrestling champ at the county fair.

Turns out, the bigger kid had been picking on some of the younger, smaller Scouts. Steve, who had decided to dismiss pacifism for a time, had taken justice into his own hands (and legs and arms). He wouldn't let the kid up until he promised, Scout's Honor, to knock it off. The other boys were cheering like Steve had just taken down Goliath. Scott stood in quiet disbelief. And when the kid finally agreed to stop bullying, Steve dusted himself off, helped him up like a gentleman, and went right back to playing.

Lesson learned, big fella.

That moment? That was First Class in every way that counted.

Head, Heart, Hands, and Health

Growing up on a farm, Dad was a 4-H alumnus—part of a tradition spanning centuries that emphasized "Head, Heart, Hands, and Health." This program taught real-world skills through hands-on learning and competitions, often culminating at county and state fairs. Dad even won the hog showing competition one year—an achievement that brought him legendary status in our family lore.

Steve found his niche in photography. Armed with a Brownie camera, he captured moments of farm life and family. Developing film was expensive, so Mom and Dad had to remind him to think before he clicked. While he never snagged a grand champion ribbon, he did win some ribbons, and seeing his photos displayed at the Tippecanoe County Fair was a major source of pride. Steve's joy came not from winning but from sharing his vision—a lesson echoing the Olympic creed: "The important thing is not to win but to take part; it's not the triumph but the struggle."

Learning to Drive (and Learning Limits)

When Steve hit 16, Mom and Dad thought, "Hey, maybe he can drive!"—you know, in the noble quest for independence. So they signed him up for private driving lessons. Steve did pretty well, honestly—there are plenty of drivers on the road who'd make Steve look like a racecar champion. But then came the final exam... and, well, let's just say Steve made a little oops moment: a fender-bender with another car. Just a tiny tap—nothing dramatic, but enough for the examiner to pull out the dreaded "Fail" card.

After that, Steve politely declined the whole driving thing. Driving made him very anxious, which was fair—anyone who's tried parallel parking on a busy street knows the anxiety is real.

Instead, Steve became a transportation connoisseur of other kinds: biking, city buses, walking, or hitching rides with whoever was willing. Honestly, he turned public transit into an art form.

He even taught me how to navigate the labyrinthine city bus routes in Lafayette every Saturday when we'd head to Market Square for bowling back before I scared the driving world by getting my license. I was a nervous wreck trying to figure out which bus to catch, but Steve? He made it look like a walk in the park—or rather, a smooth ride to the alley.

Not a Savant, but a Chess Master

The public's fascination with savants—like Raymond Babbitt in *Rain Man* (Levinson, 1988)—often eclipses the quiet talents of people like Steve. He wasn't a science genius or a musical prodigy, but he had an extraordinary skill in chess. Dad taught him the game as a child, and Steve quickly became hooked. Chess books lined his shelves, from beginner guides to advanced strategy tomes. In 1972, he avidly watched the World Chess Championship between Bobby Fischer and Boris Spassky, mirroring their moves on his board and offering running commentary to anyone in the house willing to listen. No one listened.

Steve joined the chess team at Jefferson High, and let me tell you, that raised a few eyebrows. Most people assumed he signed up because he liked knocking over plastic knights at home or moving pawns around like checkers. They didn't think he could actually play—play. You know—like with strategy and thought and... rules.

Turns out, Steve could absolutely play. In fact, he could wipe the board with most of the team before they finished their Frescas. I'm certain none of them told a living soul that the "retarded kid" beat them. I'm still not sure I ever beat him, though I maintain to this day that one game was a draw. (Steve would just smile and say, "You wanna play again?" which we all know is chess code for, *I've already mapped out your next three failures.*)

A classic chess set. Photograph by Jorge Stolfi, licensed under CC BY-SA 3.0 via Wikimedia Commons

He never gloated, never rubbed it in. Just gave you that Steve-smirk—part angel, part assassin—and reset the board like a gentleman. A quiet checkmate artist with a humble soul and killer opening moves.

My dad loves telling this story—really loves it. If he had a campfire and a captive audience, this would be his go-to tale: the time Steve, armed with his trusty chessboard and a gleam in his eye, annihilated Uncle Gordon in front of the whole family. Repeatedly.

Now, Steve didn't just like chess—he lived it. He carried his chess set around like most kids clutch their favorite toy or a blankie. Tucked under his arm like a sacred artifact, that board went everywhere. And anytime there was a family gathering, Steve went on the hunt. "Wanna play chess?" really meant, "Are you ready to lose with grace and dignity... or just lose?"

Enter: Uncle Gordon. My dad's older brother. Smart guy. Valedictorian of his class. Academic overachiever. But clearly out of his league, and he didn't know it, yet.

One fateful family gathering, Steve approached him with his usual sparkle: "Wanna play?" Uncle Gordon, assuming this was just an act of charitable uncle-ing toward his "disadvantaged" nephew, casually agreed. Big mistake.

Steve quickly set up the board with the enthusiasm of someone about to unwrap a birthday present. Gordon, only half paying attention—probably still chewing a deviled egg while talking to others—let Steve take white.

Now here's the thing: Steve was obsessed with the Scholar's Mate. If chess strategies had fan clubs, Steve would've been president, secretary, and treasurer of the "Four-Move Checkmate Fan Society." The rest of us knew this. Uncle Gordon did not.

Four moves and thirty seconds later, Steve beamed: "Checkmate!"

Uncle Gordon blinked. "Wait—what?"

Cue laughter. Cue confusion. Cue Gordon squinting at the board like it had just personally betrayed him.

Embarrassed but undeterred, Uncle Gordon asked for a rematch. Respect. He even repositioned himself in his chair like a man preparing for intellectual war. Steve, ever the gentleman, politely let him pick colors again. Gordon stuck with black. Round two.

Steve opened. Move one. Move two. Move three. Move four. Checkmate. Again.

Honestly, at this point, it was less like a chess game and more like a speed-run tutorial.

Gordon didn't laugh this time. Nope. He clenched his jaw with the determination of a man who'd never lost a spelling bee and wasn't about to let his nephew go 3–0.

Match three was the stuff of legends. Gordon leaned in, eyes narrowed, with the family in gallery-watching position. Steve leaned back, calm and ready, like a cowboy at high noon. He couldn't use the Scholar's Mate again—Gordon had caught on—but that didn't matter. About twenty moves later, Steve had Uncle Gordon checkmated yet again.

Game. Set. Match. *Mic drop.*

We cheered. Gordon sighed. Steve? He just smiled and asked if anyone else wanted to play — ready for the next victim. There were no takers after that display.

Summers on the Farm: Lessons from the Land

Steve, Susan, Scott, and I all got a little taste of farm life during those magical summer weeks spent at Grandpa Harold and Grandma Thelma's farm. Every year, for several years, we packed up our city shoes and headed out to where the corn grew taller than any of us could imagine—and where the Hoosier country accents sounded like a whole new language! Grandpa came from a long, proud line of Jones farmers stretching back over 300 years to the country of Wales, and he took great pride in running his bustling farm in the Flora and Camden area. Meanwhile, our dad had broken the family tradition by choosing city life in Lafayette, Indiana, which made us the "city kids" in Grandpa's eyes. So spending a week "living on the farm" felt like a grand adventure for us, though I can't help but think it might have been a bit of a relief for Mom and Dad, too!

I sometimes wonder if Grandma and Grandpa saw our visits the same way... Hmmmm.

The Jones family farmhouse—standing steady through time, sheltering generations and stories alike

Steve, in particular, thrived in the rhythm of farm life. He loved clambering into the corn crib, taking the tractor and combine with Grandpa for rides, exploring the giant barn, feeding the cattle and hogs, collecting eggs from the chicken coop, and getting up to all kinds of harmless kid mischief with the rest of us. One of our absolute favorite morning rituals was taking the leftovers from the day before out to the barn just to watch the magic happen: from seemingly nowhere and everywhere, at least two dozen farm cats would come racing in like a furry breakfast tornado! As kids, we thought Grandma and Grandpa must just love having so many cats around, but looking back, we know those clever cats were busy keeping the pesky mouse population in check.

When Steve was 14, he wrote a letter—lovingly guided by Mom—to Grandpa and Grandma, asking if he could come visit again. Though he was about to start ninth grade, his handwriting and phrasing echoed that of a much younger child, maybe third or fourth grade. But what the letter may have lacked in polish, it more than made up for in heart. Every word was genuine, tender, and full of the kind of sweetness that made you want to keep it forever, and Mom did.

June 6, 1968

Dear Grandma and Grandpa Jones.
I Would like to help you
on the farme. It would
be very nice to go.
I like to help with the
cattle and pigs.
It would be fun to ride
in the truck and the
tracker.
I would like to work with
~~yu~~ you.
I like to go to cruch with
you.
It would be fun to go in
to town and buy **things**.
I like to see and feed the
cats.
I would like to ride the
lownmorer. And play –
catch.
I like to hite the ball.
I **like** to play hide and
~~seke~~ seek.
I would like to play
~~h~~ kinds of games and
watch t.v.

love
Steve Keith
Jones

Just like the rest of us, Steve quickly discovered that when the sun went down in the country, the silence could almost sing—it was that peaceful. But we also discovered that when the wind blew just right (or wrong), it carried the unmistakable perfume of the hog lot straight to the house. Pee-yew! That smell could curl your nose hairs.

The Fab Four city kids arriving at the farm in the family's trusty old Ford Falcon— ready for more unforgettable adventures with the grandparents (God help them!)

We were introduced to the strange, twangy world of *Hee Haw*—and couldn't figure out why Grandma and Grandpa found it so hilarious. But they did—and somehow, that made us laugh too. Laughter, like chores and bedtime, wasn't optional on the farm.

We found out the hard way that hot water disappears fast when four kids are lining up for baths in one tub. The first one in got a spa day. Susan. The last one? A dirty, polar plunge that could shock the sass out of you.

Breakfast was always quick and cheerful—Grandpa was fiercely loyal to his bowl of Apple Jacks, eaten with a concentration that suggested he was solving farm problems and had to get back to work with every spoonful. And Grandma? She had her favorite stories, and she told them like they were breaking news. We nodded with wide eyes, pretending we'd never heard them before. (Funny how I do the same thing now with her son—my Dad.)

Steve and Scott's favorite times were the quiet trips into town with Grandpa to run some errands. "Just need some lumber," he'd say to Grandma, though they both knew what that really meant. After stopping at the hardware store, they'd make their way to the little corner diner, where he'd wink and order them each a bowl of ice cream. Grandpa enjoyed multiple scoops in his bowl. "Don't tell Grandma," he'd say, which of course guaranteed they'd never breathe a word. It was their delicious little secret, eaten slowly at the counter like two outlaws savoring their loot.

We also learned that going to my grandparents' Baptist church meant you sat still and you stayed silent. If you didn't, Grandpa's hand would remind you with a sharp thwap to the back of the head. Trust me, I got the message—more than once!

But Steve... oh, he adored the farm. Every visit was an adventure, every chore was a chance to learn, and every moment—whether it smelled funny, sounded strange, or felt like a head-thwap waiting to happen—was something brand new. And that kind of joy? That's the kind you never forget.

Growing Up and Growing Independent

My parents had countless moments of quiet pride watching Steve grow, learn, and achieve things the experts once doubted he could ever do—those little milestones most of us take for granted. The day he finally rode his bike without training wheels was like a family celebration. When he caught his first ball, read a children's book aloud, graduated from school, brought home a 4-H ribbon, and landed his first job, their hearts swelled with joy. Mom and Dad patiently taught him the life skills he'd need to live semi-independently. Every week, grocery shopping trips became lessons in finding the best deals and picking out special food items on sale. Mom even showed him how to cook simple meals on his trusty electric stove in his first apartment (which was a renovated car garage).

But there was one tiny detail they overlooked: portion control... and the mysterious art of saving leftovers.

Soon after Steve moved into his own apartment, the pounds quietly crept on—despite his daily walks and bike rides that took him everywhere from here to there and back again. Mom quickly realized why: Steve ate everything he made. Apparently, the concept of "leftovers" was either completely foreign to him or just didn't pass the 'Steve test' of belief. When he cooked a package of eight hot dogs for dinner, he devoured every single one. A box of macaroni and cheese meant for a family of four? Steve was the family of four— no sharing necessary. And forget about a simple bowl of ice cream. Steve believed in downing the whole half-gallon. While watching TV, of course. That's Grandpa's fault!

And don't even get me started on his snack food obsession. He got that from his father, just like I did. Mom usually left snack cakes and chips off the grocery list, deeming them "unnecessary," but Steve quickly found a workaround: the corner convenience store stocked his favorites—Hostess snack cakes and Seifert's BBQ potato chips— just a short bike ride away. That boy could polish off an entire bag of chips in one sitting. I've seen it with my own eyes. Wowzers.

So, portion control and the elusive art of saving leftovers soon became the next set of "teachable moments" for my parents and

Steve. These humorous little real-life lessons were proof that learning doesn't stop, no matter how old you get.

After thirty years working in higher education, I can tell you this much for sure: even college students are still figuring out how to juggle the wild responsibilities that come with independence. Steve just taught us all a thing or two about doing it with heart, humor, and a healthy appetite.

Uncle Steve

Steve's role as "Uncle" may have been his favorite title of all—especially since he never had children of his own. Whether it was Susan's kids, Matthew, David, and Benjamin; Scott's two, Brian and Sarah; Sudi's children, Salma and Sahand; or my boys, Daniel and Derek, he wore the title of uncle with pride. In truth, he was more than an uncle—he was a kind of surrogate dad.

Nieces and nephews never had to wonder where they stood with him—he adored them, plain and simple. He'd plop down cross-legged on the floor for hours, letting little hands pile toys on his lap as if he were the toy shelf himself. He clapped like an Olympic judge for every somersault and cartwheel, no matter how wobbly, and had a way of making each child feel like the most important person in the room.

At family picnics, Steve was the one sneaking cookies to the kids, ignoring their parents' raised eyebrows with that sheepish grin of his. If a toddler drifted too close to danger, he was the first to dash over, protective instincts firing. And when the games began—kickball, hide-and-seek, or just a full-throttle tag as they ran around the farmyard—Steve was right in the middle of the action, laughing louder than anyone. He was forever a child in mind—and heart, so if it was about fun, he was in.

What struck me most was how natural it was for him to connect. His nieces and nephews gave him what he treasured most—unfiltered acceptance. They didn't see labels, IQ scores, or differences. They saw "Uncle Steve," the one who laughed at their jokes, played their games long after the grown-ups had quit, and loved them without conditions. And in return, he showed them what love without calculation or hesitation looked like. His bond with them wasn't just affection—it was legacy in the making.

A Legacy of Love and Perseverance

Steve's story reminds us that intellectual disability is not a barrier to a rich, meaningful life. It's a different journey—marked by love, effort, humor, and triumphs that may seem small to some, but are huge to those who live them. It was for the love of Stephen.

PART III

LOVE, LOSS, AND THE LONG FIGHT

CHAPTER 10

WHERE VULTURES CIRCLE, PART ONE

The true measure of our society is how we
treat the most vulnerable among us.

— Anonymous

The Scavengers Who Circled Steve

Hunched posture, balding head, wings stretched menacingly across a cloudless sky, eyes fixed on whatever creature can't get up fast enough. Nature's undertaker, the vulture, is patient, persistent, and never in a rush. Because death always comes. And vultures? They're always hungry.

Vultures make a perfect metaphor for a certain type of human: scavengers who prey on the vulnerable with smiling faces and invisible talons.

Photo: Densita Kireva / Pexels (used under Pexels License)

"Like the patient and resourceful carrion feeder circling over the dead or dying, the relationship vultures in human form also hover over their victims, waiting for the right moment to swoop in and take full advantage of their vulnerable state" (Dahi, 2023, March 5).

These predators didn't live in distant forests or savannas. They lived in our town. In Steve's neighborhood. In his church, his workplace, on the bus, his apartment building—and even as a spouse. They lived in plain sight. And often, they called themselves "friends."

The Kindness Con: When Friendship Is a Disguise

Steve didn't know he was prey. Why would he? Like most people, he just wanted what we all want: connection, companionship, a reason to laugh, someone to trust. He found that trust easily—and gave his away to others even more easily. He was sincere. Loyal. Kind. And that—tragically—is exactly what made him a target.

To the vultures, Steve wasn't a person to befriend. He was a resource to exploit. My sister Susan once put it plainly: "Steve didn't have many friends who didn't take advantage of him." A brutal truth, but an honest one. Every new "friend" in Steve's life prompted a quiet family investigation. We weren't just protective—we were paranoid. We had to be.

Mate crime—a term coined in the UK—describes exactly this kind of exploitation. The Endeavour Foundation (2025) defines it as what happens when a person with an intellectual disability is "befriended" by someone who goes on to abuse or exploit that friendship. *"Mate"* may be British for *friend*—but there's nothing friendly about what actually happens. In fact, it's a deeply sinister dynamic that leaves the vulnerable even more isolated, disoriented, and often financially or emotionally devastated.

According to research, people with intellectual and developmental disabilities are disproportionately affected by this form of abuse. In one review, 80% of these adults reported having been bullied, exploited, or abused by someone they considered a friend or partner (Endeavour Foundation, 2025). For Steve, I'm sorry to say, abuse was a regular part of his life.

The Anatomy of Exploitation: A Guide for the Cold-Hearted

Steve had an innate trust that you couldn't fake if you tried. That trust, that eagerness to believe in goodness, was a beautiful thing to behold—and a devastating vulnerability to have living in a world that doesn't always deserve it. When someone asked Steve for money, or help, or companionship, he didn't think, *What's their angle?* He thought, *This person needs me.*

And so, time after time, he opened his door—and his wallet—to those he believed in. When my parents tried to explain that he was being taken advantage of, his reaction was always the same: confusion. He simply didn't see it. "But he's my friend," Steve would insist, eyes wide and uncomprehending.

The manipulation was often slow, deliberate, and persistent. Like a wolf in sheep's clothing, the mate criminal waits until the victim feels safe before striking.

As the *British Journal of Social Work* notes, "the grooming process in mate crime is subtle, often spanning months or even years, making it difficult for victims and their families to identify abuse until significant harm has occurred" (Milner & Myers, 2022, p. 1056). This is the true horror of this kind of abuse—it wears a disguise.

It is More Than Just "Mean Behavior"

Mate crime is not harmless teasing or the occasional prank. It is abuse. Serious, criminal, and often devastating abuse.

The Endeavour Foundation (2025) outlines five major categories of mate crime, all of which Steve experienced over the years:

1. Financial Abuse – Manipulating the individual to give or lend money, or to sign legal contracts they don't understand.
2. Physical Abuse – Using force, threat, or violence to control the individual or punish them.
3. Emotional Abuse – Undermining their self-worth through manipulation or guilt.
4. Sexual Abuse – Coercing the individual into sexual promises, unwanted sexual activity, or inappropriate relationships.
5. Criminal Exploitation – Grooming the person to commit crimes, often unknowingly, on behalf of their abuser.

It's hard to believe, right? Five-for-five. Steve hit the awful jackpot.

Again and again, our family had to intervene after the damage had been done. New bank accounts. New phones. New locks. New apartments. Same heartbreak. Same tears. Same exhaustion. Over and over.

Steve, despite his IDD, was a human being with a full emotional life. When he was betrayed, it hurt. Sometimes he cried. Sometimes he just went quiet. Either way, it shattered something in us, watching him realize—if only for a moment—that someone he trusted had used him.

Fighting Back: How Parents Become Private Investigators

Steve didn't like to get people in trouble. In fact, like many individuals with IDD, he feared the very idea of being "in trouble" himself. That fear—deeply rooted in childhood—made it hard for him to report abuse. Often, he felt he was somehow to blame.

My parents became experts at gentle—or not so gentle— interrogation. They developed a sixth sense for detecting when something wasn't right. If Steve seemed off—quieter than usual, less eager to ride his bike to church, more hesitant about going to work, or suddenly out of money—they started asking questions.

Sometimes Steve opened up. Sometimes he didn't. Often, they had to work backward: from an empty bank account, or a bruised face, or a concerning phone call. But eventually, the truth would leak out, piece by painful piece.

And when it did, my parents acted. They didn't wring their hands. They made calls, filed reports, changed locks, and, when necessary, took legal action.

The Lawyer Who Showed Up Like a Guardian Angel

In 1988, my parents met Ed J. Nemeth—a Lafayette attorney with a disabled brother and a lion's heart for justice. Ed handled Steve's legal cases pro bono, including one especially toxic and manipulative marriage. He called the predators what they were: "They run in packs," he told my parents. "They're everywhere."

Ed was right. He didn't just give us legal counsel—he gave us hope. And he gave Steve a chance to be protected under the law, even if the law was often slow to act. Sadly, Ed passed away in 2015, but his legacy lives on in the families he helped—ours included.

You May Have Fooled Him, But You Didn't Win

To every smiling con artist who walked into Steve's life wearing the mask of kindness: know this. You may have fooled him, but you didn't win. Because Steve was surrounded by people who saw you for what you were. And we fought back.

Now, buckle up. What follows is a wild and unpleasant ride through some of the worst moments of Steve's life—stories of betrayal, deceit, and cruelty at the hands of those who called themselves friends. These are the circling vultures in vivid detail. And once you've met them, you may not ever look at a "friendly face" the same way again.

Vultures and Lunch Money: A Stairwell Shakedown

Of all the vulture species that circled Steve throughout his life, few were more repugnant than the Stairwell Scavengers—a gang of adolescent buzzards disguised as high school boys. You see, in the 1960s and 70s, long before lunch cards and PIN numbers were invented to help keep money safe, kids went to school with cold, hard cash in their pockets. A quarter here, a dollar there—enough for a burger, maybe a chocolate milk, and some fries if you were lucky. For most kids, it was a mundane routine. But for Steve, carrying lunch money was like taping a "Free Meat" sign to his forehead.

The predators soon sniffed him out. Like flies to rot, they swarmed the "retarded kids"—their words, not ours—with a daily ritual of intimidation. Steve and a few others were ambushed in the same stairwell every day on their way to lunch. That dimly lit hallway might as well have been their feeding trough. "Hand over your money, or we'll kick the shit out of you," the vultures demanded, flapping their cowardly, featherless wings. Steve, terrified and taught to obey, handed it over. Every day. For weeks. Then he'd go hungry. And no one noticed—because no one ever suspects the vultures of stealing from the gentle lamb.

Research confirms what Steve lived: "Any child can be a victim of bullying or harassment, but children with special needs are both more likely to be bullied or harassed and also more likely to be seriously harmed by it" (Special Needs Alliance, 2025). These aren't just facts. They're autopsy reports of childhood innocence.

Legally, harassment is behavior meant to intimidate, threaten, or cause fear, while bullying adds physical or verbal abuse into the mix, plus a few psychological garnishes like name-calling and blackmail. Whatever legalese you prefer, Steve had the sampler platter—repeatedly, and often served cold. And unlike today's parents who can appeal to school boards and attorneys armed with federal disability protections, our parents were stuck with one option: call the principal and beg. "Please make the beatings stop" (Special Needs Alliance, 2025; Stop Bullying, 2025).

Eventually, an unexpected hero stepped in. (Cue the epic theme song.)

Enter the Good Samaritan, a teenage boy from our neighborhood who had a soft spot for Steve and a spine of steel. One day, he caught the vultures in mid-shakedown. There stood Steve and a couple of other targets, cornered like prey. The Good Samaritan and his friend told the thieves to give the money back.

The bullies refused. Naturally, vultures don't cough up what they've already swallowed.

Then came the brawl.

A flurry of fists and feathers erupted in the stairwell. By the time the school staff intervened, all four boys, the bullies and the heroes, were hauled off to the principal's office and promptly suspended for three days. That's right. Justice, thy name is Bureaucracy. No good deed goes unpunished when zero-tolerance policies tie the hands of school leaders. Still, in a rare moment of quiet humanity, the principal kept the Good Samaritans behind for an extra moment after the bullies had left and said, "Thank you for helping Steve." He was proud. Powerless—but proud.

And after that, Steve's lunch money was never stolen again (that we were aware of, that is).

But this was just one flock of vultures. They came in many forms. Others—mean-spirited alpha wannabes—would sometimes attack Steve just for show. A bruised ego was the price of a bruised body. These were the lowlifes desperate to prove themselves to other boys by beating up someone who couldn't fight back. What a way to win admiration—by choosing a battle you knew you couldn't lose. Darwin must've rolled over in his grave watching these specimens fake dominance through assault.

Thankfully, there were still a few decent human beings left in the student body—kids who stepped in, pulled Steve out of harm's way, and reported the violence. But those moments were rare. Our parents dreaded those phone calls from school: "Steve got hurt today. He has a cut. A bruise. We're sorry." That apology always came too late, like flowers after a funeral.

Today, there are laws—bless them—that might have protected Steve. When bullying creates a "hostile environment at school," especially when tied to a child's disability, it can cross the line into what is now classified as "disability harassment." And under Section 504 of the Rehabilitation Act of 1973 and Title II of the Americans with Disabilities Act of 1990, schools must take action (StopBullying.gov, 2025). But back then, no such legal wings shielded Steve. There were no federal mandates, no advocacy toolkits, no attorneys with IEP flowcharts. Only the occasional brave soul willing to take a punch on Steve's behalf.

Steve survived those vultures, though not without scars. But he never let it change him; he never stopped being kind. Never stopped trusting, even when he had every reason to lock the world out. And that is both the miracle and the tragedy of Steve's story. He had to survive what no child should, and still found a way to love life.

The Fake French Maid: A Vulture in Disguise

When Steve landed his job at Home Hospital shortly after high school graduation, Mom and Dad were cautiously optimistic. They helped him settle into a modest little apartment (a former garage turned into an apartment) just a few blocks away—a practical nest where he could spread his wings, close to work, and near the essentials: a laundromat and grocery store. It was a small step toward independence, a fragile hope. Little did they know, the neighborhood had its own predators circling, waiting for the moment to strike.

Next door to Steve lived a couple with their daughter, a wild card in this grim tale. At about 19 or 20 years old, this young woman, whom we'll call the "French Maid," was less of a maid than a vulture disguised as one, poised to feast on Steve's newfound freedom and vulnerability. On one of Mom and Dad's routine visits, they met this "cleaning angel" at Steve's door. The French Maid acted startled by their arrival, claiming she was "just helping clean" Steve's apartment from time to time—a story that didn't hold water. Mom, the no-nonsense matriarch, knew well who was supposed to be doing the cleaning: Steve and her. No one else was welcome with a mop in hand.

Steve, meanwhile, was caught in his usual awkwardness, stammering and stumbling over words when asked about the mysterious visitor. He hadn't done anything wrong, yet the shadow of shame hovered over him. After all, this was his first brush with a woman in his apartment—something unfamiliar and confusing. Every guy, no matter his challenges, would be unsettled by such an unexpected "guest."

But the French Maid was no innocent passerby. She was a wolf in housekeeping clothes, sharpening her claws for a long-term feast.

The first inkling of trouble came when Mom received a frantic call from the bank: Steve's checking account was overdrawn. How can that be? A sense of panic gripped her heart. Steve, the steady, hardworking man, was suddenly in financial free fall? Upon visiting Steve to investigate, Mom's trained eye caught the red flags immediately. Checks from his checkbook were missing—each one carrying a unique ID number, tracked meticulously in a registry, now suspiciously absent.

Worse yet, when Mom tried to balance the account, the numbers refused to add up. Steve's funds had been plucked clean, every penny drained and then some.

Fueled by maternal fury, Mom suspected who the vulture was, stormed next door, and confronted the French Maid directly. Her denials were slick and practiced, a protective mask for a thief. When Mom warned that such theft could land her behind bars, the French

Maid smirked and taunted in a signing tone, "You're going to jail," before slamming the door in Mom's face. The audacity! The vulture mocks the victim's family.

It was painfully obvious: the French Maid had been pilfering Steve's checks, forging his signature, and cashing them out as if they were her own paychecks. This was no mere slip or misunderstanding—it was cold, calculated check fraud. Steve, blissfully unaware, was the unwitting victim—a sinister exploitation where trust is weaponized against the vulnerable (Endeavour Foundation, 2025).

Mom contacted the bank, which confirmed the forgery. The missing checks had indeed been processed, but none bore Steve's authentic signature. The bank's fraud department sprung into action, gathering evidence to build a case. Check forgery, legally defined as the act of altering a written document with intent to deceive and defraud, is a serious felony (Indiana Code § 35-43-5-2, 2023). Here, the French Maid's signature forged on Steve's checks was a perfect example.

The case landed swiftly in the hands of law enforcement and local prosecutors. Police served a warrant and arrested the French Maid at her parents' home, the very nest she fled to when the walls closed in. No more taunting laughter from her then—just the grim reality of consequences. If only she'd remembered Mom's warning about jail time.

Her trial lasted mere hours. The French Maid tried to spin a tale of permission, claiming Steve had "given her" the authority to write checks to herself for cleaning services. The judge, however, was not buying this shabby defense. Guilty as charged, she received the minimum one-year sentence in jail.

Steve lost money, yes, but the theft also stripped away a layer of his trust. This episode was a grim chapter in the ongoing saga of exploitation he faced. Yet, the family's fierce protection ensured the vultures learned the hard way: when you mess with Steve, you mess with a set of parents that refuse to let their son be preyed upon.

Paul—The Parasitic Pal

Some vultures don't circle in the sky. They walk right into your living room, sit on your couch, and call you "buddy" for years while they rob you blind with a smile. They say things like, "Steve, you're the only one who understands."

That's Paul for you. A long-time friend of Steve's. A classmate. A fellow traveler in the slow lane of life's cognitive freeway. And, eventually, a textbook mate-crime perpetrator (Dahi, 2023).

Paul and Steve met in junior high school—both students with intellectual disabilities, both trying to find their place in a world that rarely had time or patience for kids who needed a little more support. They bonded the way some boys do: awkwardly, authentically, and completely.

They stayed close through high school and even graduated together, wearing the same cheap polyester robes and beaming with pride that no one could ever understand unless they've seen someone fight through the storm of special education and come out the other side.

After graduation, Paul got married—to a young woman with IDD, just like him. Eventually, they had some kids. Steve was there through all of it. They were, to all appearances, the kind of loyal friends you hope your kid grows up to have.

But Paul was more than just a friend. Over time, he became something darker.

He couldn't hold a job. Not for long. Every time I saw him, it was the same story: "Got a new job," he'd say. And by the next time I saw him, he'd already been fired. Sometimes it was because of his disability he'd say, and sometimes—let's be honest—it was because of his attitude or absenteeism. Or maybe all three. But while he was always unemployed, he was never broke. Not really. Not as long as Steve had money.

See, Paul learned something after high school graduation: Steve had a steady paycheck and a good heart. And Paul had a gift for emotional manipulation. A skill, really. The man could guilt you into writing him a check with tears and trembles so convincing you'd swear he missed his calling as a televangelist.

"My kids won't have a Christmas unless you help, Steve."

"We don't have groceries."

"We're going to lose our apartment."

Steve, who never said no, couldn't say no to Paul either. Over and over again. And not just little things. I once walked into Steve's house during the holidays and found what looked like a cheesy movie on a shoestring budget: Paul, his wife, and their kids, unwrapping presents, beaming with gratitude, practically singing "Joy to the World." But here's the kicker—Steve had bought every single one of those gifts. Santa Steve. With his own money. From his own wallet. For someone else's kids, because Paul convinced him they couldn't do it, so Steve had to.

And Steve was proud of it.

That's the heartbreaking part. Steve wasn't just being used—he was being rewarded emotionally every time he was taken advantage of. He felt like a hero. A provider. And try as we might, it was almost impossible to convince him that his so-called friend was treating him like an ATM with a heartbeat.

Paul had learned all the tricks. When Steve hesitated—and that happened more as we tried to teach Steve to stand up for himself—Paul would layer on guilt like gravy on stuffing.

"Come on, Steve. Don't let my kids go hungry. You're better than that."

Yes, Steve was better than that. But that's the problem with being better than that. You don't always see it when the vultures come pecking.

The abuse went on for years, I'm sorry to say. Friendship crime isn't always loud or violent. Sometimes it's just a series of whispered lies and fake tears designed to bleed someone out over time (Endeavour Foundation, 2025). My parents knew what was happening. I knew. We all tried to intervene. But Steve was stubborn—not in a mean way, just in that loyal, devoted way that made you want to scream into a pillow. He believed in his friend.

And then came The Saturday.

I pulled up to Steve's place, and right there, in front, was Paul's battered station wagon. My heart sank. I walked in, and there they all were—Paul and family—getting ready for a fun afternoon at Columbian Park. The park was practically in Steve's backyard, a little local gem with rides, a petting zoo, a swimming pool, carnival games, and cheap hot dogs. A great place for a family. Or, apparently, a great place to spend someone else's money.

After they left, I casually asked Steve why Paul had stopped by. Steve stuttered. Lied. Fumbled. It was like watching a fourth-grader hide a frog behind his back. Eventually, he confessed: Paul had asked for money. Again. For the park. And groceries later.

I felt something ancient rise in me, something primal and furious. I wasn't mad at Steve. Never Steve. I was mad at the man who had grown fat on my brother's generosity for far too long.

I parked myself at Steve's place and waited for Paul to return. And when he did, it was just him. His family was in the car, waiting. Steve let him in, and within ten seconds, I told Paul, flat-out, that it was over. He would never again ask Steve for a dime. I was polite, but only in the way a storm is polite before the lightning hits. My sons can attest to this vocal gift I possess.

Paul looked stunned. Then caught. Then insulted. Then angry. And then he swung.

Poor bastard.

I ducked the punch—thanks to the Bruce Lee films I watched with Steve—and tackled him. Steve, God bless him, pulled me off before I could do real damage. Paul got up, and I told him I was calling the police. He sprinted out like a roach in a spotlight. I hadn't even dialed. The dial tone was still humming when I looked out the window and saw his station wagon peel away like it was running from the truth.

We didn't see him again for a while.

But fate wasn't finished with Paul. No, sir. Not long after, his wife reported him for the repeated sexual abuse of one of their children. She testified in court. He was convicted and sent to prison. A few years—frankly, not nearly enough. His parents washed their hands of him. His wife divorced him. The people in his life wanted nothing to do with him.

And yet.

When he got out of prison, the first place he went was Steve's apartment. The one place where the locks were still open, the lights were still on, and the fridge was still full. Steve, God love him, let the vulture back in.

Paul claimed the one bed for himself. Steve was demoted to the couch.

My dad, by some miracle of timing, stopped by that same week and saw Paul lounging like a Roman emperor on Steve's couch. Dad—far calmer than I would've been—told Paul that the lease didn't allow for him to stay there. It was a lie, but a noble one. Paul actually complied. Packed up. Gave back the key (yes, he had a key—of course he had a key after Dad assumed he had a key). And walked out of our lives for the last time—we think.

After that, my parents moved Steve to a new apartment. Quietly. Without telling anyone.

Especially not Paul.

We don't know what happened to Paul after that. We don't care. Chances are, Steve saw him again but didn't dare tell us.

The Poker Predators: Vultures in Scrubs

Vultures don't always swoop down from desert skies. Sometimes, they wear orthopedic shoes and hospital name badges—smiling, joking, pretending to be your pal as they drain your dignity five bucks at a time over chicken salad sandwiches. In Steve's case, the vultures flocked to a lunchtime poker game at Home Hospital. It was a feeding frenzy masquerading as friendship.

Like many people with IDD, Steve never had a full grasp of financial concepts. "Money in, money out" made some sense to him, but the nuances of budgeting, interest, and saving for a rainy day might as well have been astrophysics. He understood math, but not money math.

Thankfully, Steve had Mom, a woman whose maternal instincts came with a degree in unlicensed forensic accounting. She was Steve's banker, accountant, and guardian angel with a check register. She didn't just manage Steve's finances—she taught him. Or tried to.

Mom would sit with him, week after week, coaching him on simple principles: when payday comes, you cash your check, you pay your bills, you buy groceries, you save a little, and you don't give your paycheck to the first guy who says, "Wanna play poker, buddy?" He had a checking account. A savings account. A budget. And every one of those was a two-person operation with Mom's name on the paperwork—because where there's money and disability, there are predators.

Still, Steve had some autonomy. He cashed his own checks from time to time—this was the pre-direct deposit era, after all, when getting paid meant physically walking into a bank. He carried cash. He had a weekly allowance, and as long as he was on track, Mom let him enjoy a little freedom.

Until Saturday, he was broke.

Mom showed up that morning for their usual routine—groceries, laundry, maybe lunch. But Steve didn't want to go. He seemed sheepish, even evasive. That was strange. He loved grocery shopping. It was his weekly outing, a ritual. Something was off.

"Why not, Steve?" she asked gently.

He avoided eye contact. "I-I d-don't have any m-money," he mumbled.

Now that really made no sense. It wasn't payday yet, sure—but his checking account should have been enough to cover groceries, maybe even a treat or two. Something wasn't adding up. So Mom, using her time-tested technique of maternal interrogation (part cross-examination, part gentle guilt trip), coaxed out the truth.

He lost his money. In a poker game.

Wait—what? A poker game? Steve?

Where? When? How?

The answers came out in fragments, hesitant and embarrassed. The poker games were almost a daily ritual at work. Lunchtime, in the breakroom. "The guys" played and invited Steve to join. Not out of generosity. Not to include him in their social circle. No—they invited him because he was, in their eyes, a walking ATM with a developmental disability. The perfect mark. The sucker. The fish at the table.

And these guys didn't just fleece Steve—they made it easy for themselves. When he didn't have cash for the game, they drove him to the bank to get some. How thoughtful, right? Vultures with chauffeur service.

This wasn't friendship. This was exploitation, plain and dirty. A textbook case of abuse, where people with disabilities are targeted and abused by those pretending to be their friends (Endeavour Foundation, 2025). They didn't need threats or fists. All they needed was Steve's trust—and that, tragically, he gave freely.

Imagine the scene: Steve sitting at a breakroom table, his warm, open face lit up with excitement because he thought he was included. He believed they liked him. He believed he was finally one of the guys. Meanwhile, they peeked at his cards. Lied about their hands. Told him two pair beat three pair if they were spades. Convinced him to bet big. Pressured him to stay in when he should've folded. Laughed when he left the table with empty pockets and no clue what just happened.

When Mom found out, she was livid. Fire-breathing, scorched-earth furious. Dad had been married to Mom long enough to know when she's on fire, you don't try to put her out, you get the hell out of the way. On Monday morning, she marched to the phone and called Home Hospital's Human Resources department. She reported the poker game and the vultures who ran it. She didn't care if they were custodians or surgeons—if they played poker with her son's trust, they were going to answer for it.

To HR's credit, they acted swiftly. Steve's supervisor was brought in and told the story. And that man—Carl—who genuinely cared about Steve and had no idea what was going on—was pissed. Carl called my Mom and Dad the next day to inform them that the poker-playing parasites had been reprimanded, "chewed up one side and down the other." The ringleader was put on probation. And, in what must have felt like a bad sitcom ending, the vultures offered apologies.

Apologies. No restitution. No returned money. No offer to fix what they broke in Steve's sense of belonging or trust. Just a few sheepish "sorry, man" muttered in the hallway between elevator rides.

How much did Steve lose? Hundreds? Maybe more? We'll never know. But what he really lost was something harder to calculate: his confidence, his faith in others, his pride. The damage went deeper than his wallet.

And yet—because life sometimes offers bittersweet redemption— this story has a surprising coda. Carl, Steve's supervisor, the one who stood up for him and punished the vultures, never forgot him.

Years later, when Steve was dying, Carl (still his supervisor) showed up again—this time not as a boss, but as a friend. He came to Steve's bedside. He stood at his funeral. He mourned him. He made sure a small plaque honoring Steve and his 30+ years of hospital service was put on a wall in the main lobby.

Because some people, some rare people, understand that being human means protecting the vulnerable, not exploiting them.

So, what do we learn from this story? That not all vultures fly. Some play cards. Some drive you to the bank. Some smile in your face while picking your pockets. This is just one flock of scavengers in the saga of Steve's life.

The Bus Lady: A Case Study in Public Transit Predation

For someone like Steve, public transit—those crowded buses and noisy city streets—can be a hunting ground just as treacherous as any stairwell or hospital breakroom.

When he wasn't riding his bike or walking, Steve rode the city bus to appointments, bowling, the mall, and friend visits. He liked the independence of it all. The routine. The dignity. The occasional hot dog from a corner stand. Riding the bus made him feel like part of the world—like everyone else.

But the bus also brought him face-to-face with a different kind of predator: the Bus Lady.

She was a regular. A little too chatty, a little too eager to be friendly. At first glance, she seemed harmless—just another eccentric rider with too many opinions about her ailments and astrological signs. But her true gift wasn't conversation. It was manipulation.

She knew how to spot the kind-hearted, the trusting, and the quietly vulnerable. Steve—gentle, generous, and always eager to connect—fit her target demographic a little too well.

It started small. Friendly chatter. Compliments. Questions about his job and family. Then came the requests: a few bucks for lunch, bus fare to the next stop, help with her groceries. Steve, being Steve, obliged. He believed her stories. Why wouldn't he? She said she was his friend.

But the strings got tighter. His wallet got lighter. And Mom noticed.

Something was off. His usual weekly spending didn't add up. The math wasn't mathing. Why was he nervous when she asked where his money was going so quickly each week?

What the Bus Lady didn't count on, though, was Jackie.

Jackie was Steve's usual driver—a woman with a heart of gold and a face that said, "Don't even think about it." I imagine her gaze could melt asphalt, and her voice could stop a con artist in their tracks. She didn't suffer fools; she had seen too many. And she sure didn't suffer predators.

She'd been watching. Watching the way the Bus Lady always sat next to Steve. The way she latched onto him like static cling. The forced conversations. The cash quietly handed over. Jackie saw it all through her rearview mirror—and she didn't like what she saw.

One day, she stopped Steve just before he stepped off.

"She takin' advantage of you, Steve," she said, gently but firmly.

"Nawww," he said, with that shy little smile. "S-S-She just needs help with some stuff."

Jackie was more than a bus driver. She was a silent guardian in a reflective vest, wielding her brake pedal like a broadsword. She tipped Steve off, looped in the transit authorities, and made sure he was never alone with that woman again.

Not long after, the Bus Lady vanished from the route. Whether she was banned, banished, or simply discouraged by being called out, we never found out. Maybe she slithered off to find another target.

Either way, she was gone. But the impact lingered.

What she did wasn't just annoying or opportunistic—it was textbook mate crime: targeting Steve's kindness and social isolation to extract money and attention under the false pretense of friendship (Endeavour Foundation, 2025). Like many predators, she cloaked her exploitation in the language of care and concern. And if anyone dared question her, she'd likely whine, *"I was just being nice."* Of course, she was.

After this incident, my Father tried yet again to teach Steve that he can't hand out cash like candy to whoever asks.

"Steve," he said gently, "when people ask for your money, they're not being your friend. They're taking advantage of you."

Steve, in his full Wolfman Jack glory,
chillin' with Grandma Thelma (most of you will have to Google who Wolfman Jack was)

But Steve—simple in the best way—just said, "But Dad... you t-t-taught us to help people who n-need it."

What could Dad say after that? It was one of those rare times he didn't have words.

Even after being used, Steve didn't lose his way. He didn't harden. He didn't fold into bitterness. He held fast to the very values that made him vulnerable—and made him *strong*.

This whole episode was a brutal reminder: people with intellectual and developmental disabilities face unique risks in public spaces. The very things that make them beautiful—trust, openness, compassion—also make them targets.

That's why we need better training for transit staff. Stronger safeguards. More community vigilance. And more people like Jackie.

We never forgot her. Steve didn't either. She wasn't family. She wasn't paid extra. She was just a bus driver with eyes wide open and a moral compass pointed true north.

When Steve died—far too soon—it was Jackie who showed up to the funeral home for the showing. I was blessed to meet her.

She signed the guest book, stood quietly at the casket, tears in her eyes. Steve meant something to her. She didn't say much. She didn't have to. Her presence said everything. But we did talk a little, and she shared this story with me.

In life, she showed up to protect him. And in death, she showed up to honor him. It was for the love of Stephen.

CHAPTER 11

WHERE VULTURES CIRCLE, PART TWO

"It is easier to abuse or exploit someone if you inherently believe that people with disabilities are less human, less valuable or don't contribute to society."

— Disability Justice, Abuse and Exploitation of People with Developmental Disabilities

---

The Stories You'll Never Hear

There are too many stories to tell about Steve being manipulated or abused, and even more we'll never know. My mom once said, "These stories are just some of what we learned about. I know there are more we never found out about."

That's the part that gnaws at me. The idea that Steve suffered in silence more times than we can count. That he smiled through betrayals. That he blamed himself when he should have blamed them. That he was afraid of being in trouble, when in fact, he had done nothing wrong.

But this continuing chapter isn't just about what Steve endured. It's about what he survived. It's about what our family fought for. It's about what still needs to change.

The Queen Vulture

In the long parade of colorful characters who drifted in and out of Steve's life, a few seemed to show up with more take than give. But none had quite the staying power—or flair for reappearing at inconvenient times—like his first wife, Elaine. (Spoiler alert: Yes—his *first* wife. In the next chapter, you'll enjoy how Steve will find love again, along with a second marriage and true happiness.)

In the summer of 1985, Steve met Elaine through friends (not her real name—because, you know, lawsuits and all that). To the best of our knowledge, Elaine was never diagnosed with an intellectual disability or any mental health disorder. That will make this story all the more egregious.

Steve was thirty-one and she was twenty-one when they met. Elaine had a young five-year-old son from a previous teenage relationship, and, at least in Steve's mind, things clicked right away.

That Christmas, Steve brought Elaine and her little boy home to meet his family. We rolled out the welcome mat—Midwestern style—which meant offering second helpings of all the holiday favorites and, perhaps more impressively, adding them to the family gift list. For our clan, that was practically a marriage proposal. The little fella tore into his presents like a squirrel discovering espresso beans, paper flying everywhere. Elaine smiled politely, thanked us warmly, and for a moment, it felt like maybe, just maybe, this could work.

But the shine wore off quickly. We started noticing the boy's nervous flinches whenever Elaine's voice sharpened and she approached him. She tried to hide her anger when he acted out, but the mask slipped often enough to reveal that "discipline" in her world went well beyond timeouts. Her child was scared of her in those moments. Steve, ever the gentle soul, handled both child and mother with quiet patience—soothing tantrums without raising his voice, defusing tension without lifting a hand. You could tell this wasn't the first time he'd been the buffer, and honestly, he showed more fatherly grace than many so-called "normal" dads.

We waved off the warning signs, convincing ourselves they were none of our business. Then, months later, came the curveball: Steve and Elaine were engaged.

And then—another curveball. Steve's hard-earned $10,000 in savings, built up through his work at Home Hospital and with some financial planning help from Mom and Dad, vanished almost overnight, swallowed up by engagement rings, wedding bands, and whatever shiny thing caught Elaine's eye before the "I dos." That money represented years of sweat and sacrifice.

And the hard truth was this: Steve wasn't just the groom—he was the bank. Elaine never worked a day or brought home a paycheck during their marriage. Every bill paid, every meal on the table, every little luxury came from Steve's pocket alone. He was the provider, the safety net, and, ultimately, the only source of income.

I wish I could say that the draining of Steve's savings account was when our alarm bells finally went off. But no—we were too hopeful, too eager to believe this was Steve's shot at the family he'd always dreamed of.

The wedding went ahead at an outdoor venue, sunshine and optimism on full display. I officiated—partly because I was a newly minted minister, but mostly because, as Steve's brother, my fee was a steal. (It was free.)

Elaine's family? Nowhere to be seen. They were just a couple of states away, but they didn't show. No one asked too many questions at the time—we were too focused on Steve's wide grin and the hopeful glow in his eyes.

But warning signs never stay quiet for long. Steve stepped fully into the role of father—making sure her son was fed, clothed, and on the bus—Elaine slipped more and more into late nights at the local tavern, missed morning breakfasts, and unexplained absences.

One early morning on their way into Lafayette for work, Mom and Dad spotted her leaving a house with a man who most definitely wasn't Steve. They didn't tell him right away—maybe out of fear of breaking his heart, maybe to avoid igniting a family storm—but they felt the truth pressing in. Steve was in a bad marriage.

This circus lasted nearly three years before Steve finally told Dad, "I'm done." Dad called his friend, attorney Ed Nemeth, and the divorce wheels started turning. That's when Elaine played her last big card: she announced she was pregnant with Steve's child and demanded child support. Steve, in his blunt honesty, said to Dad, "That's not my baby." When Dad pressed, Steve stunned him with the reply: "We-we-we never had sex."

As awkward and unbelievable as that sounded, it was true. A court-ordered DNA test confirmed the child was 99.99% not Steve's. Elaine hadn't even bothered to fake marital intimacy. When the results came in, Steve grinned and said to Dad, "See! I told you it wasn't mine."

Elaine's courtroom misadventures didn't end there. Not long after the divorce, Nemeth saw her name on another case, this time trying to secure support for her first child. The judge, connecting the dots with Nemeth's help, dismissed it without hesitation. Scoreboard: Nemeth 2, Elaine's petitions 0.

You'd think that would be the last of her. But Elaine was like a bad sitcom character—always making a surprise reappearance just when the plot had moved on. One Thanksgiving, Dad went to pick up Steve for the family gathering, with Susan, in from town, riding shotgun. As Steve walked out of his apartment, Dad noticed him talking to someone inside. On the drive back, Dad asked, "Who were you talking to?" Steve hesitated, stammered, and sheepishly muttered, "E-E-Elaine."

Turns out her latest relationship had booted her out, and she had shown up at Steve's door—kids in tow—looking for a place to stay. And of course, Steve, with his boundless kindness, had let her in. Dad fumed. Susan sat stiff and silent, her lips pressed into a hard line. Steve just gazed out the window, retreating into his own world while the tension swirled around him.

Eventually, Elaine drifted out of Steve's life for good. Many years later, Mom and Dad saw her son on the local evening news—grown now, heading to prison. A sad ending, but hardly surprising.

Elaine wasn't just a disruption; she was a case study in what Dahi (2023) describes: exploitation in relationships involving people with disabilities often goes unnoticed because "society underestimates both their vulnerability and their capacity for being targeted by those closest to them" (p. 57). Steve's story was both heartbreaking and absurd, a reminder of how deeply trust can be misused, and how even in betrayal, he clung to kindness.

Birds of Prey

Of all the vermin that slithered into Steve's life under the guise of friendship, none left quite the stench of malevolence like the one known, ironically, as Bird. Yes—Bird. Not the kind that chirps sweetly outside your window, but more the kind that perches on the shoulder of the Grim Reaper and whispers, "Hey man, I know a guy who gets paid every other Friday." Bird, it turned out, was less of a nickname and more of an omen.

After years of working reliably at Home Hospital, and long after his divorce, Steve had to relocate when the hospital merged with St. Elizabeth's. That meant a new apartment in a new part of town so he could be close enough to ride his bike to work. The new place seemed harmless enough at first. Fresh start. New neighbors. New challenges, sure, but Steve was nothing if not adaptable. But as life would have it—and by "life" I mean the universal magnet that draws sociopaths to vulnerable souls—Steve's apartment just so happened to be above a woman whose boyfriend was freshly sprung from prison.

Steve, true to form, made the tragic mistake of being friendly. He met Bird through the downstairs neighbor and, in typical Steve fashion, probably greeted him with a handshake, a smile, and a story about where he worked and when he got paid.

You know, just to be polite.

Bird, of course, zeroed in on Steve like a heat-seeking missile. This wasn't his first rodeo at exploitation. Within days of their meeting, Bird figured out Steve's payday routine. Every other Friday, Steve cashed his paycheck, deposited most of it, and kept a small allowance in his pocket for food, fun, bowling, and video arcades. Just like Mom taught him. Just like a loving, trusting, good-hearted adult with IDD would do.

And Bird? Well, he decided Friday was now his payday, too.

He started showing up like clockwork. At first, he'd knock. Ask for "a little help." His girlfriend was "sick." They were "behind on rent." A car repair. A utility bill. A dying relative who apparently required exact change to survive. Classic manipulation. Exploitation masked as friendship, a silent epidemic that targets people with intellectual and developmental disabilities. People like Steve, who are more likely to be trusting and less likely to distinguish a friendly favor from predation (Dahi, 2023).

But as with most parasites, Bird didn't stay subtle for long.

When Steve finally summoned the courage to say no—likely after rehearing the warning words from Mom and Dad—Bird dropped the act. And then he dropped his fist.

He punched Steve.

In the face.

That single act of violence wasn't just about the bruising—it was about control. It was about teaching Steve a lesson: *I can hurt you whenever I want. And next time, it might be worse.* The physical pain was only the beginning. The real cruelty was psychological—the unspoken threat that hovered over every payday like a dark cloud: Pay me, or I'll kick your ass.

This wasn't just a mugging or theft. It was a systematic ritual of coercion, designed to exploit Steve's deepest vulnerabilities: his fear of conflict, his inability to lie convincingly, his desire to keep the peace at all costs. It was emotional terrorism with a side of blunt force trauma.

Steve started handing over the money. Not because he wanted to, not because he was helping a friend, but because he was afraid. And fear, when it's carved into someone who already lives with cognitive limitations, doesn't just hurt—it hollows.

Let's not mince words: this was a hate crime. A grotesque betrayal of trust, and a perfect example of how predators like Bird use not just lies, but brute violence, to rob people with disabilities of their autonomy, safety, and dignity. As the Special Needs Alliance (2025) reminds us, individuals with developmental disabilities are far more vulnerable to abuse and far less likely to report it, particularly when the abuser is someone who claims to be a friend or caregiver.

Steve didn't report Bird. Of course, he didn't. He tried to cover for him. Said he "bumped into a door." But when my parents saw the swelling on his cheek and the scabbed cut that told a different story, they gently dug deeper. And when Steve's shaky voice finally confessed the truth, my parents collectively felt something crack inside, again.

Mom wept this time. Dad? Dad burned.

He stomped down the apartment steps like a man on a mission, ready to confront Bird face-to-face. Fortunately for Bird, he wasn't home. Either he and his girlfriend were out, or they'd heard the footsteps of justice and decided to play dead behind the curtains.

But my father wasn't done.

Steve had the woman's phone number—because, of course, he did, being the trusting, friendly neighbor he was—and Dad, a few hours later, dialed it like it was a war drum. Bird picked up the phone, not knowing that the man on the other end wasn't just a dad—he was an Army-trained sharpshooter with a son who'd just been assaulted. Dad didn't yell. He didn't curse. He made a simple statement of fact:

"If you ever lay a finger on my son again, or come near his door, I will take you down."

Bird laughed. "What the hell does that mean?"

"It means I served two years in the Army as a sharpshooter. I don't miss."

Bird stopped laughing.

And just like that, he flew off. The next payday came and went. No knock. No scam. No bruises.

But my parents weren't about to trust the silence.

Enter Attorney Ed Nemeth—legal bulldog, protector of the vulnerable, and longtime friend to the Jones family. When Nemeth learned Bird was out on probation, he filed a petition to revoke it with all the efficiency of a man who knew exactly what kind of trash he was dealing with.

It worked.

Bird was carted back to jail, that familiar roost he knew so well, and a restraining order was issued. Nemeth told my parents this wasn't just about punishing Bird—it was about warning all the vultures in the vicinity. Word gets around, especially in circles of scum. And just like that, the apartment complex that had become a feeding ground for predators went quiet.

At least, for a while.

Because if there's one thing we've learned, it's that when one vulture gets caged, another starts circling.

The Landline Leech: Another Vulture Circles In

Just when we thought the skies were momentarily clear at the apartment complex, when the last greasy-feathered grifter (yes, I'm talking about Bird) had finally flapped his way into a jail cell, the next predator began circling. This one moved into the apartment complex like a shadow without a conscience. His perch? Directly above Steve.

It's almost like the universe had put out a Craigslist ad that read:

"Free rent, free utilities, and a trusting neighbor with intellectual disabilities. Predators welcome. No morals required."

He showed up with a friendly smile and the usual empty pleasantries. To Steve, who had been taught all his life to "love thy neighbor," especially friendly neighbors, this new guy seemed like a potential friend. But we know what vultures look like now, don't we?

We will call this one Landline—because that's where his thievery began.

Before cell phones ruled our pockets and minds, there were only landlines. You remember those—cords you could trip over, phones that rang like alarm clocks from hell, and operators who still occasionally had to manually patch your call through like they were in a World War II command center.

Landline took full advantage of Steve's trust—and his analog vulnerability. On one of his very first visits, Landline knocked on Steve's door and told him a lie so ridiculous it deserved a standing ovation for audacity. He said the phone company instructed him to run his own phone line through Steve's apartment so it could "connect properly."

Let that sink in for a moment. Imagine a new neighbor knocking on your door and saying, "Hey, the gas company told me I need to drill into your stove to get my oven working." Would you go along with it? Of course not. But Steve did. Because he'd been taught to help others, to trust people, and to assume good intentions. And also—let's be honest—because he had an intellectual disability that made discerning ulterior motives exceptionally difficult (Razzano et al., 2005).

So, Steve—ever the good guy—said yes. He allowed the vulture upstairs to run a phone cable through his wall and connect it to his phone system.

Now, Landline had free, unrestricted, unlimited access to Steve's phone line. No bills. No limits. No conscience. He started making calls. Not just a few. Dozens and dozens of calls. To everywhere and everything. Long-distance calls to distant cities. International calls. And then… the 1-900 numbers.

For those unfamiliar with 1-900 numbers, they were essentially the gateway to sin in the 1980s. Want someone to tell you your future? Call a psychic on a 900 number. Want someone to talk dirty to you while you ate Cheez-Its in your boxer shorts? Call a sex hotline. Want to hear a woman pretend she was vacuuming in a French maid outfit while telling you you're "special"? $4.00 a minute, buddy. Just pick up the phone.

And Landline picked up that phone—a lot.

Steve didn't know. He didn't suspect a thing. Why would he? He wasn't making the calls. But when the bill came? Oh boy. Cue the orchestra's dark, dramatic music.

Mom was sitting with Steve, like she often did, going through his bills and helping him balance his checkbook, another one of the many tasks she undertook to help Steve learn financial responsibility. She opened the phone bill, expecting to see the usual amount—maybe $30, $40. Instead, her jaw hit the kitchen table. The bill was over $1,000.

In today's dollars, that's a down payment on a car. Back then? It was panic-inducing. Steve, fending off accusations that phone sex was his favorite hobby, calmly explained that his neighbor had been using his phone, too. That was all Mom needed. You could practically hear the "Ah-ha!" theme music kick in, like she'd just cracked a prime-time detective case.

Mom called the phone company immediately. She explained everything. Their response was classic: sympathetic but firm. They were very sorry, but the bill still had to be paid. That's the thing about corporations—they can "understand" your situation and still demand their money.

A technician was dispatched to investigate. He crawled through the apartment, traced the cables, and confirmed it: Steve's phone line had been illegally tapped. The calls weren't his. The crime was clear. Wiretapping—also known as call redirection in hacker circles (and also as "being a complete bastard" in our family circle).

The technician cut the line at no charge. But justice? That was going to require more than wire cutters.

Enter Attorney Ed, the family's go-to legal eagle—a man who had, by this point, developed a sort of Pavlovian response to the words "Someone's stealing from Steve again." He filed charges: illegal telephone tapping, wire fraud, and misrepresentation.

In court, Landline's defense was bold. Stupid, but bold. He produced forged documents—yes, forged—allegedly bearing Steve's signature, claiming that Steve had consented to the phone line connection. The signature looked like it had been traced with a crayon by someone with vertigo. The judge looked over the document, chuckled quietly, and tossed it aside like it was a bad punchline. "Nice try," he basically said, before declaring Landline guilty.

But wait! Then came an unexpected gut punch.

Despite the crime—despite the evidence, the forged papers, the violation, the betrayal—Landline didn't serve jail time. The judge classified it as a misdemeanor instead of a felony, handed Landline a fine, and sentenced him to some community service. No jail. No restitution. No apology.

Why? Because the court, in its infinite wisdom, decided that Steve "should have known better."

Let that rot in your gut for a second.

Steve should have known better? Yes, that bewildered our attorney Ed as well, who had already explained Steve's IDD diagnosis.

Maybe he should have known better…if he didn't have an intellectual disability. Maybe…if he hadn't spent his life believing the best in people. Maybe…if someone had taught him to be cynical instead of kind.

But he didn't know better. Because that's what happens when you grow up with developmental differences. You trust. You try. You believe. And then you pay the price for someone else's sin.

These are crimes of betrayal—emotional abuse disguised as companionship, financial theft dressed up as friendship.

After the short court case, Landline disappeared back into the shadows of the apartment complex, avoiding Steve like a snake that slithered too close to a bonfire. We assume his lawyer told him to keep his distance. Good call—pun intended.

Another vulture exposed. Another legal win. Another emotional loss.

How many times would this happen?

Too many.

God's Violent Emissary

Of all the predators Steve encountered—the exploiters, the takers, the users—few were as convincing as this next one. This particular vulture didn't swoop down from a marriage altar, a poker game, or an adjacent apartment. No, this one came sanctified, stamped with a cross, and cloaked in the righteousness of "service to the Lord," armed with a Bible in one hand and a battering fist in the other.

Steve didn't know the difference between Baptists, Methodists, Presbyterians, or any other flavor of Sunday salvation. He didn't need to. He believed in God. He believed in people. He believed in kindness, in helping others, and in the healing power of church potlucks (oh, how he loved to eat). To Steve, being a Baptist simply meant being the person he was raised to be—faithful, friendly, and forgiving. So when he stumbled across a local Baptist Church—just a bus ride from his apartment—it felt like home. Same Baptist name, same cross, same Jesus. Familiarity counts when your life is filled with uncertainty.

And for a while, it was good. This Baptist church welcomed Steve. The pastors greeted him by name. They told him God had a special purpose for him. They gave him tasks—small ones he had done before, but important to him: setting up chairs, handing out programs, collecting the offering. People smiled at him, thanked him. It made him feel needed. Useful. Worth something. And what human being doesn't want to feel that way?

But in churches—just as in the secular world—not everyone who walks through the doors is there for redemption. Some come to be fed, yes—but not spiritually. They come to feed on others.

Enter the "ministry opportunity."

One day, the church decided to help a homeless man who had been attending. This man needed food, clothing, shelter, and apparently, a host. The pastors, so enraptured by their own righteousness, didn't so much vet the man as they did assign him a Savior: Steve.

Now, let's pause here. Steve was no case manager, no social services expert, and not equipped to handle the complex needs of an itinerant stranger. He had IDD, which affected his reasoning, his discernment, and his ability to navigate threats. But did that give the pastors pause? Did it spark a deeper conversation about Steve's own vulnerabilities? Of course not. They saw an opportunity for ministry. Steve saw someone in need. And the vulture saw shelter and a meal ticket.

So, with full pastoral blessing and not a single background check, the man moved in with Steve.

It didn't take long for heaven to turn into hell.

My parents got the call from Steve's supervisor, Carl, at the hospital—the same one who had stopped the poker games and always had Steve's back—who discovered Steve sleeping overnight in a supply closet. Not once, but for several nights. Why? Because the holy houseguest had taken over Steve's apartment, his bed, and his peace of mind. And when Steve didn't give him what he wanted, the man lashed out violently. He hit Steve. Threatened him. Controlled him. Roughed him up, as the phrase goes, which does far too little to convey the sheer cruelty of the act.

Steve was terrified. He stopped going home after work. He couldn't even rest in his own space. He feared for his safety—bruised, both literally and emotionally, by the very man he thought he was helping, in the name of Jesus. Steve didn't want to tell Mom and Dad—not again.

Let's be clear here: the church, in its infinite lack of discernment, had placed a vulnerable man with IDD into a cohabitating arrangement with a complete stranger—a violent stranger. All in the name of Christian charity. Jesus said: "I needed clothes and you clothed me, I was sick and you looked after me… whatever you did for one of the least of these brothers and sisters of mine, you did for me" (Matthew 25:36-40, New International Version). But what happens when the "least of these" is the one being beaten in his own home?

Eventually, our Father—God bless the Old Testament "wrath" in him—stepped in. No miracles, no gentle rebukes, no police or Attorney Ed. Just old-fashioned justice. Dad evicted the holy squatter with all the mercy of a thunderclap. No apologies. No second chances. Steve's abuser was homeless once again. And for the first time in days, Steve could breathe.

The aftermath was painfully ironic. Steve, not wanting to upset anyone or expose his own suffering, told the pastors that the man had just… disappeared. Gone in the night. Raptured, perhaps. The pastors nodded, smiled, and praised Steve for being such a "good servant." They had the gall to call him a blessing to others.

A blessing?

He had been bruised, used, and confused in the wreckage of their failed ministry experiment. He had paid the rent, bought the food, suffered the violence, and endured the fear. And still, they called it love. They called it service. They wrapped their failure in pious platitudes and sent Steve home with a pat on the back and not one ounce of accountability.

Let this be a lesson: not all vultures have feathers. Some wear choir robes.

The Bank Teller: Vulture in Business Casual

If you've ever watched a real vulture eat, it doesn't just nibble. It grips. Rips. Tears. With cold precision and complete indifference to the cries of the dying prey it's feasting on. This bank teller—freshly hired, fresh-faced, newly trained, and probably still fresh off her high school prom—might not have intended to sink her beak into Steve, but sink she did. And what she tore into wasn't flesh, but confidence, dignity, and hard-won independence.

It was a Friday. Payday. A sacred holiday of sorts in my parents' routine with Steve. Every other week, like the rising of the tides, Mom and Dad picked Steve up from his apartment and took him to the same bank branch they'd used for years. It was a well-oiled process: park in front, Steve takes his check inside with the deposit slip, deposits it like a pro, keeps some money for personal spending, and comes back beaming with pride. Then off to the grocery store where he could stock up on Pepsi, Little Debbie snack cakes, and whatever new chips were on sale that week (if Mom would let him).

Steve had learned the ropes. Mom had taught him—patiently and thoroughly—how to endorse a check, fill out a deposit slip, and politely ask the teller for "a little bit back in cash." It was more than just a transaction. It was a badge of independence, something he could do without needing assistance, without being treated like a child or a charity case.

That Friday started like any other. Same bank. Same parking spot. Same warm feeling that everything in the world was, at least for now, safe and predictable. From the back seat, Steve said to Mom, "I got it, Mom. You and Dad can wait here."

Proud. Confident. Capable.

So he went in. And time dragged.

Ten minutes passed. Then fifteen. Then twenty. Something was off.

About the time Mom started to go in, Steve came out. His posture was deflated. Shoulders hunched. Head down. He climbed into the back seat of the car like he had just flunked a test he didn't study for.

"I wondered what took so long," Mom said.

Steve, voice tight and stumbling, replied, "Th-they wouldn't c-c-c-c-c-cash my paycheck." He was stuttering as hard as his heart was pounding. Cue the sound of the parental emergency siren.

Mom got out of the car like she was about to reenact the climactic scene of *Erin Brockovich*. She marched toward the bank with Steve reluctantly trailing behind, likely whispering silent prayers that she wouldn't cause a scene. Dad—well, something deep inside said, "Stay in the car."

Inside, Mom was greeted by the teller responsible for the debacle. According to Mom's later report, this girl looked "barely older than my Tupperware." Her tone was smug, her words clipped, and her reasoning was... breathtaking in its absurdity.

She explained that she couldn't process Steve's paycheck deposit for a number of reasons. She delivered them like commandments etched on a golden stone tablet.

My mother, all five feet of her, stood as tall as a redwood.

"Let me explain something to you," she began, in that tone that makes telemarketers hang up and teenage boys start mowing the lawn. "My son is a regular customer here. You see that account number? That's his. He comes in every payday. He has deposited checks here for years, without issue. Everyone in this branch knows him. They like him. And not once—not once—has he ever had trouble until today."

The young teller blinked.

Mom continued. "He showed you his ID. He gave you a deposit slip. He wasn't asking for a loan. He was depositing his paycheck. He works hard. Harder than most people I know. And you treated him like a criminal."

At this point, another teller—an older, familiar one—finally emerged from the back, perhaps drawn by the sound of moral decency reawakening inside a commercial bank.

"Oh, Steve!" she said warmly, waving him over. "Come on over here, hon. I'll take care of you."

And she did. She processed his deposit, gave him his cash, and chatted casually about the Colts, the weather, and how his bowling team was doing in the league. Steve's shoulders relaxed. His smile returned. He walked out of that bank feeling whole again, restored by kindness and consistency.

Later, another teller discreetly confirmed what we suspected: the new girl had grilled Steve with so many unnecessary questions that he became overwhelmed. His speech impediment, mild under normal circumstances, had worsened as he struggled to respond. Instead of reading the situation with any empathy or training, she labeled him "suspicious."

Suspicious? Suspicious of what, exactly? Having an intellectual disability? Having trouble with words? Carrying his paycheck from Home Hospital like he did every other Friday?

It wasn't about policy. It wasn't even about ignorance. It was about power. She saw Steve not as a human being but as an inconvenience. A test case. A punching bag for her newly acquired "banking authority."

As researchers at the Endeavour Foundation (2025) have noted, people with intellectual and developmental disabilities are at heightened risk of mistreatment, not just through overt scams or abuse, but through "everyday systems" that are stacked against them. These aren't always dramatic crimes. Sometimes they come in the form of denial, delay, suspicion, or passive microaggression hidden behind plexiglass and policy.

Mom likes to believe she hexed that young teller with a glance as they left the bank that day. Maybe she did. What we do know is that she was never seen at that branch again. Maybe she was transferred. Maybe she was warned. Or maybe she was just there temporarily in training.

How did that happen? Well, interestingly, a good friend of my parents—one of their town and travel buddies—happened to serve on the Board of Directors for that bank. When he heard the story from my parents, he was appalled. He apologized on behalf of the bank (unnecessarily) and promised to "handle it."

My parents hadn't told him to escalate the matter—they just needed to vent. But sometimes, venting turns into change. We hope so. All we know is the teller wasn't at that branch anymore.

Two weeks later, it was payday again.

Mom, tentative but hopeful, asked Steve as they pulled into the bank lot: "Want me to go in with you this time, honey?"

Steve didn't stutter. Not one syllable. "No, Mom! No!" Dad laughed out loud.

See? When it really mattered, Steve could say no with authority.

He was still learning to navigate a world full of predators disguised as professionals—but he did so with courage, humility, and just enough stubborn pride to insist on walking back into that bank again. On his own.

And that, more than anything, is what made him stronger than most.

The Bootlegging Brother: A Confession with a Chaser of Grace

Even family members can be unintentional vultures, which brings us—awkwardly and unflatteringly—to me: the teenage brother who needed a bootlegger. I've saved this shameful story for last, not for dramatic effect, but because it still makes me cringe.

Senior year swagger, 1979—looking like I could be the bootlegger, but Steve took care of that for me

Like most seventeen-year-olds with more hormones than judgment, I was convinced the universe spun on its axis solely to accommodate *my* adolescent needs. Susan and Scott could attest to this. I was the star of my own coming-of-age movie—unfortunately, it was directed by impulse, scored by bad decisions, and poorly lit with moral ambiguity.

Enter Steve. My amazing, generous, trusting big brother. At twenty-four, Steve was living in his small garage-turned-apartment near the hospital. He had his own place, his own life, and—most importantly to my teenage mind—his own legal ID.

Meanwhile, I had just discovered the high school party scene. It turns out I had a unique talent for becoming popular: not because I was charming or talented or even all that interesting, but because I had a secret weapon—Steve.

With pre-party cash in hand from my wide-eyed, underage classmates, I would call Steve up with the subtlety of a mob boss:

"Hey, bro, want to help me run an errand?"

And just like that, my kind-hearted, always-up-for-an-adventure brother would hop in the car, ride shotgun, and unknowingly become the designated bootlegger for a bunch of suburban party animals.

Over time, I imagine the liquor store clerk began to develop a few theories about Steve. Theory A: Steve had a hollow leg and drank like a fish. Theory B: Steve was the most sought-after guest on the Indiana party circuit. Either way, he was consistent. Friendly. Loyal. And entirely unaware that his little brother was making him an accomplice to teenage mischief and a minor felony. Good God, what was I thinking? (Well, I suppose I wasn't.)

Here's the thing: Steve never hesitated. He was proud to help his brother. And I—foolish, selfish, blinded by adolescent nonsense— never stopped to consider the risk I was asking him to take. Supplying alcohol to minors is, to this day, *not* considered best practice—even in the anything-goes cornfields of 1970s Indiana.

Am I proud of this? Not even a little. Even now, decades later, I shake my head at that version of myself. Not because I was a reckless teen (that's practically a rite of passage), but because I used Steve's trust, his love, his eagerness to help, for my own gains. Mate crime.

And yet, redemption isn't about rewriting history—it's about learning from it. I've wrestled with whether to include this story in this chapter, and I finally decided that I had to, because sometimes, the people who love us the most are the ones we unintentionally take advantage of. Not necessarily out of malice. Not necessarily out of cruelty. But out of blindness and immaturity. And families of vulnerable people need to know this: sometimes the circling vultures aren't strangers or outside friends. Sometimes, heartbreakingly, they're us—the ones in the inner circle.

I've long since asked Steve's forgiveness—and God's—quietly, through prayer and memory—and I believe both have given it. Steve was always quick to grace. He'd probably just laugh and say, "Hey, at least I never had to g-g-go to one of those d-dumb parties."

Touché, Steve. Touché.

When Trust Is Weaponized: The Silent Scourge of Mate Crime

People with intellectual and developmental disabilities (IDD) are frequently targeted for exploitation by abusers posing as friends, partners, or helpers who manipulate and rob their victims (Endeavour Foundation, 2025). It's often invisible at first, disguised as affection, camaraderie, or concern. But behind the scenes, it's always the same: control, exploitation, and abuse.

The warning signs are disturbingly common and eerily familiar to anyone who knew Steve or persons like him:

1. A sudden influx of new "friends" who seem to steer the ship of your loved one's life (Endeavour Foundation, 2025).
2. Manipulative guilt trips—"If you really care about me, you'll buy this," or "Don't tell anyone, they won't understand."
3. Paying for everything in the relationship—meals, rides, gifts—until the victim's bank account is thinner than the empathy of their abuser.

4. Changes in mood, behavior, hygiene, even physical signs of distress.
5. Fear. Shame. Silence.

Steve experienced all of this. Even from me. Others were more malicious, more covert, and more violent.

That's why prevention is key—not just teaching people with IDD about money and trust (though we must do that), but equipping families and communities to recognize the red flags and step in early. Every incident, no matter how small, should be investigated. Friendship crime doesn't just happen—it escalates if left unchecked. And too often, it ends in total devastation (Endeavour Foundation, 2025).

Steve didn't see himself as a victim. He didn't carry himself with bitterness or with suspicion of others (although the suspicion part would have been helpful). He loved people. He trusted people. That was both his glory and his vulnerability.

He lived with purpose, rode his bike to church in the rain, hugged strangers with conviction, and sang off-key with the enthusiasm of a thousand choirs. He didn't understand manipulation because he wasn't built that way.

And while vultures came—too many to count, too many we didn't see coming, too many we don't even know about—they didn't win.

Steve loved, and he was loved in return. That kind of light doesn't go out just because a few scavengers tried to cash in on it.

I needed to tell these stories—including mine—for the love of Stephen.

CHAPTER 12

THE HEART HAS NO IQ: LOVE, LOSS, AND THE LIFE STEVE BUILT

The best and most beautiful things in the world cannot
be seen or even touched, but just felt in the heart.

— Helen Keller

Hearts, Hormones, and Hindsight: Steve's Journey Through Love and Loss

Celebrating love—
Steve and Cathy's wedding, 2005

et's get something straight, right from the start: people with intellectual and developmental disabilities are sexual beings. Yes, you read that correctly. They aren't celibate angels living in some antiseptic world devoid of desire, attraction, or heartbreak. And they certainly don't need our pity or our prudishness.

Steve, my brother, had sexual desires. And guess what? He acted on them in entirely human ways—albeit with some awkward discoveries along the way. Like the time Mom found his secret stash of adult materials. Let's just say it made for an eye-opening moment of motherhood. If I had been there, I probably would have choked from laughing so hard at my mother having that conversation with Steve.

Sex, Rights, and the Church Hypocrites

If awkward family discoveries were our only hurdles, we'd all be sleeping a lot easier. But things were (and still are) much more sinister when it comes to the sexual and reproductive rights of people like Steve. Did you know that as of 2022, 31 U.S. states and Washington, D.C., allow for the forced sterilization of disabled individuals, without their consent? Yes, in the land of the free, a judge can decide that someone like Steve doesn't have the right to reproduce (National Women's Law Center, 2022).

What's the origin of this monstrosity? Indiana—yes, my home state—was the first to pass a law allowing the sterilization of people deemed "unfit" to reproduce. In 1907, this practice became part of our legislative record. And although it was declared unconstitutional by the Indiana Supreme Court in 1921 (Indiana Historical Bureau, 2025), the ideology behind it has proven stubbornly undead, like a bad horror movie villain who just keeps crawling out of the grave.

Case in point: One lovely Sunday morning in the 1970s, during a Bible study at our beloved First Baptist Church in Lafayette, a so-called Christian and "enlightened" university professor declared that "all retarded kids should be neutered." In church. In Sunday School, no less. I still don't know how my father didn't leap across the classroom table to wring his neck. According to Dad, he wanted to. Apparently, Jesus saves... but the professor didn't get the memo about 'love thy neighbor.'

My parents never once considered sterilizing Steve. Not even for a second, even though it was suggested to them. In fact, they fiercely protected his dignity and personhood in a society that routinely tried to deny him both.

Let me share how Steve experienced romantic love—the way it lifted him to the clouds, and the way it yanked him down to the earth with equal force.

Love in the Time of Tilt-a-Whirls

When Steve was a teenager, love struck him like a Tilt-a-Whirl bar to the gut. Literally.

Charlene, a sweet girl from his high school special education class, became Steve's first official girlfriend. They were both seventeen, and Steve was smitten. I was only 10 and could definitely see it, and was so happy about it. To prove his devotion, Steve took her to the annual Fairfield Manufacturing Family Day at Indiana Beach in Monticello, a super fun day that I looked forward to every year (thanks for working there, Dad!). Now, Steve's girl, Charlene, loved carnival rides; Steve... not so much. But love makes you do dumb things—like riding the spinning Tilt-a-Whirl and the terrifying Sky Ride despite a debilitating fear of heights. Steve turned so pale he could have passed for a snowman in July, but he soldiered on like a hormonal knight in shining armor.

That's the thing people often miss: love among people with IDD is just as real and raw as anyone else's. And just like anyone else's, love can be euphoric and cause tremendous pain.

Sadly, Charlene's father died, and she and her mother decided to return to their home state of Florida. It was as if someone had quietly pulled the sun from Steve's sky. Mom and Dad clued us in that he was hurting. The light in his eyes dimmed a bit, his easy laughter vanished, and the steady rhythm of his days stumbled. Now, don't get me wrong, he didn't lose his appetite for food. Never his appetite. But the Steve we knew, the one with daily energy who greeted us with a smile big enough to fill a room, seemed to retreat somewhere far away, but just for a while. He missed her—not in the casual way people say they miss someone, but in the bone-deep ache that leaves a person hollow.

And yet, as life has a way of doing, love came around again.

Love on Layaway: The Curious Case of Elaine

Unfortunately, you already met Elaine in the previous chapter, *Where Vultures Circle, Part Two*. Whatever anyone else might say about her—or about the choices that followed—one thing remained unshakably true: Steve loved her. His love had no boundaries, no conditions. It was patient to a fault, and it endured far more than it should have.

Steve and Elaine

Three years. That's how long the marriage lasted. Three long years—though, if we're being honest, at least two years and eleven months too long.

In that time, Steve was manipulated, drained of what little money he had, and mistreated in ways both emotional and isolating. And yet he stayed, holding on as long as he could. Because Steve, in the truest sense, was always determined to make things work. He always put others before himself—especially her child.

Where Elaine faltered, Steve tried to fill the gaps. He never yelled, never raised a hand. Instead, he loved with the quiet steadiness that defined him. In his own way, he became a father to that boy. And when the marriage finally crumbled, Steve didn't just mourn the end of a relationship. He mourned the loss of a child he had grown to cherish as if he were his own.

I'll never forget the day he confided in me, long after the dust had settled. Speaking about the wreckage of that marriage, his voice softened, and he said simply, "I sure miss that little guy." Of course he did. That was Steve—his heart was never the part that failed.

Resilience in Recovery

It would take sixteen years for Steve to emerge from the wreckage and court battles of the Elaine experience. Sixteen years of being single. Sixteen years of building back his self-worth and his peace. My parents helped him move into a new apartment on Union Street after the divorce, just down the road from the hospital. Slowly, joy returned to his life.

He bowled in a community league and became a team captain. He found a couple of new church families at another Baptist church he found. He made friends through a community center for adults with IDD. He even survived a hospital merger and downsizing like a seasoned professional. Steve was back. His laugh was back. His energy was back. His confidence was back.

His smile—that radiant, goofy, Steve-smile—was back.

And though he didn't date anyone for those sixteen years, we all knew that he still carried love in his heart. No bitterness. No resentment. Just love and a hurting heart.

The Right to Be Human

Steve's life, with all its ups and downs, serves as a powerful reminder that individuals with IDD are not asexual curiosities or burdens in need of control. They are lovers. Friends. Parents. And sometimes, survivors. They are human.

People like disability lawyer Katie Tastrom, who is also a disabled parent, advocate for recognition of the power and capability in disabled parenting. As she puts it, her kids have learned independence early—because their mother's disability taught them life skills, not helplessness (Leary, 2018, May 7).

What the world needs is not fewer Steves, but fewer barriers to love, dignity, and choice. We need to stop treating disability as a problem to be fixed or feared, and start seeing it as a dimension of humanity worth honoring.

Because if Steve taught us anything, it's this: Love is not measured by IQ. It's measured by heart.

Love in the Time of Swisher Sweets: The Redemption of Steve and Cathy

Needless to say, when Cathy entered the picture, our family became the emotional equivalent of a pack of border collies circling the pasture. We weren't just watching—we were on watch. Vigilant. Alert. Skeptical. Think Secret Service with a green bean casserole and Indiana accents.

Why the panic?

Because Steve—our beloved, big-hearted, IDD-wired brother—had already been tripped up by love, in a cruel way. And when someone you love has a mind that's both

Steve and Cathy—a moment shared

beautifully simple and endlessly open, heartbreak doesn't just sting—it echoes. We had seen the bruises on his tender spirit before. And so we all bristled with protective instincts when Cathy stepped onto the field. I had hoped he would just stay single the rest of his life. Shame on me!

Cathy H. (Ream) Osborn was 44, and Steve was 50. They met the way many people do later in life: through friends who knew better than to leave romance up to chance. This wasn't a dating app situation—no profile pics, bios, or swipe fatigue. This was old-school matchmaking, Hoosier-style. People who knew Steve from church, the bowling league, and the community center had someone in mind. A sweet woman. A hard worker. A little quirky. Someone who "might be a good match." We rolled our eyes, of course—but it turned out they were right.

From the beginning, Cathy had that magnetic sparkle that made her hard to ignore. She was loud in all the best ways—her jewelry jingled when she walked, her voice had a musical lilt, and her laugh could startle cats out of trees. Her style was a unique hybrid of Walmart couture and dollar-store dazzle. Think rhinestone butterflies and teddy bears in sequins. Subtle, she was not. But Steve? Steve was enchanted.

And we—Steve's worried, overthinking, codependent tribe—were rattled.

We googled her. We prayed about it. We listened to our mother's worst-case-scenario whisperings. Cathy had been married twice before. That was a red flag as far as Mom was concerned. Maybe even a crimson banner waved by the Ghost of Bad Decisions Past. But Steve wasn't bothered. Maybe because he didn't judge people by their résumés or backstories—he judged them by how they made him feel.

And Cathy made him feel something he hadn't felt in a long time: wanted.

What followed was a courtship worthy of a syrupy-sweet love story full of shy glances, evening phone calls exchanged, dinners at Golden Corral, and long talks about favorite shows they shared (Walker, Texas Ranger and Wheel of Fortune, for the record). Cathy loved fried chicken. Steve loved eating—it didn't matter what, he just loved eating. They both loved each other. It was, dare I say, adorable.

On August 15, 2005, beneath the summer sun on the lawn of the Tippecanoe County Courthouse in Lafayette, Steve and Cathy were married by a pastor from Cornerstone Baptist Church. The ceremony was humble, sweet, and full of heartfelt awkwardness— the best kind. Family, friends, and a handful of well-wishers gathered to see two adults with developmental disabilities vow to share a life together. Some people cried. Some people chuckled. But everyone left with the unmistakable feeling that something pure had just happened.

That magical (and slightly nerve-wracking) wedding vows moment—
Steve looking a bit like a deer caught in the headlights

Steve could not stop smiling. And I mean it. He grinned the entire day like someone had told him he'd won the lottery and a lifetime supply of doughnuts. Cathy looked genuinely happy, too, content in a way that suggested she knew this time, she'd found a keeper. And maybe we didn't all trust her fully just yet. Can you blame us? But love, you'll recall, doesn't wait for unanimous votes.

The Honeymoon Period (Also Known As "Cathy Does a Steve 'Extreme Makeover'")

Now, let me explain something about Steve. Before Cathy, his personal aesthetic could best be described as "hospital janitor meets martial arts fanboy meets half-hearted hoarder." His prized possessions included Swisher Sweet cigars, posters of Bruce Lee, a cracked lava lamp, and a stack of porn magazines that he definitely did not get from a church rummage sale, no matter what he claimed.

Cathy changed all of that.

She didn't just move into his life—she reordered it like she was channeling Martha Stewart with a Southern Indiana twang. Suddenly, Steve was slimming down—thirty pounds melted away like cheese on a drive-thru burger. Gone were the cigars and the risqué magazines. In their place? Skin lotion. Combed hair. Glasses cleaned with an actual cloth instead of shirt sleeves. Cathy didn't just love him. She upgraded him. Perhaps my Mom was just a bit envious that Cathy fashioned Steve in the way she had tried for years.

Steve started wearing better clothes—clothes that matched, even! Clothes that hadn't been selected exclusively for their elastic waistbands or their ability to survive spaghetti night. And something else changed, too: his personality was back. Suddenly, he was adulting—hard! He was mowing the lawn, doing the dishes, and living in a house where the furniture actually coordinated—on purpose.

Of course, progress never comes without a few growing pains. Cathy, ever the reformer, may have pushed my famously patient brother just a smidge too far. At one point early in their marriage, Steve—yes, Steve—had his bags packed and was ready to hit the road. But to her credit, Cathy got wise, softened her approach, and crafted a gentler path forward. And thanks to that compromise, Steve stayed... and so did the matching throw pillows.

Studies have shown (and I love this) that adults with intellectual and developmental disabilities can experience strong and fulfilling romantic relationships when given proper support and community acceptance (Lunsky & Benson, 2001; Milligan & Neufeldt, 2001). Steve and Cathy were proof of that. Cathy had a wonderful family supporting her, and you know, Steve did as well.

The Three Amigos—brothers with Cathy in the mix.
Left to right: Scott, me, Cathy, and blissful Steve

Cathy had her own home when they married—a modest, loving space—and Steve moved in. It was a palace compared to his bachelor pad, and he treated it with the reverence of someone who had finally been given his own castle. His friends noticed the changes. His family did too. Our sweet boy-man, who once hoarded baseball-playing cards and holey socks, had become a man with a wife and responsibilities.

The Domestic Years: Routine, Resilience, and Bike Helmets

Their life together was simple and structured, like a casserole recipe passed down through the church bulletin. Cathy was up early every morning, picked up by a co-worker who also worked at Purdue, where she had a job in housekeeping. Steve worked housekeeping at St. Elizabeth's Hospital and rode his bike to and from work—a practice that kept him healthy and, we hoped, happy.

Cathy insisted he wear a bike helmet. He said he did. But we all knew better. There were reports of him "forgetting" the helmet behind the hedge after rounding the corner from the house. Helmet or not, it didn't matter. He was active. He had purpose. He had a wife waiting for him when he got home. For the first time, Steve's life felt fully formed, just like he'd seen in his parents and from his siblings, and longed to emulate.

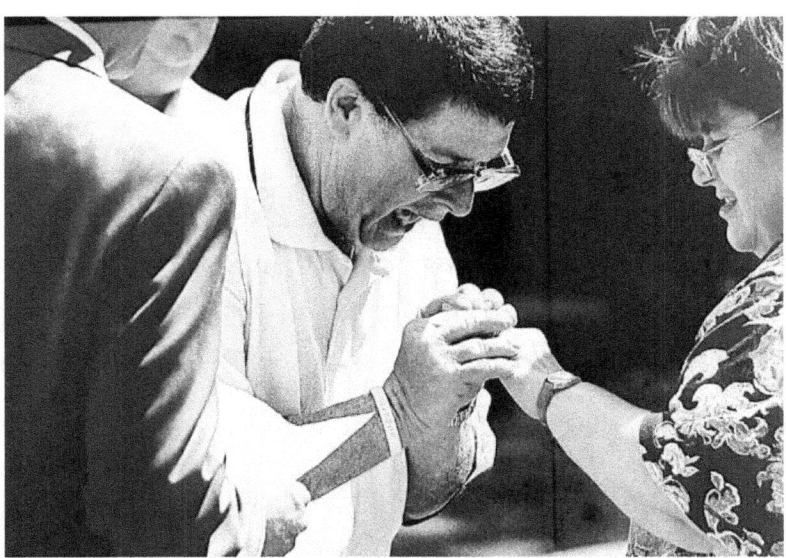

Wait—weren't we sure this ring fit earlier

They even joined their bank accounts. Steve, who had squirreled away a surprisingly large amount of money during his single years, spent it (with Cathy's help) on new furniture, a microwave that didn't spark, paint for the living room walls, and a new loveseat that no longer had duct tape holding the cushions in place. It was HGTV on a budget—and it worked. Their home reflected their new life: patchworked, imperfect, and completely theirs.

Every update Steve gave to our parents was glowing. He was happy. He had a home, a partner, a role. This was the life he had dreamed about when he used to see couples on TV and think, "Could I do that too someday?"

Yes, Steve. Yes, you could.

And you did.

Fifteen Months

They were married for just fifteen months.

Fifteen months of laughter, of growing up, of learning how to love and be loved. Of buying furniture, appliances, and nagging each other, and watching the same DVD six times because it was Steve's favorite. Fifteen months of arguing over groceries, of making up with hugs and chocolate milk, of setting alarm clocks and cooking Hamburger Helper. Fifteen months of being a husband. And for Steve, that was everything.

Then Cathy got the call—the kind of call no one ever wants to get.

We all remember where we were when we heard. How time stopped. How laughter fled the room. How cruel reality barged in like an unwelcome guest.

But this chapter isn't about how Steve died. It's about how he lived—especially during those final fifteen months, when love found him, demanded his best, and brought out his deepest joy. Cathy gave him that. And for that, we are forever grateful.

Even if we were suspicious at first. Even if we hovered like paranoid sheepdogs. Even if we second-guessed and judged and muttered about bank accounts and second marriages.

Because in the end, Cathy gave Steve what we couldn't: a shot at ordinary, messy, glorious married life. That is something sacred, and it was all for the love of Stephen.

CHAPTER 13

THE LONG ROAD TO INCLUSION: WHY WE'RE NOT "THERE" YET

(AND WHY PRETENDING WE ARE IS JUST EMBARRASSING)

Start by doing what's necessary; then do what's possible; and suddenly you are doing the impossible.

— Francis of Assisi

There's a phrase that gets tossed around in disability advocacy circles with the same resigned sigh you hear from exhausted parents watching a toddler smear spaghetti on the wall: *"We've come a long way, but we're not there yet."* And it's true. People with intellectual and developmental disabilities have far more opportunities, legal protections, and social visibility than they did a generation ago. The days of locking someone like my brother Steve away in an institution "for his own good" are mostly behind us.

Mostly.

And if you think that's enough, then you haven't been paying attention.

Steve was born when phrases like "special needs" hadn't yet been focus-grouped into polite society. He entered a world where disability often meant invisibility—unless you were being publicly pitied, pathologized, or paraded around during telethons with music so manipulative it could make a shark weep. And yet, he lived, laughed, learned, and loved louder than any of the rest of us.

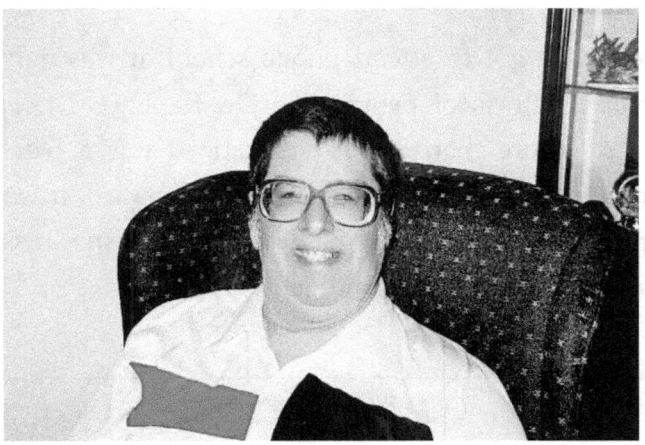

So no, this isn't just commentary. This is personal. Because Steve didn't just walk the road to inclusion—he paved it with his own two feet, often while someone was trying to redirect him back to the "special" room, the "special" job, or the "special" corner of society.

A Brief History of "Better Than It Was"
(Which Isn't the Same as "Good")

To appreciate how far we've come, let's remember how absurdly low the bar once was. For much of the 20th century, people with IDD were excluded from schools, employment, and even families. They were sent to institutions with sunny-sounding names like Willowbrook or Pennhurst—names that now live in infamy as case studies in neglect, abuse, and federal civil rights violations (Yell, 2023).

Steve was born in the 1950s, a time when the most common recommendation to parents of children with disabilities was: *"Put him in an institution and forget he was born."* But our parents, with a mix of stubbornness, faith, and what can only be called holy defiance, said no. They brought him home. They loved him. And they forced the world to do the same.

When he finally got to attend public school, it was only because of the tireless efforts of people like Dr. Kephart, Dr. Hiatt, and my parents. Before that, Steve's "education" was a patchwork of exclusion and well-meaning babysitting. Afterward, it was still far from perfect, but at least he had a desk—albeit sometimes one in a corner, or a different building altogether.

Inclusion ≠ Proximity
(Just Ask Steve)

Steve was in the school, yes. But "included"? That depended on the day.

Inclusion is not proximity. You can sit someone at the lunch table without ever feeding their spirit or inviting them into real relationship. Steve was at the table, but often alone in the conversation. He was often in classrooms, but not always in community. There were times when he was celebrated, even loved— like at First Baptist Church, Boy Scouts, or Home Hospital. And times when he was mocked, underestimated, or ignored. There were teachers who saw him as fully human, and others who saw him as an obligation, or worse—a disruption.

When Steve joined the school chess team, some people scoffed, assuming he wouldn't understand the game. Turns out, he was better than most of them. And when he won, he didn't gloat. He just smiled and said, *"Do you want to play again?"* That was Steve. Quiet confidence. Persistent grace. A living refutation of every stereotype the system had quietly absorbed.

We talk about inclusive education like it's a box to check. Steve's life reminded us it's a relationship. A daily decision to see someone, value someone, and support someone—not just seat them near the front and hope they blend in.

"We Don't See Disability"
(An Erasure Danger)

Ah, the beloved "colorblind" cousin of ableism: *"We don't see disability in this family/company/classroom."* That's usually said by someone who definitely sees disability, but also sees it as a liability, so they're pretending not to.

Steve saw right through that nonsense. He knew who he was. He knew he wasn't like everyone else. But he didn't want to be "fixed." He wanted to be included. Celebrated. Supported. If you denied his disability, you denied part of his identity—part of what made him hilarious, strong, tender-hearted, and more emotionally intelligent than some therapists I've met.

Refusing to acknowledge someone's disability isn't inclusion—it's erasure. And Steve's life was a testament to what happens when people finally stop doing that. He didn't need less recognition of his needs. He needed people to take those needs seriously, while still seeing his worth. And when they did—oh, how he flourished.

The Mission Accomplished Banner of Disability Inclusion

There's this recurring delusion, especially among policymakers and smug dinner party guests, that "we've arrived" when it comes to disability inclusion. As if the ADA was some sort of magical spell that undid centuries of exclusion.

Family and friends celebrating Steve and Cathy's special day

You don't get to fly the "Mission Accomplished" banner when adults with IDD still have employment rates hovering around 19 percent, despite 30 percent wanting to work in the community (NCI, 2022). You don't get to call it "done" when direct support professionals— people who bathe, feed, and care for people with disabilities— make less than a living wage (National Alliance for Direct Support Professionals, 2022).

Steve worked. He contributed. He paid taxes. He lent money to family members (with interest) and made liquor runs for me, his underage delinquent brother. He was not a burden on society, but society often burdened him. With inaccessible transportation. With dismissive doctors. With pity instead of power.

The "Racism Is Over" Logic, Applied to Disability

It's the same energy you hear when people say, *"Well, we had a Black president, so racism is over."* Sure. And I had a salad last week, so my high cholesterol is cured.

Saying ableism is gone because of the ADA is like saying the Civil Rights Movement solved racism. It ignores the real, ongoing systemic barriers. People with IDD—especially those from marginalized racial and economic backgrounds—still face lower life expectancy, higher rates of abuse, and reduced access to healthcare (Ouellette-Kuntz et al., 2023).

Of course, progress matters. But progress doesn't mean parity. And it doesn't mean justice is automatic.

Steve lived that complexity. As a white man with a strong support system, he had privileges others didn't. But even then, the system made him prove, over and over, that he mattered.

Steve Showed Us the Better Way

Here's the thing: Steve wasn't just a "person with a disability." He was a person with a mission. He modeled patience in the face of ignorance. Kindness in the face of condescension. Joy in the face of limitation. And perhaps most heroically, he forgave us—for our awkwardness, the ways society used him or dismissed him, for underestimating him, and for our failure to show up sometimes.

He was ahead of his time. Not just because he lived through policy shifts and cultural awakenings. But because his humble daily life—

his dignity, his resilience, his humor—called the rest of us to be better.

The Road Goes On, But We Walk It Together

So yes, we've come a long way. But to act like we've "arrived" is to betray the very people who got us this far. People like Steve.

Inclusion is not a moment in history—it's a daily, lived commitment. One that asks more of us than ribbons, posters, or inclusion marches. It asks us to build accessible spaces, fund essential supports, train inclusive educators, listen to disabled voices, and celebrate lives like Steve's not just as *inspiring*, but as *indispensable*.

The Fab Four with the woman who gave us life—Mom

Steve's story doesn't exist outside the system. It reveals the system— its flaws, its successes, its potential, and its capacity for continued transformation. If we keep telling it, keep learning from it, and keep walking forward—together—we just might get somewhere worth going, for the love of Stephen, and millions of others.

CHAPTER 14

YOU WERE MEANT FOR THIS CHILD: A LOVE LETTER TO PARENTS

"Parenting is not for the faint of heart. Parenting a child with special needs? That's not just parenting—it's a full-contact, heart-wide-open, caffeine-fueled act of holy resistance."

— **Keith and Phyllis Jones**

To the Parents on This Important Journey

Dear Parent,

If you've made it to this chapter, chances are you've already cried in a doctor's office, googled something alarming at 2:00 a.m., questioned God, explained a diagnosis to someone who still didn't get it, and discovered that you can, in fact, survive on three hours of sleep and an expired granola bar.

In short: you're one of the brave ones.

You are raising a child who needs a little more from you—and from the world—than most people realize. And while this journey comes with its own beautiful rewards, it's not the parenting path most folks picture when they flip through the glossy pages of baby books filled with pastel nurseries and milestones measured in neat, predictable charts.

Photo: Kampus Production / Pexels (used under Pexels License)

Your journey is real. It is sacred. It is exhausting. And you are not alone.

Let me walk beside you for a moment—not as an expert, but as a sibling who watched my parents stumble, struggle, succeed, and love my brother Stephen into wholeness, despite the world's insistence that he wasn't worth the effort. This chapter is for *you*—equal parts love letter, battle cry, survival guide, and warm casserole delivered to your metaphorical front porch.

To the Parents Still in the Trenches

We see you. Truly, we do.

We see you packing snacks, meds, weighted blankets, and three contingency plans just to survive a trip to the grocery store. We see you filling out forms where every box seems to say, "Please quantify all the ways your child is not meeting expectations." We see you pretending not to cry in the school parking lot. We see you answering the same question—"What's wrong with her?"—for the fiftieth time with clenched grace.

You are not doing it wrong just because it's hard. It *is* hard.

And yes, we know you've been told to "enjoy every moment." But, let's be honest: no one dreams of starting their day scraping dried therapy putty off car upholstery, or having to explain that AAC doesn't stand for "All About Crystals" to a wide-eyed new therapist fresh out of grad school. Enjoyment is optional. *Endurance*, however, is your superpower.

In truth, the "trenches" are where miracles happen. They just don't come with spotlights or applause. They come in whispers: a first word long past its expected date. Eye contact on a day you thought you couldn't keep going. A new sound. A moment of calm. A laugh. A connection.

Those wins? They're yours. You earned them. And even if it seems like no one else sees it, there are some of us who do.

You Are Not the Diagnosis

Let's talk about something nobody says out loud enough: you are not your child's case file.

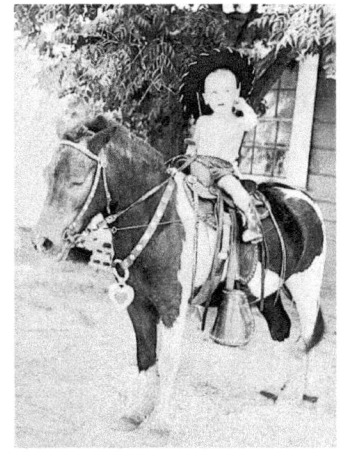

Somewhere between the evaluations, labels, appointments, and acronyms (OT, PT, SLP, IEP, WTH), you may have started disappearing. You used to be *you*. Now you're "Mom of the kid with

Little Steve riding tall in the old portrait pony photos

global delays" or "Dad who's always late to the pickup line because of feeding therapy."

But hear me: you are still *you*.

You are still allowed to have a life. A dream. A body that gets tired. A brain that needs stimulation beyond insurance paperwork. Research by Burke and Hodapp (2014) found that while parental stress is higher among caregivers of children with IDD, social support, time for oneself, and emotional self-care significantly improve mental health outcomes. Translation? You need space to breathe—not just to advocate.

So if you've ever felt guilty for binge-watching shows on Netflix, escaping to the garage, or locking yourself in the bathroom with a piece of chocolate and a glass of wine—you're not alone. You're *surviving*. Keep at it.

And your child? They are not a walking list of deficits. They are not a diagnosis. They are a person—sometimes loud, sometimes unreachable, sometimes hilarious, sometimes miraculous. In my experience, they're often all of that in a 15-minute span.

Let the world do its labeling. You? You do the loving.

What My Parents Got Right (and What I Learned Watching)

My parents didn't have a manual when Steve was born. What they had were dreams that shattered, professionals who recommended institutionalization, and a son who was not expected to live as a preemie—let alone thrive.

They were young. They were scared. They were broke. But they did something radical: they chose to love him anyway.

My mother read to Steve when he couldn't yet sit up. My father taught him coordination and thinking skills. They fought for him to attend public school years before the Individuals with Disabilities Education Act (IDEA) said he had a right to.

Keith and Phyllis with their boys, Steve and Johnny—
1955, when love was young and the road ahead unknown

They were not perfect. They yelled sometimes. They got tired. They didn't always agree. But they never gave up on Steve. And they never let him believe that he was less than worthy of joy.

And you know what? That was enough. That was more than enough.

What I learned watching them is this: children with disabilities don't need perfect parents. They need fierce ones. Humble ones. Ones who know when to fight and when to hug and when to cry behind the bathroom door and then come out swinging.

My mother used to say, "You don't have to understand everything to love completely. You just love."

And my father, with tears in his eyes after one of my interview sessions with him for this book, whispered, "He taught *me* more than anything I ever taught him."

Research backs this up: long-term developmental success is more closely correlated with family acceptance, expectations, and emotional responsiveness than with any one therapy or intervention (Dillenburger, McKerr, & Jordan, 2015).

If that's all you do—love them like your life depends on it—it will change theirs.

What I Want Every Parent to Know

Here's what I wish I could say to every parent in every waiting room, at every support group, or holding their breath in a hospital hallway:

1. There will be days when you grieve the life you thought your child—or you—would have. That's okay. That grief is real. Let it in.
2. There will be days when your child will stun you with their humor, strength, or joy. Let that in too.
3. Clinical reports can be helpful—but not infallible. My parents knew to question what didn't sit right. So should you. Trust your gut—you know your child best.
4. There is no timeline. No one is "behind" in a race that was never fair to begin with. And sometimes the slowest journeys produce the biggest wins.
5. You can't fix everything. You're not supposed to. That's not love's job. Love's job is to *stay*.
6. You will need help. Take it. No, really. TAKE IT.
7. Laughter is not betrayal. Humor is survival. In fact, some of the hardest moments in our family ended with someone snorting milk out their nose.

Your child's life has meaning. So does yours.

Even when progress is slow. Even when behaviors regress. Even when your house looks like a therapy supply store exploded.

Research by Woodgate, Ateah, and Secco (2008) found that while families of children with disabilities face chronic uncertainty, the core of resilience lies in meaning-making and strong relationships. In other words: you're building something sacred.

And please, for the love of your sanity and soul, do not waste one more ounce of energy on unanswerable, self-blaming questions like:

"Why was my child born this way?"

"Did I do something wrong during pregnancy?"

"Whose fault is it—mine, my partner's, God's?"

These are the questions that spiral us into shame, not understanding. And they are rooted in the false assumption that *something went wrong*. But your child is not a mistake to be explained. They are a person to be celebrated.

Yes, the road may be different—but it is not lesser. And your child, no matter their challenges or diagnosis, was *not* created defective.

"God don't make no junk."

And if you need that in more clinical terms: studies have shown that spiritual meaning-making and affirming beliefs about divine purpose are linked with higher levels of hope and emotional resilience in parents of children with disabilities (Poston & Turnbull, 2004).

Your child is not here as a punishment, nor are they a cosmic glitch. They are here as part of this world's rich, sacred mosaic—bearing light and love in their own way. And you? You were chosen, called, or perhaps just thrown headfirst into this—but either way, you are the right one for this child.

So, please: toss the guilt. Set down the shame. Give yourself a break, and simply breathe.

You Are Not Alone

You may feel like you're pushing a boulder uphill with one hand while filling out Medicaid paperwork and a doctor's intake form with the other. And some days, you are.

But others have pushed that same boulder. You are part of a quiet, beautiful fellowship: the parents who keep going. The ones who choose love, over and over, even when it hurts. Even when no one applauds. Even when it feels like you're the only one who remembers the appointments, the meds, the triggers, the soft words that work, the exact way the apple needs to be sliced or the whole day unravels.

Steve's smile made every milestone worthwhile, and so will your child's

You are not forgotten. You are not invisible. You are one of the great ones.

Steve's life taught me that the most powerful advocacy often looks like ordinary love, practiced over decades. You're doing that now.

You Don't Have to Do This Alone

There's a truth that rarely makes it into pamphlets or pediatric intake forms: this journey can break your heart. Even the strongest parents—those who can interpret insurance jargon before coffee and build IKEA equipment with one hand—can find themselves undone by the quiet moments. The what-ifs. The late-night scans. The birthdays that look more like countdowns than celebrations.

If your child is slowly losing their battle—or if your child has already passed on—this journey can feel impossibly heavy. And no amount of brave faces or casseroles from the church and neighbors can stitch that kind of grief back together.

That's why you need people.

Not just friends who say, "Let me know if you need anything," but people who *get it*. People who have sat in waiting rooms and funeral homes and support groups with names like "Hope After Loss." People who know that healing doesn't mean forgetting. People who won't flinch when you say your child's name—or mention their feeding tube—or talk about the way the house feels too quiet now.

Find a support group. A counselor. A pastor. A therapist. An online community. A weepy friend with tissues and takeout. Don't wait until the weight crushes you to realize you were never meant to carry it alone.

There is no shame in needing help. There is only strength in reaching for it.

You were meant for this child, yes—but you were also meant to be held while you hold them.

When our family was raising Steve, there was no internet to turn to. No Facebook groups, no late-night Google searches, no easy way to type in "help for parents like us." Mom and Dad relied on word of mouth, trial and error, and a lot of faith. Support was out there, but it often took persistence—and sometimes sheer luck—to find it.

Parents today have a different challenge. The resources are plentiful—almost too plentiful. A quick search will return hundreds of organizations, groups, and websites. The question isn't *whether* help is available, but *which* help is right for you and your child. Every family's journey is unique, and what comforts or equips one parent may not be the right fit for another.

Resources matter. Support groups, mentors, and organizations can provide information, advocacy, and encouragement when the road feels overwhelming. But at the heart of it all, the most powerful resource you have is love—the love you carry for your child, and the love that grows when you find others willing to walk beside you.

Our family discovered this with Steve: no matter how limited the options seemed, there was always someone—sometimes a teacher, a neighbor, a church friend, or a fellow parent—ready to remind us we weren't alone. My hope is that as you explore these resources, you'll find that same reminder.

Ultimately, what carries us is not just programs or policies, but people. People who see, who listen, who show up, and who help us believe—again and again—that every child is worthy, every parent is stronger than they think, and every story is worth telling.

A Mirror Will Suffice: A Tribute, With Caveats

Erma Bombeck, the iconic American humorist and columnist, wrote a short prose piece I happen to like.

Now, I'll preface this with a few caveats: the language isn't exactly modern or inclusive by today's standards. There's a distinctly Judeo-Christian undertone, which some may find comforting and others may find exclusionary. And yes, unfortunately, fathers and siblings were left out of this one, as if only moms were on duty during the night shift of worry and advocacy. But still, this piece has staying power. It offers a glimpse into the deep admiration, humor, and awe that many parents feel when raising a child with special needs.

You may love it. You may roll your eyes. Maybe both. But let's take it for what it is: an attempt, however imperfect, to celebrate the strength and sacred chaos of families like ours.

The Special Mother by Erma Bombeck
Reprinted with permission of the Aaron M. Priest Literary Agency, Inc.

> Most women become mothers by accident, some by choice, a few by social pressures, and a couple by habit. This year, nearly 100,000 women will become mothers of handicapped children. Did you ever wonder how mothers of handicapped children are chosen?
>
> Somehow, I visualize God hovering over Earth, selecting his instruments for propagation with great care and deliberation. As he observes, he instructs his angels to make notes in a giant ledger.

"Armstrong, Beth, son, patron saint, Matthew. Forrest, Marjorie, daughter, patron saint, Cecilia.

"Rudledge, Carrie, twins, patron saint, give her Gerard. He's used to profanity."

Finally, he passes a name to an angel and smiles, "Give her a handicapped child."

The angel is curious. "Why this one, God? She's so happy."

"Exactly," says God. "Could I give a handicapped child to a mother who does not know laughter? That would be cruel."

"But has she patience?" asks the angel.

"I don't want her to have too much patience, or she will drown in a sea of self-pity and despair. Once the shock and resentment wear off, she'll handle it.

I watched her today. She has that feeling of self and independence that is so rare and so necessary in a mother. You see, the child I'm going to give her has his own world. She has to make it live in her world, and that's not going to be easy."

"But, Lord, I don't think she even believes in you."

God smiles. "No matter. I can fix that. This one is perfect. She has just enough selfishness."

The angel gasps, "Selfishness? Is that a virtue?"

God nods. "If she can't separate herself from the child occasionally, she'll never survive. Yes, here is a woman whom I will bless with a child less than perfect. She doesn't realize it yet, but she is to be envied. She will never take for granted a 'spoken word.'

She will never consider a 'step' ordinary. When her child says 'Momma' for the first time, she will be present at a miracle and know it! When she describes beauty to her child, she will see it as few people ever see my creations.

I will permit her to see clearly the things I see... ignorance, cruelty, prejudice... and allow her to rise above them. She will never be alone. I will be at her side every minute of every day of her life because she is doing my work as surely as she is here by my side."

"And what about her patron saint?" asks the angel, pen poised midair. God smiles. "A mirror will suffice" (Bombeck, 1996).

Every child is worthy, every parent is stronger than they think, and every story is worth telling. This story is for the love of Stephen. Who is your story for the love of?

With deepest respect and shared love,

Stuart

PART IV

ANGELS, ENDINGS, AND ETERNITY

CHAPTER 15

ANGELS WITH NAMETAGS

A hero is an ordinary individual who finds the strength to
persevere and endure in spite of overwhelming obstacles.

— Christopher Reeve

We've seen the brave love of parents. Now let's celebrate the other heroes who show up daily with arms full of support—and yes, sometimes snacks and sarcasm too. Steve had many of them in his life, a small number of whom we've touched on already. They were the quiet champions who showed up, lifted him up, and helped him build a life filled with dignity, purpose, and joy. Thanks to them, he didn't just survive—he learned, grew, and lived more fully than anyone ever expected.

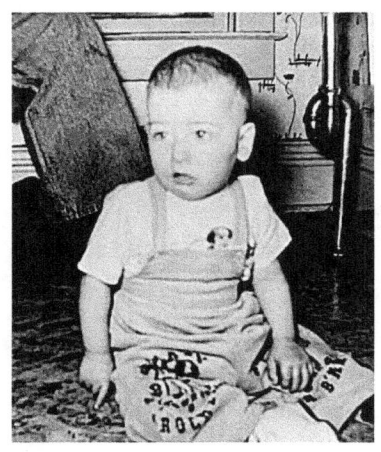

Some heroes wear capes. Others wear scrubs, teacher badges, or orthopedic shoes with arch support. And some heroes—let's be honest—smell faintly of hand sanitizer, coffee, and Crayola markers. They are teachers, therapists, doctors, aides, advocates, counselors, coaches, nurses, drivers, cafeteria workers, and quiet saints who dedicate their lives to serving individuals with disabilities.

This chapter is for them.

We don't always know their names. We don't always see them at award ceremonies or featured in glossy magazines. But we see their fingerprints everywhere—on progress reports, on smiles, on quiet victories that defy statistics. They are the people who refuse to give up, who choose to lean in, and who carry a deep sense of mission, even if their job description just says "staff."

The Courage to Show Up—Every Day

It takes a special kind of courage to walk into a classroom or therapy room every day, knowing you may face outbursts, heartbreaks, and challenges you can't fix with a worksheet or a Band-Aid. But show up they do. Rain, shine, snow day hangovers, or lice outbreaks— they're there. These remarkable people see the child who rocks, flaps, bites, or bolts not as a problem but as a person. Not as a label, but as a life. And that makes all the difference.

Ms. Clara, one of my brother Steve's teachers at the Wabash Center in the early 1960s, didn't have an advanced degree in special education—those were rare and still being accredited. What she did have was fierce patience and a sense of humor that could defuse a meltdown like a pro. When Steve removed his shirt in the middle of the classroom one spring afternoon, announcing, "I'm hot and handsome," she chuckled, handed him a popsicle stick puppet, and said, "So is this guy—keep your clothes on and introduce him to the class." That, friends, is behavioral redirection with flair.

According to my parents, Ms. Clara didn't just teach Steve; she modeled something rare and holy: unconditional acceptance. That's not found in textbooks. It's found in the people who sit on the floor with a nonverbal child for forty minutes because they know that connection sometimes starts with silence.

According to the Council for Exceptional Children (n.d.), special educators today are expected to be highly qualified professionals who can assess learning, write individualized education plans (IEPs), collaborate with multidisciplinary teams, sometimes dodge (or don't) physical harm, and work under intense accountability—all while keeping their sense of humor intact. Somehow, many of them manage to do just that.

The Helpers Among Us

Mr. Rogers, the soft-spoken saint of cardigans and kindness, once said, "Look for the helpers. You will always find people who are helping" (Rogers, 2002). That's never more true than in the world of disability services. Helpers are everywhere—quiet, calm, often exhausted, and frequently underpaid.

There are social workers who hunt down the right Medicaid waiver like they're tracking a golden snitch in a bureaucratic forest. There are aides who memorize every child's comfort item and backup plan. There are transportation workers who learn the language of echolalia just so a student won't feel alone on the way home. And there are special education teachers who design individualized plans like master architects—layering patience, creativity, and relentless hope into lessons that meet each student exactly where they are. They build bridges between students and possibilities, decoding progress others might miss, celebrating victories measured not in test scores but in breakthroughs of connection and confidence.

These are people who stay after the shift ends. Who pack extra snacks. Who know that trust is earned through presence.

Photo: Antoni Shkraba Studio / Pexels (used under Pexels License)

When Steve was at the Purdue Achievement Center, his physical therapist, Betty, had a way of turning therapy into magic. One room at the Center was her jungle gym. She transformed foam mats into mountains, ankle weights into rocket boots, and plastic cones into castles. Steve didn't think he was doing coordination exercises. He thought he was going on adventures. My mother, who watched him one day, said, "If that girl had ever run for mayor, I'd have voted for her."

Helpers are not saints, though we often call them that. They're human. They get tired. They cry in their cars. They wrestle with guilt and red tape, and sometimes the overwhelming sense that it will never be enough. But they come back. God love 'em—they keep showing up. And that is what makes them heroic.

The Advocates: No Capes, Just Clipboards and Fire

While the helpers heal and teach, the advocates fight. These are the moms with binders, the dads with spreadsheets, the self-advocates with voices that shake rooms. These are nonprofit leaders, policymakers, law students, and disability rights veterans who have read the fine print of every version of IDEA since 1975 and still carry the scars from years of budget cuts.

Judith Heumann—may her memory be a revolution—once said, "Some people say that what I did changed the world. But really, I just refused to accept what I was told I could not do" (Heumann & Joiner, 2020, p. 211). She and many others transformed obstacles into movement. Their advocacy pushed the Americans with Disabilities Act (ADA) into law, laid the foundation for inclusive education, and demanded that the world finally widen the doorway.

My family didn't know Judith personally, but we owe her. So does every child who ever rolled into a classroom instead of being pushed into a basement. So does every parent who heard, "Your child has rights," instead of, "We don't have a place for him here."

Advocates are the ones who teach us that accessibility isn't charity— it's justice. And justice, like love, is never passive.

Healers with Humor and Heart

It's not easy to deliver diagnoses, adjust braces, or track seizure patterns. But the doctors, nurses, and specialists who care for people with disabilities often do it with deep compassion and—bless them—a little humor. The best healers are those who see the whole person, not just the medical chart. They're the ones who remember birthdays, laugh at bad knock-knock jokes, and gently redirect a needle-phobic child with the skill of a magician.

Dr. Miller once told my parents, when Steve was five, "Yes, he's slow. But there's no telling what he'll be able to do, so I wouldn't put limits on him." That one line helped provide a whole new lens through which Mom and Dad could see Steve. It became a kind of mantra: *No limits. Just detours.*

Healers meet people in their most vulnerable moments and offer not just treatment but presence. That is an act of sacred care.

Spirit, Mind, and Body

I count myself incredibly fortunate to have served as vice president of enrollment at Springfield College in Massachusetts—a place that turned out to be far more than just a job. Somewhere between the flurry of strategic planning, budget meetings, and enrollment spreadsheets, I discovered something rare and profoundly human: a college with a soul.

Springfield didn't just post its mission on a wall and forget about it. It lived and breathed it: *educating students in spirit, mind, and body for leadership in service to others* (Springfield College, n.d.). They called it the Humanics philosophy. But at Springfield, "Humanics" wasn't just a buzzword—it was a daily heartbeat.

The community of Springfield College didn't serve others because they had to—they served because they wanted to. Everyone served. Because it mattered. Because people mattered. With more service hours devoted to supporting disabled, underprivileged, and marginalized communities than any other college its size, Springfield earned national recognition from President Barack Obama himself. And every single hour was given with sincerity.

Springfield College campus. Photograph courtesy of Springfield College
Used with permission.

Students didn't go to Springfield to build resumes. They went because they were builders of something else—character, community, and hope. That kind of compassion radiated across campus, and it lit something in me, too. I saw students dedicate themselves to children with disabilities—not with pity, but with presence. With joy. With purpose. More than once, I found myself selfishly thinking, *If only Steve could have been one of those kids.* One of the ones lifted up, not left out.

If we could bottle that kind of spirit and pour it into every school, every workplace, every neighborhood—my God, how different the world could be. How desperately we need more Springfields. More angels with nametags, showing up not out of obligation, but out of love.

There are so many more places like Springfield College—quiet, steadfast havens where compassion is not a slogan but a way of life. They are the not-for-profits working from cramped offices, the community centers with worn floors polished by decades of care, the clinics and hospital wards where hope wears scrubs, the ministries that embrace without judgment, and the countless other unsung heroes who stand in the gap. Seek them out for your child. Step through their doors with an open heart. These places are more than programs or services—they are living blessings, ready to shape, strengthen, and inspire a life.

A Tapestry of Love

It's tempting to think that, in order to make a difference, we need to do something dramatic like the Special Olympics, the Miracle League, or Best Buddies International. But in the world of disability support, the real difference is made in the quiet, unflashy, beautiful, everyday gestures. A bus driver waiting an extra minute. A camp counselor learning a new communication device. A high school teacher insisting that "inclusion" means more than just sharing the same room.

Each act of kindness, each choice to honor dignity, is a thread in the tapestry.

A Tapestry of Hope
(Author Unknown)

In halls where echoes softly weave,
And where a silent language they believe,
These souls, with hearts that gently mend,
On journeys of healing, they extend.

The path they walk, a winding maze,
Through shadowed corners, sunlit days,
With patient hands, they lift and guide,
Where wounded spirits, they confide.

A tapestry of hope they spin,
With threads of courage, deep within,
Each individual, a unique art,
A masterpiece etched in their heart.

From tender touch to watchful eye,
They watch and learn, they help them try,
To find their voice, to stand up tall,
In a world where challenges enthrall.

These guardians of a silent call,
They see the beauty in one and all,
A symphony of souls, they blend,
A bond of love that knows no end.

Thank You

If you're one of these angels, thank you. If you know one, thank them. And if you're raising or walking beside someone with disabilities, know that you are part of the same tapestry: woven with love, stitched with humor, and reinforced by people who refuse to let anyone fall through. Our tapestry was for the love of Stephen.

CHAPTER 16

THE DRIVE THAT WOULDN'T END

You can kiss your family and friends goodbye and put miles between you, but at the same time you carry them with you in your heart, your mind, your stomach... because you do not just live in a world but a world lives in you.

— Frederick Buechner

The call came like a thunderclap—unexpected and impossible to ignore. Terri's voice trembled as she told me what had happened: Steve had been hit by a car while riding his bicycle. I remember hearing her words but not fully understanding them, as if she were speaking through water. There was no time to process, no time to panic. Just the primal instinct: get home.

That three-hour drive—from wherever I was to where Steve lay—was not just the longest of my life; it was a journey into dread. My foot pressed harder on the accelerator with every mile, even as I told myself not to speed. But how do you keep calm when your brother—your buddy, your constant—is lying in a hospital bed with injuries no one will fully describe?

I gripped the steering wheel like a lifeline. Every thought screamed louder than the last:

Me with Steve—my lifelong protector and gentle giant

Are Steve's injuries really that bad? Will I make it in time? Is he going to die before I can see him?

Then came the denial:

No, no—he's going to be all right. He's always been tough. He's tougher than any of us. He's as tough as nails.

But underneath the determination, the truth loomed like a shadow I couldn't shake.

Brother, Playmate, Mirror

The hum of tires on the highway faded behind memories that flooded my senses like a reel of old home movies. Steve and I, kids again—sitting cross-legged in the bedroom we shared with Scott, a room barely big enough for the three single beds but somehow large enough to hold entire play worlds.

The house we grew up in was modest. The bedrooms were small, the bathroom had one sink, and some of the furniture was hand-me-down—but none of that mattered. We had each other. That was enough. The front yard had a few flowers, the backyard a ball field, and the shared bedroom a wrestling arena, a G.I. Joe battle zone, and a secret hideout all in one.

Backyard adventures in full swing—Scott, Steve, and me (left to right),
ruling our tiny kingdom of grass and sunshine

Steve was seven years older, but we had the same mental age. That's what made him my best playmate—his joy was pure and uncomplicated, always ready for a game, a laugh, a wild idea. He never said no. Not once. And I never had to pretend to be someone I wasn't.

Mom said it best once, in a quiet moment: "You and Steve were so close because you were a child, and he had the mind of one."

I carried that with me for years. It wasn't just a truth—it was a gift. I had been given a childhood partner who never grew too old to play.

Susan and Scott had their own closeness—born just eleven months apart, they moved in tandem like twins. But Steve belonged to all of us in a different way. He was the heart of our sibling constellation, shining with a light no one else could replicate.

But the present was pulling me back, the weight of that morning pressing hard.

A Knock at the Door

As Terri and I raced toward the hospital, my mind drifted to what my parents must have experienced earlier that day. They were retired now, living in the old family farmhouse—the one tucked between corn and soybean fields, with a gravel driveway that stretched out like a ribbon of memories. It was the house of roots, the house where Jones family stories began.

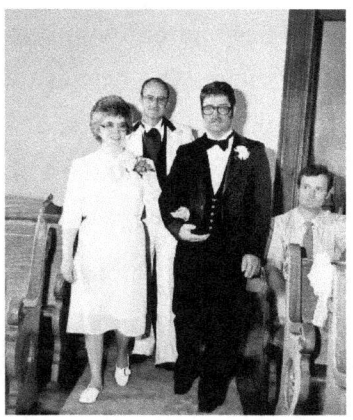

Polished, posed, and practically glowing. From left to right: Mom, Dad, Steve, and Uncle Phil (seated)

And it was there, on that same fateful morning, that a deputy sheriff from Delphi pulled in. Mom and Dad must've known immediately that something was wrong—visits like that never mean anything else.

He didn't give them details. He didn't explain. He simply asked, "Are you the parents of Stephen Keith Jones?" Then, when they said yes, he replied, "Steve has been in a bicycling accident. He's at St. Elizabeth Hospital in Lafayette. You need to go immediately."

That's all. Just go.

What do you pack for news like that? What do you say to each other on the way to the hospital, driving through the Indiana countryside in a silence too loud for comfort?

Cathy's Journey

While Mom and Dad were receiving that devastating news, hospital staff were desperately trying to find Cathy, Steve's wife. She was at work, cleaning a building on Purdue University's sprawling campus. It should've been easy—but in those moments, everything conspires to slow you down.

They couldn't find her because she was exactly where she always was—doing her job, quietly and faithfully, in the background. Eventually, a coworker reached her. Her boss drove her straight to the hospital because, like Steve, Cathy didn't drive.

When she arrived, Mom and Dad were the ones who had to tell her. It's hard enough to lose one child while fearing the death of another. But to then have to break a spouse's heart with that news? That's a cruelty no parent should bear.

First came disbelief. Then came the sobs. Then came the walk to Steve's room.

What she saw is what we all saw. And none of us would ever unsee it.

The Silent Room

When I stepped into that hospital room, it was as if the world stopped turning. Nothing mattered except my brother.

Steve lay there, bandaged and broken, surrounded by machines that beeped and pulsed with an artificial rhythm. His head was wrapped like a mummy, the bandages stained with blood that had no business being outside his body. His face bore abrasions and lacerations. Even the pillow showed signs of the violence he had endured.

I stood frozen.

The medical team moved in and out of the room, adjusting monitors, checking IVs, whispering to each other. Their hands were busy, but their eyes—those told a different story. A story of hopelessness. Of inevitability.

Terri wrapped her arms around mine, trying to anchor me. But I couldn't feel my body anymore. My eyes were on Steve. My heart was somewhere unreachable.

Why isn't he smiling? Why doesn't he ask to play chess or tauntingly pat my face like he always did? Why doesn't he joke, or call me a name, or ask me to turn on the TV?

The room was full of noise—the hum of machines, footsteps, whispered voices—but Steve's silence was the only sound that pierced me.

"He's One of Ours"

News traveled fast at the hospital. Steve wasn't just a patient—he was a beloved member of the entire team. He had a presence, a spirit that made people pause and smile. He was a bright light in a place often defined by pain and healing.

One by one, his coworkers came to his room. Nurses. Doctors. Janitors. Administrators. They introduced themselves to our family, shared their stories, their laughs, their tears. Everyone had something to say about Steve—how he made them laugh, how he noticed them when no one else did, how he made their day a little lighter, what a dedicated worker he was.

One doctor in Steve's room, unaware my parents were standing nearby, said softly to a nurse, "He's one of ours. Take good care of him."

Those four words—that meant everything.

The Ones Who Couldn't Get There: Three Journeys, One Goodbye

Scott

Scott also received the call no brother should ever have to receive.

He was at his office in Michigan, seated at his desk as Vice President of The Christman Company, preparing for a meeting with senior corporate leadership. When Dad's name flashed across his cell phone, Scott hesitated—just for a moment—and let it go to voicemail. He figured he'd return the call once the meeting prep was done. But then the office landline rang.

He picked it up.

It was Dad.

His voice was trembling. Broken.

Steve had been hit by a car early that morning on his way to work. He was in emergency surgery. The prognosis was grim.

Just like that, Scott's world stopped turning.

Scott and Donna

He dropped everything. The meeting, the agenda, the carefully planned schedule—all of it evaporated in an instant. He packed up his things and prepared to take the meeting by phone from his car as he drove toward Indiana. He realized this wasn't going to be a quick trip. He wouldn't be back in a day or two. He ran home, threw clothes into a suitcase, and called his partner, Donna, who was out of town, to tell her what had happened. That he was on the road. That he was heading south, trying to outrun fate.

Donna would not be able to get there in time to see Steve, nor would Scott's children, Sarah and Brian. Even though Scott's support team couldn't be there physically, they called, prayed, and sent love through every means they could. Steve was their uncle, but he was more than that. He was a presence.

He alerted Christman's executive secretary that he had a family emergency and would be calling into the afternoon meeting from the road. He had seven long hours of highway ahead.

But then something happened—something that cracked the stoic shell he'd been holding together.

Christman called back.

"Family first," they told him. "We've already rescheduled the meeting. Don't worry about calling in."

They even offered to book him a flight and a rental car—anything to get him to Indiana faster.

That gesture, simple and deeply human, broke Scott open. It was the first time the tears came. Not silent ones, either. Real, heavy, gut-wrenching tears. Because now it was real. Now it was too real.

He declined their offer. He needed the drive. The miles would give him space to breathe, to grieve, to brace for whatever waited at the end of the road. Just like me, Scott would spend those hours tangled in memories of the big brother who had always been there—laughing, teasing, protecting, loving.

Later, he'd find out that Christman had sent a company-wide message about the emergency. No emails. No calls. Just support. A few colleagues reached out anyway, hoping to offer a kind word. And in that sea of corporate responsibility, something sacred surfaced—grace.

Susan

If Scott's journey was heavy with emotion, Susan's was heavy with emotion and delay.

My sister Susan was in Arizona, serving as a prison psychologist when everything began to unravel. Mom and Dad tried to reach her. So did Scott. No answer. Finally, he managed to contact her husband at the time, Deane, who was in Wisconsin. Through him, word finally reached Susan.

Jon and Susan

But by then, the clock was already against her.

Her journey—from the sun-scorched desert of Arizona to Wisconsin to gather her husband, and then on to Indiana—spanned more hours than Steve had left. She was doing everything she could. Racing time. Willing the planes to fly faster. Begging the universe to bend just this once.

But the universe was unrelenting, and Steve slipped away before she could reach him.

Susan's grown sons—Matthew, David, and Benjamin—were scattered across the country, unable to be there in person. Still, they sent more than thoughts and prayers. Their love ran deep, and though miles apart, their presence was felt. It lingered in the quiet moments, in the memories they carried, and in the invisible thread of devotion that bound them to their Uncle Steve.

Sudi

Sudi's absence was different. Not rushed. Not delayed. Just... removed.

She was out of the country at the time, traveling for work as an engineer, unaware of the tragedy unfolding back home. By the time our parents reached her, it was already too late. Steve's final moments had passed. The goodbyes, the gathering, the honoring—they all came and went without her.

Mehdi and Sudi

She grieved from afar, quietly and alone, carrying the weight of loss in a silence all her own. Separated by distance and circumstance, she mourned in the only way she could: privately, inwardly, and with her husband Mehdi, daughter Salma, and son Sahand by her side.

There would be no final words of farewell offered to Steve. No embraces, no hospital bedside. Just an aching absence where connection should have been.

And yet, in her solitude, she still bore the same sorrow we all did. Love doesn't require proximity or bloodline. Nor does grief.

Holding Vigil

We set up camp in the ICU waiting room, which quickly became both a sanctuary and a prison. The hours crawled by with cruel slowness. Word traveled fast—among aunts and uncles, cousins, lifelong friends, and neighbors. One by one, they came and went, dropping everything to be with us. Some brought casseroles of compassion, others arrived with baskets of prayers. Every hug, every shared tear, every whispered "we're here" was a lifeline.

Terri and Me

Steve held on. Machines kept him alive. Tests were run. Vitals monitored. But nothing changed.

The doctors had told us they needed twenty-four hours. That was the tipping point—either Steve's brain would show signs of life… or it wouldn't.

So we waited. We prayed. And we waited again.

That evening, just after seven, Scott arrived at St. Elizabeth Hospital. He had made the drive in record time, pushing the limits without apology. When he walked through the ICU waiting room doors, he was met with the full weight of our gathered sorrow—Mom, Dad, Cathy, Aunt Josie, and a few cousins sitting in weary silence. Aunt Josie, as tender as ever, took his coat but not without first pulling him into a deep hug that said everything no one else could.

Scott made his way to Mom and Dad. They embraced, the three of them standing in a silent triangle of grief and shared resolve. They spoke in hushed tones—catching him up, preparing him—and then he went in with them to see Steve.

When Scott came back out, I was waiting. He looked at me, and for a moment, we were just two brothers, standing in a world that had been turned upside down. We stepped toward each other and embraced—not one of those stiff, awkward pats on the back—but the kind of hug that shakes loose everything you've been trying to hold in. We wept in each other's arms, no words needed. I have never seen him cry like that; it broke my heart even more.

Then, as brothers do, we straightened up. Cleared our throats. Brushed away the tears. Put the armor back on before anyone else could see the chinks in it.

Later that night, the hospital chaplain gathered us for a family prayer. We circled up, linked hands and arms, and bowed our heads. Our tears came softly, mingling with whispered pleas and desperate hope. We were clinging to a miracle that had not yet come—for the love of Stephen.

CHAPTER 17

GOODBYE, MY BROTHER

Grief is the price we pay for love.

— Queen Elizabeth II

The Decision

The next morning, the family gathered once more in that dreaded waiting room.

What do you wait for in a place like that? Hope? A miracle?

None of us had slept; the long night had drained what little strength we had left.

Exhaustion hung heavy in the air. Desperation was written on every face.

I was there with reinforcements. My sons, Daniel and Derek, wanted to come—as did Derek's girlfriend, Kyleigh. We all sat. We all waited. The moments lingered—hard and long.

Finally, the doctor entered the room; he didn't need to speak—we already knew.

Still, he said delicately, "There's been no brain activity. None at all in the last 24 hours."

Steve was gone. Machines were breathing for him, technology keeping his heart beating. But Steve—our Steve—was no longer there.

Supported by Mom and Dad and with impossible strength, Cathy made the decision to discontinue life support. My parents looked at my brother Scott and me. We agreed.

There was no miracle. No surprise recovery. No awakening.

Now, there was only goodbye.

Goodbye, My Brother

We took turns stepping into Steve's room for our final goodbyes.

Cathy went first, a small circle of her family and friends gathered around her like a shield.

Then Mom and Dad went in together, leaning on each other in that quiet way they did when words weren't enough.

Scott stayed back. He shook his head and said he couldn't do it again—his goodbye had been yesterday, and that was all his heart could manage.

Mine hadn't come yet.

I wanted to go last, so I stayed back. I'm not sure why—I just knew I needed to. I dreaded the moment.

I had never done anything like this before—never said goodbye to someone I loved so deeply while they were still slipping away.

With Terri and my family at my side, we walked into Steve's room. We were silent. There were simply no words from any of us.

Steve looked the same, but nothing was the same.

The machines hissed and beeped in those final moments, but the sounds now felt intrusive—out of place. They were trying to sustain what was slipping away.

I walked to him, bent down, and draped my arm across his chest, my hand gently cupping his neck. I laid my head next to his. I tried to hold him tight.

And I began to sob.

"I love you, Steve," I whispered. "Thank you for being the best big brother and playmate a boy could have. I'll never forget."

And I never have.

Science says he couldn't hear me. Logic agrees. But love says otherwise. And I believe love.

The Last Silence

We joined the others already gathered in the waiting room—hushed, weary, and waiting for the final word. My Mom looked at me, and tears welled in her eyes. In a soft, compassionate voice, she asked, "Are you okay?"

She needed to be reassured.

I looked at her and gently replied, "I will be." That was the best I could do.

The doctor returned, his voice quiet—almost reverent.

"He's gone."

Stephen Keith Jones died on Wednesday, December 20, 2006. He was 52 years old.

It was a shitty Christmas that year.

The Helmet That Wasn't Worn

Steve wasn't wearing his bike helmet that day. Cathy had always insisted he wear it, and usually he did. But on that dark December morning— for reasons we'll never know—it was strapped to his handlebars instead of his head. Maybe he'd taken it off for just a moment, or maybe he never put it on at all in defiance of those who always told him he had to.

Generations gathered once more— Steve and Dad standing tall behind Grandma Eva and Mom at another cherished family reunion on the farm

Steve had a stubborn streak— he came by it honestly. Like the rest of us Joneses, he valued his independence and the right to feel the wind in his hair, even if just for a few blocks. Perhaps that small act of rebellion felt like freedom to him. And maybe—just maybe—it cost him everything.

Would the helmet have saved his life? We'll never know. And that not knowing is its own kind of torment.

The Impact

Later, the official paperwork would distill it all down to three sterile words: closed head injury. That was the medical term the death certificate used—tidy, clinical, cold. What it really meant was that Steve had suffered a traumatic brain injury: a violent jolt to the skull that caused his brain to whip forward, crashing against the inside of his skull with devastating force.

Bruising. Swelling. Bleeding. Tearing. A cascade of damage hidden from sight. The doctors understood it in terms of neurology and trauma. We understood it in terms of heartbreak.

The reality was simpler—and far crueler. Steve had been struck from behind by a car as he rode his bicycle to work. His unprotected head hit the cold concrete curb with brutal force. He was knocked unconscious immediately and never regained consciousness. Ironically, he fell to his death right in front of a fire station. Though he received immediate medical attention, by the time the ambulance arrived, he was already unconscious, his brain swollen and damaged beyond repair. Nothing and no one could save him.

And though the loss was unbearable, I clung to one small thread of mercy: Steve did not suffer. There was no long agony, no cruel stretch of pain or confusion. He was simply—gone. In an instant. Some families are not so fortunate. I know that. I have seen that. For those who have watched a loved one linger and suffer, I hurt for you. But in our case, that small grace mattered.

All his life, Steve fought to be seen—really seen—for who he was. Every day was an act of defiance against invisibility, against the world's tendency to look past people like him. That's why it felt both poetic and unbearably cruel that, in the end, it was not being seen that killed him. One driver's failure to notice the man right in front of him ended a lifetime of striving to be noticed.

The Question Without an Answer

We left the hospital numb. For me, it all still felt somewhat surreal. We gathered back at the farmhouse where Mom and Dad lived—and where so many beautiful memories of Steve resided—it was his favorite place. My sister Susan finally arrived, her husband Deane quietly by her side. The house had quickly filled with people stopping in: family, friends, church members—all trying, in their own quiet ways, to support our shattered parents. When Susan walked through the door, she was met with open arms and aching hearts.

My father pulled her into a hug—the kind only grief can make truly tight.

Through sobs and trembling breath, Susan managed to ask the question that so many of us had already whispered to ourselves: "Why did God let this happen?"

My father, a man of faith forged in hardship, looked into her tear-filled eyes and said simply, "I don't know. But God knows."

That was it. No sermon. No platitude. Just truth. Sometimes faith is not about having answers—it's about surrendering to the mystery.

"Trust in the Lord with all your heart and lean not on your own understanding" (Proverbs 3:5, New International Version).

A proud day in uniform—Steve (right)
celebrating Air Force graduation with his nephew Ben Jaeger

We clung to those words, not because they answered everything, but because they steadied us in the storm—for the love of Stephen.

CHAPTER 18

SEE YOU IN PLAYLAND, STEVE

*Life, in its sorrowful wisdom, teaches us the worth of what we can
no longer hold. The world was gentler, kinder, brighter with you
in it, my beloved brother. You are—now and always—wrapped
in love, carried in hearts, and missed beyond measure.*

— Dr. Stuart Jones

The Frosted Glass and the Blind Spot

He was doing what he always did—riding his bike to work at St. Elizabeth Hospital, where he had worked faithfully for over thirty years in housekeeping and laundry. Steve loved that job. It gave him purpose, routine, and community. He took it seriously. He was proud of it.

Left to right: Grandma Fife, Scott, Steve, and Uncle Gordon

But on that early morning, just before 6:00 a.m., a man in his thirties was driving a Pontiac Grand Prix, running late. His windshield was still partially frosted. It was dark. He was in a hurry. And in that sliver of fogged glass—his blind spot—was my brother.

The police report would later conclude: "Limited visibility due to darkness and frost were contributing factors." Steve had already made it through the intersection and was riding near the curb when the driver turned left, never seeing him, even with reflectors on his bike; the frosted glass made it impossible to see him at all.

No screech of brakes. No swerve. Just the sickening sound of impact.

"It was probably a low-speed crash," Lt. Weaver would say, "but when you're on a bike, it doesn't take much speed."

No alcohol was involved. No reckless driving. Just a human mistake with a human cost.

A Tale of Caution: A Frosted Pane and a Life Forever Changed

Would you pause for a moment—for me, and for Steve?

Picture this: it's early morning in the depths of winter. The air bites at your cheeks, your breath fogs the air, and your windshield is coated with a stubborn layer of frost. You're already late—maybe for work, maybe for school drop-off, or maybe just for life.

So, in your hurry, you make a quick decision: scrape just enough of the frost to see straight ahead. The defroster will do the rest, right? You justify it to yourself, believing it's only a temporary compromise. After all, you're careful. You're a good driver. What could possibly go wrong?

But here's the uncomfortable truth: when you drive with a windshield half-covered in frost, you are piloting a two-ton machine while essentially half-blind. Your field of vision may be reduced by

50% or more. In that moment, you've traded full visibility and full responsibility for convenience.

You may not realize it, but that decision could cost someone their life.

It cost Steve his life.

That cold December morning, someone else made that same decision. Steve, who had already survived so much—born premature, having lived a life of challenging disability, enduring injustices, surviving traumas, and yet always choosing joy—was biking along the side of the road. And then, in an instant, everything ended.

I am aware that the death certificate called it a *closed head injury*, as the official cause of death. But the deeper, haunting cause? Someone didn't see him. Someone drove forward into the frosty haze, never thinking that a man's life was just beyond their field of vision.

And that someone couldn't take it back.

A few years after Steve died, my wife Terri and I were attending a funeral for a dear friend in North Manchester—another unexpected death, another moment when grief made time stand still. While waiting in line to pay our respects, we ran into Karen, a friend from a town we once lived in. She had read about Steve's accident when it happened. The obituary, the articles, the letters to the editor that followed—they stayed with her. And so did Steve, though she never met him.

She looked at me with empathy in her eyes and said, "Every time I don't want to scrape the frost or snow from my windshield, I think of your brother and how important it is to see clearly."

It was just one sentence. But I can't tell you how much that meant to me—more than I could ever have imagined. Steve's life—and death—had become someone else's caution.

His story had made someone see.

If I ever meet you someday, I hope you'll say the same as Karen. I hope you'll think of Steve.

Here's what the data tells us:

According to a 2023 Google Consumer Survey, nearly 70 percent of all vehicular accidents in the United States are linked to hazardous winter weather conditions—snow, icy roads, blowing wind, or obscured vision due to fogged or frosted windshields (Google Surveys, 2023). Impaired visibility is a key factor in these accidents, and yet, too many drivers overlook its importance.

In fact, 37 percent of American drivers surveyed identified the humble ice scraper as the most essential tool for winter driving. More important than cell phones. More essential than gloves, flashlights, snow brushes, or even kitty litter for traction. But tools only work when we use them properly and completely.

If that scraper is in your hand, use it like someone's life depends on it. Because it just might.

And while we're talking about safety, let's talk about another detail that still keeps me up some nights: Steve wasn't wearing a bicycle helmet.

According to the United States Department of Transportation (2025), head injuries are the leading cause of death in 70–80 percent of fatal bicycle crashes, and yet only 18 percent of riders regularly wear helmets. That statistic isn't just alarming—it's devastating. A helmet isn't a fashion choice. It's a line between life and death.

So please, I beg you: wear your damn helmet. If not for yourself, then for your loved ones.

Make your kids wear theirs. Your partner too.

Keep one in the garage and one in the trunk.

Insist. Even if they roll their eyes.

Because someday, if you don't, you might find yourself sitting down to write a book about someone you loved and lost—someone who died not because of one massive failure, but because of a series of small choices that added up to tragedy.

Let Steve's story be your caution. His life deserves that kind of legacy.

Mercy, Forgiveness, and Boundaries

The driver wasn't charged, and our family didn't press charges. We didn't see the point. Our faith shaped that decision—and Steve's faith would have too. One life had ended; why destroy another?

We later learned from the police that the driver was overwhelmed with remorse. He didn't know how he would live with what he'd done. My father sent a message through the officers: "You are forgiven. Do not let this destroy you. Steve would not want that." My sister Susan would later reach out to him as well, assuring him there was no anger, no hatred on our part. Upon hearing that, he wept.

These were powerful moments of mercy—some of the purest expressions of grace I've ever seen. My father and sister were right:

I wasn't angry. I didn't want vengeance. Honestly, the driver wasn't even on my mind. Steve was.

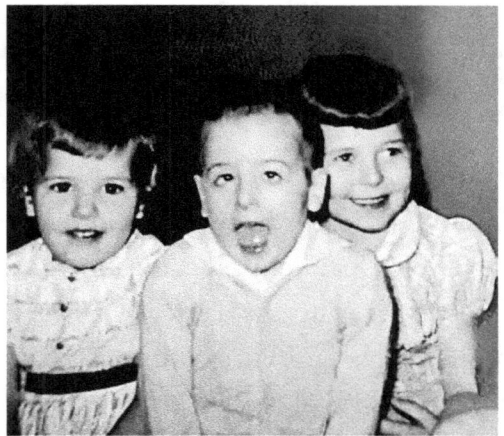

Steve, age three, already stealing the show—
flanked by cousin Gaye (left) and cousin Jo Lynn (right)

When the driver expressed his desire to attend Steve's funeral, my father gently declined.

"We have a lot going on right now," he told him. "We are grieving. We simply cannot minister to you at this time."

The driver sent flowers to the funeral—a very kind gesture. I remember seeing them as I looked at all the arrangements. I was confused about who had sent them, and when I learned it was the driver who hit and killed Steve, I was honestly moved.

And that, too, was grace—grace with boundaries.

A G.I. Joe Farewell

As naïve or childish as it might sound, my brother Steve and playland were one and the same. Growing up, rarely was there playtime without Steve. Whether it was toys in the bedroom or kick-the-can with neighborhood friends outside, play and Steve went hand in hand.

That's why I felt compelled to say goodbye to my childhood playmate in a way that was both fitting and symbolic.

The day before the funeral, I climbed into the attic and dug through old boxes until I found them—the beloved G.I. Joes we played with as kids. Most were worn, their joints loose from years of mock battles and backyard adventures with me, Scott, and Steve. But I found one that still stood tall. I dressed him in full uniform—boots, helmet, rifle, everything. My hands shook as I opened the old footlocker that held Joe's tiny gear. It was like unlocking a time capsule from a boyhood that now felt galaxies away.

Terri helped me line a box with soft fabric. We turned it into a tiny casket. I placed the soldier inside—a final gift from one brother to another. I wrapped the box like a Christmas present, just the way we used to tear through wrapping paper together at Christmas, squealing with excitement. I imagined Steve unwrapping it in heaven, stuttering with joy, wide-eyed and laughing like a boy again.

I slipped it beneath his forearm and hand in the casket, so he could hold it.

It made me smile—and it made me ache.

Steve was my playmate.

And now I was giving him one last toy. We'd play G.I. Joes together again—someday.

A Showing and a Funeral Overflowing with Love

I've always agreed with my brother Scott about the strange things people say when standing over a body at a funeral.

"He looks so good."

"They did such a nice job."

"He looks just like himself."

But the truth? Steve didn't look good to me. He didn't look like himself. He lay still. Waxen. Like a figure sculpted in his image, but not Steve— not the one who radiated energy, mischief, and joy with every breath he took. The vibrancy we had known was gone. The spark extinguished. The body before us bore his features, but not his light.

Because of the severe trauma to his head from the fall, there was real concern about whether we should have an open casket. But Cathy, ever thoughtful and steady in the storm, offered a suggestion that was both practical and profoundly personal: Steve should wear his favorite Indianapolis Colts sweatshirt and his Colts hat—the emblems of a team he loved with almost religious devotion. The hat would

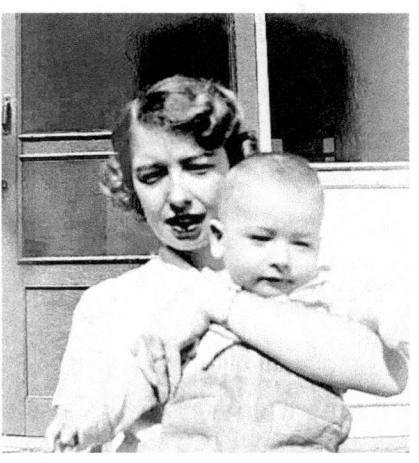

Mom with Steve, her firstborn and the baby who would teach us all the meaning of resilience

gently cover the damage to his skull. The sweatshirt would remind everyone of who he really was—casual, loyal, and full of heart. It was the perfect solution. It felt right. It felt like Steve.

There was something else that mattered, too. Steve was never without his glasses. They weren't just for sight—they were part of his face, his identity. But the pair he wore that morning had been lost at the scene of the accident. Thankfully, Cathy found another pair tucked away, and she made sure he had them on. With his glasses, his Colts gear, and his gentle hands folded in peace, Steve looked—at best— presentable. Serene. But to me, he still didn't look like my brother. Not really. The life had gone out of him. The spark was missing—the spark that made him unmistakably, irreplaceably Steve.

The funeral showing was held just days before Christmas. The cold outside was sharp and unforgiving, but inside the Hippensteel Funeral Home, the air was warm—not from the furnace, but from the quiet power of presence. Love filled the room like a gentle fire, thawing the numbness of grief. Our family gathered, aching but united, to lean on one another and to be held up in return.

The line of people stretched out the door. It surprised me; it surprised all of us.

Doctors and nurses from the hospital where Steve worked.

Teachers who once had him in class. Classmates from his special education days.

Church friends. Bowling league buddies. Two city bus drivers who knew him by name, Jackie, was one, as you know. Bank tellers (not that one). Neighbors.

Friends from every corner of his life and our lives.

My sons, Daniel and Derek, came too—not just to grieve, but to walk beside me in the shadow of heartbreak. Their quiet presence spoke volumes. They came bearing their own memories and their cousins' too—standing in for those who couldn't be there but loved

Steve deeply. Derek, who had long admired his uncle's radiant joy and gentle strength, and Daniel, who remembered the playful heart and steady calm Steve brought to every gathering. They didn't have to say a word. Their grief, like mine, ran silent, ran deep.

More than 300 people came to grieve. 300!

Fifteen more families sent flowers. Two churches sent floral arrangements. Even the local bowling alley, where Steve loved knocking down pins, sent a bouquet.

It was overwhelming.

It was humbling.

It was healing.

As we stood there—tired, tearful, and strangely grateful—we saw it clearly: Steve had touched more lives than we had ever known. No, he didn't cure cancer. He didn't win accolades or headline the news. But his kindness, his quiet strength, his joyful, unguarded spirit—it lingered. In stories. In smiles. In the very air around us.

Steve made people smile—then and now.

He made them feel seen.

And for that, they came.

They stood in the cold. They waited in line. They came for love. Yes, all for the love of Stephen, the boy, and man, who was never broken.

A Final Journey

Cathy had asked Scott and me to serve as pallbearers. Of course we would—it was an honor. To carry our brother to his final resting place felt only fitting, a final act of love for the one who had carried us so many times through the hardest seasons of life. Scott had only one request of Cathy: that he and I walk at the head of the casket. And we did.

Me at Steve's grave, remembering a life of unconditional love, resilient strength, and a legacy that echoes beyond the stone

Together with four of Steve's closest friends with intellectual and developmental disabilities, we carried him with tenderness, step by step, to his final resting place at Tippecanoe Memorial Gardens in West Lafayette.

It was there we laid him down. Not just to rest—but to rise.

And as cold winds whispered through the trees, and the winter earth looked barren, and the last prayers were spoken, I held onto the image of Steve—bike helmet tossed aside, the wind on his face and through his hair, pedaling toward freedom.

He's free now.

Long after his passing, his light hasn't faded. It lingers—in places, in people, in the quiet moments we never expected. My parents, Scott, and I have returned to the hospital a few times since his passing. Once, for a memorial service honoring staff who had died. Another time, to see the plaque they placed in Steve's honor. And each time, when veteran staff who knew Steve smile at the mention of his name, it fills our hearts with something sacred—peace, pride, and the quiet assurance that he mattered.

Scott, ever the steady one, is the most faithful among us in tending to Steve's resting place. He takes special care of the small headstone that marks where his brother lies. No season goes by without a beautiful wreath—carefully chosen, lovingly placed. It's a simple act, but it speaks volumes. A brother's devotion. A love that didn't end at goodbye. A brother who will always be his wingman.

See You in Playland, Steve

Is there anyone you know who has the power to turn back the hands of time?

If you do—please, tell me.

Because if there were a way, even the faintest glimmer of a chance, I would do everything in my power to go back to the moment before the accident that took Steve from us.

I'd race against the clock. I'd scream into the wind. I'd stand in the middle of that road if I had to.

I miss him too much. Every day. The ache is still there, like a song that won't stop playing in the background of my life.

My brother, Scott, captured Steve beautifully when he recalled:

> "My big brother Steve was truly one of a kind—the best of the bunch—the kindest soul I have ever known. His heart was boundless, always ready to give, always willing to help, even when it cost him something. Steve's quiet strength and unwavering generosity inspired all of us who were lucky enough to know him.
>
> Though some tried to take advantage of his goodness, and others were cruel, I believe that life will hold them accountable in its own way. But for those of us who loved Steve, who saw the light he carried even in the darkest moments, he will live forever, etched deep within our hearts and woven into the very fabric of our souls.
>
> Steve wasn't just my brother. He was a beacon of love and resilience, a reminder that kindness is the truest form of strength."

For me, having a brother like Steve isn't common. Thank God for him. And thank God we got to have him. What a rare, wild, sacred gift he was. Steve wasn't just my brother—he was a light in a sometimes shadowed world. He was mischief and music, resilience, and laughter, tenderness wrapped in unexpected strength. We were all better for having known him, for having loved him, and for being loved by him in return. We thought he'd always be close by—never too far from a visit or a phone call or a familiar laugh echoing through the house. But now that he's gone from our sight, I choose to believe he's closer than ever, walking with us as that proverbial angel on our shoulders—his good-natured chuckle carried on the wind, his grace showing up in unexpected kindnesses, his love laced into the quiet moments we often overlook.

God must have known that I would need someone like Steve to help me get through the chaos of childhood. The world can be a tough, confusing place when you're young and trying to make sense of it all. But somehow, without even trying, Steve made it easier. He lit up the darkness with his laughter and his games, his silliness and his soul-deep warmth. His joy was like a fluorescent nightlight in the hallway—always on, always  glowing—helping me find my way when things felt uncertain or hard.

Without ever intending to, he gave me the kind of brotherly love that heals things words never can.

Play was never just play with Steve. It was freedom. It was an escape. It was where we made sense of the world. Whether we were kids pretending to be kings and cowboys or adults rolling dice and keeping score, the games were just the wrapping paper—what we were really unwrapping was joy. In a world that sometimes felt heavy, Steve gave me levity. When life hurt, he gave me laughter. And when the grown-up world crept in too soon, Steve pulled me back to that silly sanctuary we made together—just us two.

My only regret is that we didn't get more time. That we didn't get to keep playing. There were still games to play, wrestling matches to finish, Bruce Lee movies to re-enact, cards to shuffle, chess pieces to move, pins ready to be knocked down. There are moments now when I look to my side, instinctively, expecting him to be there—elbowing me, teasing me, grinning that grin—but he's not, and it stings every time.

I believe—truly, deeply, with all that I am—that this isn't the end. I believe in a life after this one. Yes, I believe in heaven. And I believe that Steve is there now, more himself than ever before—free from every limitation this world tried to put on him. He's waiting, but not in sadness. No, Steve's waiting like a kid waits at the door for his best friend to come over. Eager. Smiling. Buzzing with anticipation.

Me with my beloved brother, holding a lifetime of memories. This memoir has been for the love of Stephen

I can see him there now. He's got the chessboard set up just how he likes it. His bowling ball's polished and ready to knock down some pins. The dice are out for a marathon game of Risk, and the cards are perfectly shuffled, probably in a lopsided stack, waiting for a game of Hearts. His baseball glove and bat are sitting on the bench beside him. And that grin—God, that grin—is stretching from ear to ear. He's bouncing on his heels, eyes twinkling, voice bubbling up with that sweet familiar stammer: "Yuh-yuh-you wanna play?"

Yes, Steve. I do. I always will. With all my heart—yes, I do.

I'll see you in Playland, dear brother. We've got so much to catch up on. And this time, there'll be no end to the fun. I love you, Stephen.

"So with you: Now is your time of grief, but I will see you again and you will rejoice, and no one will take away your joy" (John 16:22, New International Version)

EPILOGUE

I was raised, like so many others, with the simple but profound teaching: "Treat others the way you want to be treated." Known as the Golden Rule, it was more than just a nice idea in our household—it was the rhythm of daily life, the unseen thread holding our family's character together. Rooted in Christ's teachings and wrapped in everyday kindness, it wasn't merely religious—it was relational. It was about decency. Dignity. Humanity.

My mother gave the Golden Rule a softer spin—something between Jesus and Bambi: "If you can't say anything nice, don't say anything at all." In other words, zip it, just like Thumper's mom said (Disney, *Bambi*, 1942). We learned early that kindness wasn't just a virtue for Sunday mornings. It was a way of moving through the world, echoing the biblical principle of treating others as you'd like to be treated (Matthew 7:12, New International Version).

But there's a chasm between knowing the Golden Rule and living it—between quoting it and letting it change you. When you grow up watching your brother be stared at, laughed at, dismissed, excluded, or talked down to just for being who he is, the rule stops being a cute moralism. It becomes a mission. A vow. A fire in your chest that won't go out.

Steve taught me—taught all of us—that kindness is not weak. It is courageous. That true compassion costs something. That justice is not an abstract policy; it is how we treat the most vulnerable people in the smallest moments, when no one else is watching. He taught me that the words we use, the glances we give, the assumptions we make—they matter. And they either build someone up or quietly chip away at them.

He showed us that the world's definition of value—success, intelligence, productivity, perfection—is not only narrow. It's wrong. We don't need more perfect people. We need more whole-hearted people. More people like Steve—who loved without filter, forgave without grudge, and gave joy without hesitation. He didn't deliver TED Talks. He didn't start nonprofits. But he changed lives with his presence. With his laugh. With his loyalty. With the way he kept showing up, even when the world told him he didn't belong.

I believe—with every fiber of my being—that Steve was not the exception. He was the example. The reminder that every single person we pass on the street, ignore in the checkout line, or underestimate at a glance carries a story. And often, those stories are braver, harder, and more beautiful than we can begin to imagine.

So let me ask you to do something. It's simple, but not easy.

The next time you see someone who seems "different"—whether it's the way they walk, speak, behave, or simply exist—pause. Catch the reaction that rises in your chest. Maybe it's discomfort. Maybe it's judgment. Maybe it's fear. Then gently push past it. Forgive yourself for having it. And choose something better.

Look again. See deeper. Because you might be staring at someone who, like Steve, has faced rejection every day of their life—and yet still smiles. Still trusts. Still hopes. You might be looking at a hero, disguised as a stranger. And if you're lucky enough to speak with them, listen. Really listen. Because they may not have all the right words. But they just might know the right thing to say.

The English clergyman John Watson—writing under the name Ian Maclaren—once said, "Be kind, for everyone you meet is fighting a hard battle" (Watson, as cited in Brown, 2012). That's not just a poetic quote. It's a survival strategy for a society that is fraying at the seams. Kindness isn't a luxury anymore. It's our last, best chance to become who we were meant to be.

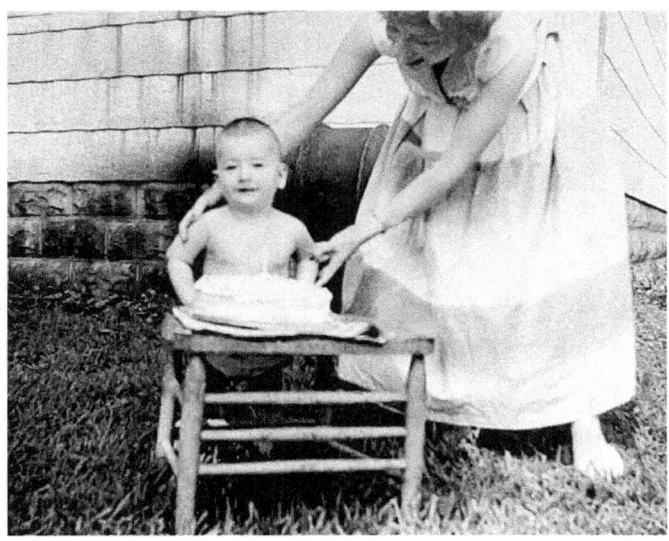

My brother fought so many quiet battles. Physical pain. Cognitive limitations. Social cruelty. Loneliness. And still, he brought light into every room he entered. Still, he laughed. Still, he loved. He was dealt a hand that most of us would consider unfair, but he played it with more courage and grace than most of us can summon on our best days.

What would this world look like if we treated every person the way we would have treated Steve? What kind of churches would we build? What kind of classrooms, workplaces, communities, and even government could we create?

My plea is this: let your life be a place where someone like Steve feels safe. Seen. Valued. Let your presence be the kind that lifts burdens instead of adding to them. Let the way you treat others—especially those who are overlooked, misunderstood, or marginalized—be the part of your legacy that matters most.

This isn't just about my brother. This is about your neighbor. Your student. Your coworker. Your congregant. Maybe even your child. And it's about you. Because the way we treat the most vulnerable isn't a reflection of who they are.

It's a reflection of who we are.

One of my father's friends from Illinois sent him a story while I was working on this book—a simple story that hit him and me like a thunderclap. It reminded me of Steve. And of what's possible when people decide, even for one moment, to choose grace.

In the story, a boy named Herbert—who had significant disabilities—wanted to play soccer with the other kids. His father, hesitant but hopeful, asked if he could join. The boys, after a moment of uncertainty, said yes. They let Herbert take a penalty kick. When the moment came, they gave him the ball, cleared the path, and made sure he scored.

He didn't kick hard. He didn't run fast. But the goal counted—not because the ball crossed the line, but because the hearts of those boys crossed a line, too. From exclusion to inclusion. From competition to compassion. From indifference to dignity.

That night, Herbert's father watched his son be held high by cheering teammates. And he knew that, for one day, his son had been a hero. A part of something. Seen. Celebrated.

Herbert died that winter. But that memory lived on. And so did the lesson: *sometimes, the most important goal in life is not to win, but to love* (Author unknown, n.d.). I also like what Iyanla Vanzant, said, "The goal of life is not to win. It is to play the game with love. The rules of the game are: have a strong desire to win, believe that you are worthy of winning, have faith that you will win, and, as long as you are alive, never believe that the game is over" (2017).

Steve never asked to be a symbol. He just wanted to belong. He just wanted what we all want—to be loved, to be known, to be treated as someone who matters.

And because of who he was—and how he lived—he became something more: a teacher. A mirror. A quiet revolution of the heart.

Let his story shape the way you live yours. Let his life remind you that love is not a feeling, but a choice—made in a thousand tiny moments, when you choose understanding over judgment, grace over fear, dignity over dismissal.

Steve changed me. He changed everyone who truly knew him. And if you let him, he just might change you, too.

If enough of us carry that change into the world—if we truly live for the love of Stephen—maybe, just maybe, the next child like Steve won't have to fight so hard to be seen.

Maybe their life will start from a place of belonging, not struggle.

Maybe the Golden Rule will stop being an aspiration…and finally become our way of life.

In the Introduction to this book, I shared my hope that this book would invite you to look again—at disability, at difference, at dignity—and to discover, as my family and I did, that while love is not always easy, it is always right. Thank you for joining me on this journey, for the love of Stephen.

REFERENCES

Access Press Staff. (2025). *History note: The foundation for special education was laid in 1975.* Access Press. http://accesspress.org/history-note-foundation-for-special-education-was-laid-in-1975

Achievement Center for Children. (n.d.). *UA 16: College of Education records* [Box 3, Folder 4]. Purdue University Archives and Special Collections, Purdue University Libraries.

American Association on Intellectual and Developmental Disabilities. (2023). *Definition of intellectual disability.* https://www.aaidd.org/intellectual-disability/definition

American Psychiatric Association. (2022). *Diagnostic and statistical manual of mental disorders* (5th ed., text rev.; DSM-5-TR). https://doi.org/10.1176/appi.books.9780890425787

Annual message to Congress on the state of the union. (1955, January 6). The American Presidency Project. https://www.presidency.ucsb.edu/documents/annual-message-the-congress-the-state-the-union-12

Author unknown. (n.d.). *A tapestry of hope.* https://www.example.com

Author unknown. (n.d.). *Each child is different* [Poem]. In *PoemHunter.* https://www.poemhunter.com/poem/each-child-is-different/

Author unknown. (n.d.). *The story of Herbert and the soccer game.* Retrieved [Month Day, Year], from https://www.example.com

Bank of America. (2024). *Understanding check fraud and forgery.* https://www.bankofamerica.com/security/check-fraud/

Bombeck, E. (1996). *Forever Erma: Best-loved writing from America's favorite humorist*. Kansas City, MO: Andrews McMeel Publishing. Reprinted with permission from the Aaron M. Priest Literary Agency.

Bratten, E. (2025). *Growing up with a sibling with a disability*. The Clay Center for Young Healthy Minds. https://www.mghclaycenter.org/parenting-concerns/growing-up-with-a-sibling-with-a-disability

Brown, B. (2012). *Daring greatly: How the courage to be vulnerable transforms the way we live, love, parent, and lead*. Gotham Books.

Buck v. Bell, 274 U.S. 200 (1927).

Bujnowska, A. M., Rodríguez, C., García, T., Areces, D., & Marsh, N. V. (2019). Parenting and future anxiety: The impact of having a child with developmental disabilities. *International Journal of Environmental Research and Public Health, 16*(4), 668. https://doi.org/10.3390/ijerph16040668

Burke, M. M., & Hodapp, R. M. (2014). Relating stress of mothers of children with developmental disabilities to family–school partnerships. *Intellectual and Developmental Disabilities, 52*(1), 13–23. https://doi.org/10.1352/1934-9556-52.1.13

Centers for Disease Control and Prevention. (2024, January 16). *What is intellectual disability?* https://www.cdc.gov/ncbddd/developmentaldisabilities/facts.html

Cole, N. K. (Performer). (1961). *Too young* [Song]. Capitol Records.

Council for Exceptional Children. (n.d.). *Who are special educators?* https://exceptionalchildren.org/about-us/who-are-special-educators

Dahl, R. (2023, March 5). *The dark side of relationships: Understanding relationship vultures*. Psychology Today. https://www.psychologytoday.com/us/blog/the-relationship-insight/202303/the-dark-side-of-relationships-understanding-relationship-vultures

David, L. (Writer), & Seinfeld, J. (Writer). (1992, November 12). *The Nose Job* (Season 3, Episode 9) [TV series episode]. In L. David & H. West (Executive Producers), *Seinfeld*. Castle Rock Entertainment.

Dillenburger, K., McKerr, L., & Jordan, J. A. (2015). Lost in translation: Public policies, services, and parental stress related to autism spectrum disorder. *Journal of Autism and Developmental Disorders, 45*, 1562–1574. https://doi.org/10.1007/s10803-014-2293-3

Disability Justice. (n.d.). *Abuse and exploitation of people with developmental disabilities*. Disability Justice. https://disabilityjustice.org/justice-denied/abuse-and-exploitation/

Disney. (Producer), & Hand, D. (Director). (1942). *Bambi* [Film]. Walt Disney Productions.

Dykens, E. M. (2006, April). Toward a positive psychology of mental retardation. *National Library of Medicine*. https://pubmed.ncbi.nlm.nih.gov/16719637/

Dykens, E. M. (2006). *Psychopathology in children with intellectual disability*. Cambridge University Press.

Education for All Handicapped Children Act of 1975, Pub. L. No. 94-142, 89 Stat. 773 (1975). https://www.govinfo.gov/content/pkg/STATUTE-89/pdf/STATUTE-89-Pg773.pdf

Eiesland, N. L. (1994). *The disabled God: Toward a liberatory theology of disability*. Abingdon Press.

Encyclopædia Britannica. (2025, August 25). *Iran hostage crisis*. In *Encyclopædia Britannica*. Retrieved from https://www.britannica.com/event/Iran-hostage-crisis

Encyclopedia of Indianapolis. (2025). *Special education*. https://indyencyclopedia.org/education-special

Endeavour Foundation. (2025). *Mate crime and disability: What is it and what can you do?* https://www.endeavour.com.au

Eunice Kennedy Shriver National Institute of Child Health and Human Development. (2023, March 31). *Intellectual and developmental disabilities (IDDs)*. U.S. Department of Health and Human Services, National Institutes of Health. https://www.nichd.nih.gov/health/topics/idds

Frost, R. (1993). *The road not taken*. In E. C. Lathem (Ed.), *The road not taken and other poems* (pp. 1–2). Dover Publications. (Original work published 1916)

Global Down Syndrome Foundation. (2025). *The history of the "R-word" and intellectual disability*. https://www.globaldownsyndrome.org/r-word-history/

Goddard, H. H. (1912). *The Kallikak family: A study in the heredity of feeble-mindedness*. Macmillan.

Goffman, E. (1963). *Stigma: Notes on the management of spoiled identity*. Prentice-Hall.

Goleniowska, H. (2012, July). Erma Bombeck: The special mother. *Downs Side Up*. http://www.downssideup.com/2012/07/erma-bombeck-special-mothers.html

Google Surveys. (2023). *Winter Driving Habits Survey Report*. Google Inc. United States Department of Transportation. (2025). *Bicycle Safety Statistics and Helmet Use*. https://www.transportation.gov/bicyclesafety

Goudie, A., Havercamp, S., Jamieson, B., & Shar, T. (2013, August). Assessing functional impairment in siblings living with children with disability. *National Library of Medicine*. https://pubmed.ncbi.nlm.nih.gov/23897909

Gould, S. J. (1996). *The mismeasure of man* (Rev. ed.). W. W. Norton. Schalock, R. L., Borthwick-Duffy, S. A., Bradley, V. J., Buntinx, W. H. E., Coulter, D. L., Craig, E. M., Gomez, S. C., Lachapelle, Y., Luckasson, R., Reeve, A., Shogren, K. A., Snell, M. E., Spreat, S., Tassé, M. J., Thompson, J. R., Verdugo, M. A., Wehmeyer, M. L., & Yeager, M. H. (2010). *Intellectual disability: Definition, classification, and systems of supports* (11th ed.). American Association on Intellectual and Developmental Disabilities.

Grandin, T. (n.d.). *I am different, not less*. In *Goodreads quotes*. Goodreads. Retrieved August 30, 2025, from https://www.goodreads.com/author/quotes/1567.Temple_Grandin

Grandin, T. (2010). *The way I see it: A personal look at autism and Asperger's*. Future Horizons.

Haley, E. (n.d.). *Grief has no expiration date*. What's Your Grief. https://whatsyourgrief.com/grief-has-no-expiration-date/

Heumann, J., & Joiner, K. (2020). *Being Heumann: An unrepentant memoir of a disability rights activist*. Beacon Press.

Howe, S. G. (1976). *On the causes of idiocy* (Original work published 1848). Arno Press. Kahneman, D. (2011). *Thinking, fast and slow*. Farrar, Straus and Giroux.

Indiana Code § 35-43-5-2. (2023). *Forgery*. Retrieved from https://iga.in.gov/legislative/laws/2023/ic/titles/035#35-43-5-2

Indiana Disability History Project. (2025). *Early schooling*. http://www.indianadisabilityhistory.org/exhibits/show/learning/earlyschooling

Indiana Historical Bureau. (2025). *Sterilization in Indiana: A history of eugenics and state policy*. Indiana State Library.

Jürgens, M., & Heston, J. (2018). *Siblings of individuals with developmental disabilities: Family dynamics and long-term adjustment. Journal of Family Social Work, 21*(4), 274–289. https://doi.org/10.1080/10522158.2018.1469567

Kahneman, D. (2011). *Thinking, fast and slow*. Farrar, Straus and Giroux.

Kephart, N. C. (1960). *The slow learner in the classroom* (1st ed.). C. E. Merrill Books.

Kurth, J., & Morningstar, M. E. (2020). *High-leverage practices in inclusive classrooms: Research-based strategies for all students*. Council for Exceptional Children.

Landman, K. (2020, May 11). Growing up alongside a sibling with a disability. *The New York Times*. https://www.nytimes.com/2020/05/11/parenting/children-sibling-disability.html

Leary, A. (2018, May 7). *Disabled moms get real about parenting with disabilities*. Romper. https://www.romper.com/p/disabled-moms-get-real-about-parenting-with-disabilities-8907952

Levinson, B. (Director). (1988). *Rain Man* [Film]. United Artists.

Long, A. (2023). Wabash Center: Agency is an integral part of life for those with special needs. *Greater Lafayette Commerce*. https://issuu.com/greaterlafayettecommerce/docs/glm-july2023-web-pages/s/31039834

Lunsky, Y., & Benson, B. A. (2001). Association between perceived social support and strain, and positive and negative outcomes for adults with mild intellectual disability. *Journal of Intellectual Disability Research, 45*(2), 106-114.

MacTaggart, J., Jaye, R., & Swanger, J. (1984). *God don't make no junk: Psalms for teenagers*. Westminster Press.

Marono, A. (2024, January 14). *Why do people judge others based on appearances?* Quora. https://www.quora.com/Why-do-people-judge-others-based-on-appearances/answer/Abbie-Marono

Milligan, M. S., & Neufeldt, A. H. (2001). The myth of asexuality: A survey of social and empirical evidence. *Sexuality and Disability, 19*(2), 91-109.

Milner, P., & Myers, F. (2022). Understanding and responding to mate crime: Social care, safeguarding, and the rights of adults with learning disabilities. *British Journal of Social Work, 52*(3), 1045–1062. https://doi.org/10.1093/bjsw/bcab045

Morgan, P. L., Farkas, G., Hillemeier, M. M., & Maczuga, S. (2018). Disproportionality in school discipline: An evidence-based discussion. *Exceptional Children, 84*(2), 204–222. https://doi.org/10.1177/0014402917748300

Murasko, M. (n.d.). *Special* [Poem]. Marla Murasko: Parenting Special Needs with a Purpose. https://marlamurasko.com/special/

National Alliance for Direct Support Professionals. (2022). *The Direct Support Workforce Crisis: 2022 Update.* https://nadsp.org

National Core Indicators. (2022). *In-Person Survey: 2020–21 Final Report.* https://www.nationalcoreindicators.org

National Women's Law Center. (2022). *Forced sterilization of disabled people in the United States: A primer.* https://nwlc.org/resource/forced-sterilization-of-disabled-people-in-the-united-states/

The New England Journal of Medicine. (2000). The influenza pandemic of 1957: A revisit. *The New England Journal of Medicine, 342*(18), 1346–1353. https://doi. org/10.1056/NEJM200005043421807

New International Bible. (2011). *Holy Bible* (New International Version). Biblica. https://www.biblica.com/

Ouellette-Kuntz, H., Cobigo, V., & Balogh, R. (2023). Health disparities and preventable deaths in adults with intellectual disabilities. *Journal of Disability Policy Studies*, 33(1), 42–53.

Poston, D. J., & Turnbull, A. P. (2004). Role of spirituality and religion in family quality of life for families of children with disabilities. *Education and Training in Developmental Disabilities, 39*(2), 95–108. https://www.jstor.org/stable/23879926

Purdue Alumnus. (1964, November 1). Finding and filling the gaps...ID's mental and physical growth. *Purdue Alumnus Magazine, 52*(2).

Razzano, L. A., Cook, J. A., Burke-Miller, J. K., Mueser, K. T., Pickett-Schenk, S. A., Grey, D. D., ... & Onken, S. J. (2005). Clinical factors associated with employment among people with severe mental illnesses: Findings from the Employment Intervention Demonstration Program. *Journal of Nervous and Mental Disease*, 193(11), 705–713.

Rivera, G. (1972). *Willowbrook: The last great disgrace* [Television broadcast]. ABC News.

Rogers, F. (2002). *The World According to Mister Rogers: Important Things to Remember*. Hachette Books.

Rosa's Law, Pub. L. No. 111–256, 124 Stat. 2643 (2010). https://www.congress. gov/111/plaws/publ256/PLAW-111publ256.pdf

Rotatori, A. F., Obiakor, F. E., & Bakken, J. P. (2011). *History of special education*. Emerald Group Publishing Limited.

Schalock, R. L., Borthwick-Duffy, S. A., Bradley, V. J., Buntinx, W. H. E., Coulter, D. L., Craig, E. M., Gomez, S. C., Lachapelle, Y., Luckasson, R. A., Reeve, A., Shogren, K. A., Snell, M. E., Spreat, S., Tassé, M. J., Thompson, J. R., Verdugo, M.

A., Wehmeyer, M. L., & Yeager, M. H. (2010). *Intellectual disability: Definition, classification, and systems of supports* (11th ed.). American Association on Intellectual and Developmental Disabilities.

Seligman, M. E. P. (2006). *Learned optimism: How to change your mind and your life*. Vintage Books.

Shivers, C., & Plavnick, J. (2014). Sibling involvement in interventions for individuals with autism spectrum disorders: A systematic review. *Journal of Autism and Developmental Disorders, 45*(3). https://doi.org/10.1007/s10803-014-2222-7

Smedes, L. B. (1993). *Shame and grace: Healing the shame we don't deserve*. HarperOne.

Smith, D. D., Tyler, N. C., & Gallagher, P. A. (2022). *Introduction to special education: Making a difference* (9th ed.). Pearson.

Smith, J. (Trans.). (2020). *The papyrus of Thebes*. University Press. (Original work published ca. 1200 BCE)

Smith, L. A. (2020). *Disability in the ancient world: Myths, medicine, and marginalization*. Oxford University Press.

Special Needs Alliance. (2025). *Bullying and children with special needs*. https://www.specialneedsalliance.org/the-voice/bullying-and-children-with-special-needs/

Springfield College. (n.d.). *Mission and Humanics*. https://springfield.edu/about/mission-and-humanics

Stiker, H.-J. (1999). *A history of disability* (W. Sayers, Trans.). University of Michigan Press. (Original work published 1982)

Stoneman, Z. (2005). *Siblings of children with disabilities: Research themes and directions. Mental Retardation, 43*(5), 339–350. https://doi.org/10.1352/0047-6765(2005)43[339:SOCWDR]2.0.CO;2

Stop Bullying. (2025). *Disability harassment and bullying*. U.S. Department of Health and Human Services. https://www.stopbullying.gov/resources/laws/federal

StopBullying.gov. (2025). *Bullying and youth with disabilities and special health needs*. U.S. Department of Health and Human Services. https://www.stopbullying.gov/resources/facts/youth-with-disabilities

Taylor, J. L., & Shivers, C. M. (2011). *Predictors of helping profession choice and volunteerism among siblings of adults with mild intellectual deficits*. American Journal on Intellectual and Developmental Disabilities, 116(4), 263-277. https://doi.org/10.1352/1944-7558-116.3.263

Ted Staff. (2013, June 28). Remembering educator Rita F. Pierson. *TED Blog*. https://blog.ted.com/remembering-educator-rita-f-pierson/

Terry, T. L. (1942). Extreme prematurity and fibroblastic overgrowth of the persistent vascular sheath behind each crystalline lens. *American Journal of Ophthalmology, 25*(2), 203–204. https://doi.org/10.1016/S0002-9394(42)92494-9

The Arc. (2025). *Siblings*. https://thearc.org/get-involved/siblings/

The Halo Benders. (1994). *God don't make no junk* [Album]. K Records.

Trent, J. W. (1994). *Inventing the feeble mind: A history of mental retardation in the United States*. University of California Press.

Tyldum, M. (Director). (2014). *The Imitation Game* [Film]. Black Bear.

United States Conference of Catholic Bishops. (n.d.). *Respect life*. https://www.usccb.org/committees/pro-life-activities/respect-life

United States Department of Transportation. (2025). *Zero is our goal. A safe system is how we get there*. https://highways.dot.gov/safety

U.S. Congress. (1975). *Education for All Handicapped Children Act of 1975*, Pub. L. No. 94-142, 89 Stat. 773.

U.S. Department of Education. (2017). *A guide to the Individualized Education Program*. https://sites.ed.gov/idea/parents-and-families/iep-process/

U.S. Department of Education. (2020). *A history of the Individuals with Disabilities Education Act*. https://sites.ed.gov/idea/IDEA-History

Vanzant, I. [DrIyanlaVanzant]. (2017, March 9). *"The goal of life is not to win. It is to play the game with love..."* [Status update]. Facebook. https://www.facebook.com/DrIyanlaVanzant/posts/the-goal-of-life-is-not-to-win-it-is-to-play-the-game-with-love-the-rules-of-the/3673657796000392/

Woodgate, R. L., Ateah, C., & Secco, L. (2008). Living in a world of our own: The experience of parents who have a child with autism. *Qualitative Health Research, 18*(8), 1075–1083. https://doi.org/10.1177/1049732308320112

World Health Organization. (2023). *Intellectual disabilities.* https://www.who.int/publications/i/item/9789240080539

Yell, M. L. (2023). *The law and special education* (6th ed.). Pearson.

Zemeckis, R. (Director). (1994). *Forrest Gump* [Film]. Paramount Pictures.

ABOUT THE AUTHOR

Author, Dr. Stuart D. Jones

Stuart D. Jones, Ph.D., hails from the south side of Lafayette, Indiana, where he grew up knowing that every story, especially family stories, deserves to be told. *For the Love of Stephen* is his heartfelt debut book, a labor of love inspired by his brother's remarkable life.

Dr. Jones's journey is as rich and varied as the chapters in his book. He holds a Ph.D. in Education with a concentration in Higher Education Leadership from Northcentral University in Arizona, an M.A. in Divinity from Christian Theological Seminary, a B.A. in Interpersonal and Public Communications from Purdue University, and a high school diploma from Jefferson High School. Stuart blends the best of scholarship with deep personal insight.

Before becoming a nationally recognized leader in higher education for his work in enrollment, financial aid, and student success and retention, Stuart spent over a decade serving Indiana congregations as an ordained pastor—wearing many hats, from youth and music minister to senior pastor. For more than 30 years, he has shaped the future of college students and institutions alike, leading record-breaking student enrollment efforts at universities across the Midwest, South, and Northeast.

Front row, left to right: Stuart, Ira, Terri, Derek, Jovie, and Kyleigh
Back row, left to right: Cassie, Lily, Daniel, and Rosalie

Stuart's leadership has earned him prestigious honors such as the Noel-Levitz Marketing and Recruitment Excellence Award and runner-up recognition from the American Association of Collegiate Registrars and Admissions Officers. As an in-demand speaker and college consultant, he shares his expertise nationwide, helping universities thrive in a rapidly changing educational landscape.

Beyond academia and leadership, Stuart is a devoted family man—married to Terri L. Jones, and a proud father of Daniel and Derek, father-in-law to Cassie and Kyleigh, and grandfather to a lively crew of four young granddaughters: Ira, Lily, Rosalie, and Jovie. When he's not writing or teaching online oral communication courses, you might find him indulging his passions as a wine enthusiast, family genealogist, collector of award-winning movies, antique hunter, or frustrated golfer.

In *For the Love of Stephen*, Stuart combines his professional academic acumen with personal warmth, inviting readers into an inspiring story about love, resilience, and the power of family—told with heart, humor, and hope.

Stay in Touch

Stuart welcomes thoughtful, insightful, respectful conversations, shared stories, and connections from readers moved by *For the Love of Stephen*. If you have reflections to share, questions to ask, an event to invite him to, a podcast you'd like him to be on, or simply want to reach out in the spirit of compassion and understanding, you're warmly invited to email him: **fortheloveofstephen@yahoo.com**.

A family picnic in 2023, though missing our beloved Steve. Pictured left to right: Keith and Phyllis, Donna and Scott, Jon and Susan, Stuart and Terri

Stuart knows a *thing or two* about public speaking—after all, he's been teaching it to college students for years, and speaking to audiences even longer. He welcomes invitations to speak with book clubs, advocacy groups, educators, religious and service organizations, and anyone interested in the themes of *For the Love of Stephen*—intellectual disability, inclusion, resilience, and love. He also welcomes your podcast invitation.

Whether in person or online, Stuart brings heartfelt storytelling, professional insight, a touch of humor, and a dynamic speaking style that makes every event engaging and memorable. He would love to connect with your group or podcast listeners to share stories, spark conversation, and inspire reflection.

Feel free to reach out to discuss scheduling a visit: fortheloveofstephen@yahoo.com.

Visit his website: www.authorstuartjones.com
Follow him on Instagram: @AuthorStuartJones
Like and connect with him on Facebook: AuthorStuartDJones

DISCUSSION QUESTIONS FOR
FOR THE LOVE OF STEPHEN

I. Personal Reflection and Connection

1. **What moment or story from Steve's life impacted you the most, and why?**

   How did it challenge or affirm your understanding of disability or family?

2. **What moments in the book made you laugh out loud? What moments brought you to tears?**

   How do humor and grief coexist in this story?

3. **How did your view of intellectual and developmental disabilities (IDD) evolve while reading this book?**

   What assumptions were challenged?

4. **Do you know someone like Steve?**

   How might this book help you engage with that person more thoughtfully or compassionately?

II. Ethical and Social Commentary

5. **The author writes: "Steve was not a saint, but he was a teacher."**

   What lessons do you think Steve taught those around him, and what did he teach you as a reader?

6. **How do societal labels and language shape our treatment of individuals with disabilities?**

   What role does language play in dignity, and how should it evolve?

7. **In what ways does the book critique the systems— educational, medical, social, or religious—that failed Steve?**

   What responsibility do these institutions hold today?

8. **How did Steve's story illuminate the concept of *ableism* for you?**

   How might we unknowingly contribute to ableist thinking or structures?

9. **Compare ableism to the myth that racism "ended" with the Civil Rights Movement.**

   Why do you think people are so eager to believe that the work is done? How might this mindset actually harm progress?

10. **Steve's story of being repeatedly exploited by those who claimed to care for him is heartbreaking and infuriating.**

    What did that chapter reveal about the vulnerability of people with intellectual and developmental disabilities in our society? What systems or attitudes allowed these "vultures" to thrive—and what must change to prevent this kind of abuse in the future?

11. **How does Steve's life expose the gap between being "included" and truly belonging?**

    Share an example from the book where inclusion felt superficial or hard-won. What does this tell us about the difference between physical presence and emotional acceptance?

12. **"We don't see disability" is framed as a form of erasure, not enlightenment.**

    Have you ever heard (or said) something like this? What might be a better way to acknowledge difference without diminishing dignity?

13. **Steve's quiet resilience and unexpected wisdom challenge societal stereotypes of people with IDD.**

    What part of Steve's story stood out most to you, and how did it shift your thinking about intelligence, contribution, or value?

III. Family, Faith, and Identity

14. **How did the Jones family embody resilience?**

    What stood out to you about their parenting, sibling support, their choices, or their faith?

15. **The book frequently references scripture and faith. How did spirituality shape the family's journey?**

    Do you think faith communities today are more inclusive? Why or why not?

16. **What role did siblings play in Steve's life?**

    How do you think having a brother like Steve shaped Stuart, Susan, or Scott's identities and worldviews?

IV. Education, Advocacy, and Action

17. **How can educators and schools better serve students with IDD today—beyond basic inclusion?**

    What does authentic support look like?

18. **The memoir references historical shifts in disability rights.**

    How far have we come—and how far is there to go?

19. **If you were to advocate for someone like Steve today, what would your first step be?**

    What kind of allyship does the author model?

20. **What does the title *For the Love of Stephen* mean to you after finishing the book?**

    What kind of love does this story ask us to give — and to whom?

www.ingramcontent.com/pod-product-compliance
Lightning Source LLC
Chambersburg PA
CBHW061554120626
46550CB00004B/1481